Lightning Slinger
of Andersonville

Front cover and second title page photo taken from the cover of *Railroad Magazine*, May, 1942, edition. Used with permission of Harold H. Carstens, President, Carstens Publications, Inc., which currently holds the rights to the magazine.

Back cover photo of Mr. Dunn by Ruby Hodgman.

Cover design by ThomasMax (Lee Clevenger & R. Preston Ward)

ISBN-13: 978-0-9822189-2-1
ISBN-10: 0-9822189-2-3

First Printing, June 2009

Published by:

ThomasMax Publishing
P.O. Box 250054
Atlanta, GA 30325
www.thomasmax.com

Lightning Slinger
of Andersonville

By Paul B. Dunn

ThomasMax

Your Publisher
For The 21st Century

Also by Paul B. Dunn from ThomasMax Publishing

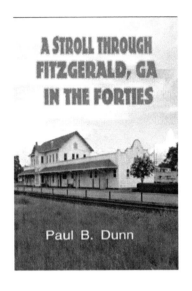

A Stroll Through Fitzgerald, GA, in the Forties, $ 14.95

Take a mythical stroll through the streets of Fitzgerald in this historic yarn as the author recalls his youth in the Colony City of Fitzgerald. Includes photographs and introduction by Sherri Butler of the *Fitzgerald Herald-Leader*. Paul B. Dunn's first published book was released in 2005.

Tremble Chin, $ 14.95

This true saga recounts the story of Teddie O'Dunn's wife, who earned the nickname of the book's title. A small woman, what she lacked in stature, she gained in spirit. Poverty, disappointment with her family, tragedy, and poor health demanded every spark of her spirit as the years passed. She married a penniless Southern lad whose only assets were the clothes on his back and an indomitable will to work and succeed. They faced the storms of life together. The only thing that ever trembled on that frail little Yankee woman was her chin.

This book is dedicated to the memory of my father,
Teddie Dunn

Table of Contents

The photograph above is from Teddie O'Dunn's school days in front of the schoolhouse in Andersonville. Teddie is in the second row, next to the last from the right.

Chapter 1

The Dunns' Arrival at Andersonville

Anyone that knew anything about Georgia Railroads, could recognize a Central of Georgia Railroad passenger train locomotive whistle in the 1890's. The sound was so shrill that the whistle sounded more like the scream of a panther.

One cold December night, in 1902, Miss Maggie Callen, the agent-operator at the Central of Georgia Depot at Andersonville, Georgia sat at her desk, awaiting the night passenger train that ran nightly from Albany, Georgia to Macon, Georgia, and on to Atlanta. It had already left Americus, Georgia, as she had read the telegraph key that was mounted on her desk. The agent had sent his "OS" (on sheet) to the train dispatcher in Macon. She knew that the train would soon be blowing its station blow for her station at Andersonville. The nine miles between the two towns could be run in 10 minutes.

Little did she realize that a special passenger would arrive that night, a mother clutching a baby in her arms and her brood of eight children. The child Sallie Ann Dunn clutched to her bosom was named Teddie, her baby, who was now a year old. She was the wife of W.T. "Bill" Dunn, the recently arrived Track Foreman of the "section" between Americus and Andersonville. Bill Dunn had brought his family from Mobile, Alabama down on the Louisville and Nashville Lines. He came from a along line of Irish track men that never stayed long anywhere. He had "landed" this job in Georgia, and claimed the railroad foreman's, "section house" that stood beside the tracks, just a bit back from the tool house that fronted the mainline, just a bit beyond the Depot and the town. The railroad company furnished him three "hands", to maintain the tracks on his section. He was a stern capable man, nearly 40 with a coal black head of hair above a fine red beard. He seldom smiled, and demanded the best performance of his children. He seemed to favor his eldest son, W.T. Jr., known as "T." T was 15 now and would soon be apprenticed to his father on the track gang.

Bill Dunn was waiting on the station platform for his family. His pipe was set in his mouth, and his breath smelled of whiskey, as he had taken his nightly "sip" that was so typical of the Irish trackmen. He had put his ear to the steel rail, and could detect the approaching passenger train bringing his family to the new section, long before he heard the shriek of the locomotive's steam whistle, that would split the silence of the cold December night. There it was! The long station blow and soon the beam of yellow light of the engine's headlight piercing the darkness of the night. He saw the sparks fall from the coaches' wheels as the airbrakes held the brake "Shoes" snugly to the coaches' steel wheels. The train groaned to a stop before the lamp lighted station platform. The train's porter opened the vestibule door and the uniformed conductor dropped the stepstool to the wood floored platform with a clop sound. Bill Dunn stepped from the darkness to greet his wife and children, two girls and six boys, one of which was almost a man, W.T. Junior. He spoke to his father, and helped his mother and her baby down the coach steps. The big girls, Minnie and Ida followed, then the boys piled off, there was Emmitt, Claude, Charlie, Henry, and Grady, all strapping boys, some still in short pants. The older boys grabbed the hand baggage and piled it on the station "float" or wagon and rolled it into the depot's warehouse, to await tomorrow's daylight. Then they bunched around their parents, as the train sped away to the next station at Oglethorpe, Georgia. Not only had the train's wheels began to turn at this little station at Andersonville, but the unseen wheels of fortune had also begun turning. They would soon be spinning away to shape the future lives of the family group that was trudging up the track to the home that Sallie Ann and Bill Dunn would never leave.

The railroad house was built of good lumber, it was level, strong, painted yellow, as all "company" buildings were. The foreman's house was larger than those of the "hands." It had a well, on a back porch, no plumbing, inside or outside, no electricity. But, there was a "two hole" dry toilet, with a "path." The large kitchen had a cast iron cook stove, and a dinner table in the center of the room. An open fireplace was in the parlor or setting room. The two bedrooms were small, and there was a "shed" room, with bunks for boy children. There was a garden plot, "stock" pen and shed, out behind the house. It was a homely house, but practical. When a foreman moved to a section, the railroad would furnish a boxcar to move his household goods or personal furnishings. This boxcar had been placed on a nearby spur/track by a local freight train the day before. Bill Dunn was fortunate to have this good job, although he had little time to spend around the house. He was out at daybreak, down at the company "tool house" where his hand, "pump car" and track tools were kept. There was oak water kegs, spike hammers, bolt wrenches, lining bars, gauge bars, eye-levels, shovels, weed slings, bank hooks, augers for both steel or wood, ballast forks, signal flags, rail torpedoes, and a four wheel "hand-car." The "track jacks" were stacked in a corner as was rain gear to protect the foreman and his hands from the elements, last but not least was a barrel of kerosene that had many uses from furnishing fuel for the hand lanterns used to light a work area for night track repairs, and lights for the lamps on the signals and switch stands. Even the lamps in the depot and company houses were lit with kerosene. As you see a railroad could not operate without kerosene. The foreman had to keep a record of all these items, not to mention time reports for him and his hands. He was responsible for the maintenance of his section of track, and the appearance of the right-away along the line. A foreman was prohibited from using hand tools, or doing any manual labor. His job was to get the work out of his "section hands" and use his expertise and common sense to maintain a safe and neat roadway. He reported to an official known as a road-master, who in turn reported to a general road master. These officials were promoted through the ranks, and usually had been section foreman that excelled at their sections and had a good record. These officials were not out on the line of road to make friends, but to get the most performance out of their "gangs." Woe be to the foreman that let weeds and bushes invade his tracks, caught asleep, fishing in a creek, reading a newspaper, strong drink on his breath, a curve out of "line," his tool house cluttered, short of tools, or sand on grade crossings. He was on duty around the clock, Sunday being his only day of rest, only if an emergency didn't rear its ugly head in the form of a washout, derailment, a run through switch, or a broken rail. As you can see, Bill Dunn was married to his gold watch, his "switch key" and the railroad. He was the bread winner.

Sallie Ann ran the home and bore his children. She was fortunate to have older sons that took care of the garden and helped her with the heavy chores, like firewood, and kept an eye on the younger boys. Her girls were good girls. Ida was good at sewing and did the patching and made curtains for the windows. She seemed to love to work buttonholes, and make patterns. Minnie excelled in the kitchen, but spent time down at the depot with Miss Callen, "low and behold," she seemed to have inherited a love for the railroad, learned the Morse Code, and mastered the telegraph key, down at the depot at Mobile, Alabama, before the move to Andersonville.

Sallie Ann Appleton Dunn was orphaned by the Civil War up in Tennessee as a child. She was found abandoned in the road that a rebel soldier who was walking home to, after the surrender of General Lee and his tattered army in Virginia. The veteran went by the name of Appleton and adopted her into his family and she was raised as one of his own children. She took his family name to become Sallie Ann Appleton. She had married W.T. Dunn back in Tennessee. He was the youngest son of an Irish immigrant that had married a Cherokee girl. He was the youngest of six boys of that union.

Bill was too young to go to war, but was embittered by cruel hardships that were brought on poor rural people by the union invaders during the last days of the Great Civil War. All his older brothers returned to a devastated south. They all worked in the Irish Track gangs that rebuilt the railroads of the south. They took great pride in the fact that they were Irish-Indian decent, and their knowledge of track building. Bill Dunn had married Sallie Ann as a teenager, she was no stranger to hard work and hard times. She had survived both with her health and cheerful spirit. She sang as she went about her duties, and gave her children her tireless devotion to duty and her indomitable will to survive. She had only those qualities to give her children, as her worldly goods were few.

Chapter 2

Teddie Dunn

The offspring of this couple were tough as pine knots and would tackle any job, with great strength and cheer. In every litter of animals or people there is usually a "runt." That dubious honor fell on Sallie Ann's baby boy, Teddie, the one she clutched to her bosom the night they unloaded at Andersonville. He had not grown off as her other children had. He failed to "flesh up" as the others had but had no afflictions, "just a runt." Teddie had been named for the popular president, the "Bull Moose" Teddie Roosevelt. Little Teddie had a long way to go to live up to his namesake, as he fought for life and health. He was an alert, "hell bent" toddler, learned quickly; he even seemed to think he was a small edition of a bull moose. His mother sang to him, and treated him with all the remedies of the mountain people. His sister Minnie nicknamed him "Bones."

His brother Grady soon grew into a gangling boy. If he grew to his large hands and feet he would be a giant. The railroad company tried to make it a little bit more convenient for their employees that lived in rural villages along its lines, where its trackmen lived. They ran a special "Pay Train" usually with only a coach with a strong safe in one end of that special coach, divided by an iron grill, two men, a paymaster sitting behind that grill that had a window and an entry door that was locked. The other man was a uniformed guard, pistol on his belt, sawed off shotgun in the cradle of his arm, and a serious look on his face. The workers gathered in the open end of the coach waiting for their names to be called. The paymaster knew their payroll I.D. number which he glanced at, and after verification, they were handed their pay envelopes containing gold coins. The employee then was required to sign a ledger to show receipt of his pay. Many men could not sign their names but "touched the pen" to witness their name, as the paymaster signed for him. The pay train was pulled by a light-fast steam engine, and at the rear of the train was a caboose with its "marker lamp" turned for the mainline, and served as quarters for the conductor and his flag man. The pay train was superior to other trains, and "burnt" the rails.

The men on the sections had named the pay train as all "Fast Special Trains" bore a name. No train was more important to the trackmen, and they had named it the "Flying Eagle," for the Eagle on the gold coins they found in the brown paper envelopes that soon littered the ground beside the tracks assuring that the hard earned money did not fall into the wrong hands. "Hard" money was scarce in the 1890's and those railroad folks were proud of their jobs and some kind of regular income. As the pay train sped away with its whistle shrieking, the merchants of the village as well as the saloon keeps would do a "brisk" business for the next few days and nights. A month was a long time to wait on your pay and the men wanted the "Eagle" to fly, and it did! The train crew that ran the "Eagle" were senior men that took pride in the train's appearance and performance. As the days drug by, the men wanted the pay train to "fly" as its name sake did.

The other coach that lacked the "fan fair" of the pay train was the "Grab." It was not a special train, only one long obsolete passenger coach, remodeled into a rolling storehouse. The local freight trains would handle the Grab next to the engine, which would "set it out" on "spur" tracks along the line of road. A store keeper, a clerk that had Spartan living quarters in this long coach, with windows and a big side door with steps that could be let down for the "railroad folks" to enter. Only these people could trade on the Grab as no cash money changed hands. The goods, only staple groceries such as flour, molasses, salt pork, salt, lard, sugar, spices, hard candy, baking powder, tobacco, a few canned goods, salt mackerel fish, and chicken feed were stocked. One section of shelves held dry goods, work shoes, work socks, overalls, bolts of calico and cotton blue denim cloth, thread, pins and needles, "long handle" underwear, red and blue handkerchiefs. Necessities were Calomel, Epson Salts, Croton Oil, Caster Oil, mustard plasters, corn plasters, soap, starch, and red devil lye. Women, wives and daughters of the workers climbed those steep steps and charge the bill to their men folks pay I.D.# to be taken out of their next pay check. You understood that stores were not on every corner, and railroads traversed lonely stretches of rural Georgia.

As I am telling of "special trains" this could be a good time to tell of the special trains that had the little town of Andersonville as their destination. The town had been around for a long time. It was a thriving village before the War Between the States. The red clay hills, when first cleared were fertile and cotton thrived on large plantations.

Peaches seemed to like the climate of Central Georgia and its frosty spring mornings. Creeks were in every bottom and there was no snow and ice to contend with in the winter time, and it was served by a first-class railroad that connected it with the capital of the confederacy at Montgomery, Atlanta, and the seaport of Savannah. Andersonville had the dubious honor of being selected as a prison site for the thousands of union soldiers that were captured at the beginning of the war in Virginia. A large track of land was enclosed in a stockade of pine logs and was built to receive the trainloads of union prisoners of war that were shipped in boxcars to spend the duration of the war as guests of the beleaguered rebel war department.

Andersonville saw much activity during the late years of the Civil War. The invasion of Georgia, the Fall of Atlanta, the "burnt earth" march of General Sherman to the sea at Savannah left Georgia destitute. No battle was fought on the rolling red clay hills around Andersonville. Starvation stalked these Georgia hills. A shot wasn't fired. The grim reaper was the victor over captor and captive alike. General Sherman and his northern army could have swept down a days march with his victorious army and freed thousands of starving northern prisoners, but he chose to let them suffer and die in the stockades at Andersonville. After the war ended Andersonville was spotlighted nationally as an atrocity. Captain Wertz, the confederate commander of the prison camp was hanged as a war criminal. His statue was erected in the Andersonville town square by the southern organizations. There were other prison camps scattered over the eastern U.S. There was atrocities at both union and confederate prison camps; starvation, disease, war wounds claimed many lives. Andersonville prison camp received by far the most notoriety after the war was over, and was made into a national cemetery by congress. There were row upon row of headstones erected on the rolling red clay hillside that supported oak and pine trees. The northern states, whose sons lay buried there, erected monuments in their honor. A large house was built by the federal government as a home for the superintendent that maintained and groomed the larger cemetery on the outskirts of the town of Andersonville. It went on as a rural southern town, a stop on the Central of Georgia Railroad. The only difference was that the national cemetery would always bear its name, and Andersonville National Cemetery would be on the lips of millions of northern veterans, and the families of the fallen soldiers, that lay sleeping beneath the sod, that was clipped and groomed in their honor. This sad scene guarded by granite angels and towering red oak trees, surrounded by miles of brick walls so carefully laid by Italian immigrant masons, and stonecutters that camped beside the springs under the oaks. The Central Railroad built "special" tracks to bring the bricks, manufactured at Macon, from the same red clay. Flat railroad cars brought Georgia marble and granite slabs from the hill country of North Georgia. The stone cutters chisels and strange language brought new sounds to the hills that surrounded Andersonville and its residents. The Dunn brothers watched all this activity, played among the white headstones and heard the war stories told around the village stores by the now aging Civil War veterans. They took all this activity right in their stride.

Sister Minnie had left home to take a railroad job on the Plant systems developing Atlantic Coastlines line that connected Montgomery, Alabama with Albany, Georgia and Waycross, Georgia through Southeast Georgia's "pine barren." She was employed as agent-operator at Pearson, Georgia.

Ida Dunn was grown up and had moved her sewing machine into a small vacant store house on the Andersonville town square. Her store was popular with the women folks of the area. Brother T Dunn had served his apprentice on the section gang of his father and he himself had a "section" on the Central of Georgia at Lizella, Georgia, just outside of Macon. The years were passing. Little Teddie still seemed to be "hide bound" and thin. He followed his older brothers, as they tramped the woods, fields, and creek banks around the town. Sallie Ann Dunn made a home for her younger children with the help of Ida.

Bill Dunn had a "spat" with his road-master one day; his boss smelled whisky on Bill's breath and he was relieved of his position as Section Foreman. He left his family there at Andersonville and soon was employed by the Seaboard Airline Railroad which was building a line from Abbeville, Georgia to the new "Colony City" of Fitzgerald that had sprung up seemingly overnight.. In 1896 Bill Dunn was gone for weeks at the time, as the large "extra" gang of track layers camped beside their work. The Dunn family had to move from the Central's section house. Bill had rented a shack of a house on the outskirts of Andersonville for his family that by now had its roots set deep in those red clay hills.

Chapter 3

Bill Dunn's Demise

Miss Maggie Callen sent word that a telegram had arrived, addressed to Sallie Dunn and it was urgent. Miss Maggie had copied the "wire" and knew its contents. Typhoid fever had broken out at the work camp, along the new Seaboard line and Bill Dunn had met something tougher than he was He was dead in three days time. His remains would be arriving in the noon train's baggage coach at Andersonville Station. Sallie Ann walked to the station and burst into tears as she read the death notice. Ida had heard the news and rushed to the station to meet her mother. She supported her mother, as she always had through the hard times.

Bill Dunn had not been an easy man to live with, his serious ways and his temper had made their life no "bed of roses." Most men that had survived the Civil War were hardened, drank too much, and ruled their women folk and children with an "iron hand." She understood those things and he had worked hard to support his family. That day the train arrived at Andersonville the shrill whistle of the engine seemed to split the air with its mournful sound. Sallie Ann had Teddie by the hand as he was usually into everything. The older boys knew the sad news of their father's misfortune, but Teddie had trouble letting the news soak into his young mind.

The train came to a stop, the side door of the baggage coach rolled open. The pine coffin was slid out of the coach onto a waiting "float" that slowly rolled across, the board platform to the black hearse pulled by a fine black horse that stomped and slung its head. The undertaker had driven from Americus to handle the burial of Bill Dunn.

Ida Dunn had arranged with the town's banker and store owner to advance the money for a decent, Christian burial for Bill Dunn in the open grave beside a nearby church graveyard that awaited his lifeless body. Little Teddie realized, as the pine coffin was loaded into the hearse, that his father was gone. His young mind wondered how they would survive without his father's pay envelope. Teddie was only eight years old, but he became a man as he saw the father, that he never seemed to please, lowered into the grave, and the red clay soil mounded on top. He saw the brave look on his mother's face as she was surrounded by her older children.

The look of determination was on their faces. Emmitt was absent from the family group. He had left home some time before as a teenager to seek his fortune in the West. Most of the tears were shed by Teddie, and they were tears of terror. About all Bill Dunn had left his family was an individual spirit, a timeless will to work, and excel at whatever they attempted to accomplish.

The Dunn's were not church goers, but were moral people. Railroad people seldom knew where they would be on Sunday morning and trains ran on Sunday just as they did on weekdays. No sooner than the last shovel of dirt was placed on Bill Dunn's grave than the prominent store owner approached the now widowed Sallie Ann, put his arm around her shoulders, and offered his condolences and credit at his general store, there on the town square at Andersonville.

Many things changed that day at the cemetery there in that little church yard. They were not physical changes, but lives would never be the same in the Dunn Family. "T" Dunn stepped into the shoes of the father that had taught him his skills of track laying and maintenance. He was a responsible young man and accepted the responsibility that fate had placed on his broad shoulders. He had seen the evils of strong drink, and was thoughtful of his mother and siblings. He went to a banker and made arrangements to buy a ten acre farm tract near town. Charlie and Grady were good to their baby brother, Teddie; they took him wherever they went. They tramped the hills and gullies around the national cemetery, set bird traps and fished set-hooks in Camp Sweetwater and Hog Crawl Creek.

The widow Dunn made a home for Ida, the younger boys and herself in the little farmhouse.

There was no such thing as pensions in those days and poor folks just had to "bump thunder" to get by. The fish and game that the boys brought in supplemented the basic southern foods that sustained life after the war. Salt pork, cornmeal, grits and cane syrup was always on the menu. Ida brought a few dollars home from her store.

One hot July day an old man walked up in the yard leading a rather boney old milk cow by a rope tied to the cow's halter. She had a little red bull calf at her side. The old man tied the cow to a hitching post in the shade of a half dead old mulberry tree that grew beside the house and called for Mrs. Dunn. She stood in the kitchen doorway, wiping her hands on her apron. She asked his business bringing that old cow and calf in her yard. He wiped the sweat from his forehead, as it was a hot summer day, and announced that he had led the pair from Ellaville, several miles away to deliver it to her. She drew a bucket of water from the well on the side porch, and then took a gourd dipper from the nail it hung by and offered the hot, tired old man a cool drink of water. She then set the bucket before the cow. Cows don't lap water, but the sucking sound she made as she drank pleased Sallie Ann Dunn. The old "stockman" wiped the sweat from his face which extended to his bald head as he began to explain his business. "Lady," he answered, there was a tall, serious young man, who said his name was W.T. Dunn, traded me out of this cow and calf. He gave me a twenty dollar gold piece for her and one extra dollar if I would deliver her to his widowed mother over at Andersonville. The young fellow shore made a good trade, but I earned that dollar for delivery!

He went on to tell her that the spotted cows name was Nezzie, and her bull calf was named Pete. Her "hooks," or hip bones showed high and her teats were too long, but she was good natured and gave about two gallons of rich milk daily if she was fed good.

Sallie Ann Dunn, tears streaming down her cheeks that had began to wrinkle, found her voice and said, "Bless Pat." I don't know if I would have made ends meet without my oldest son." The old "stockman" coiled his lead rope over his shoulder and trudged back to where he had come from.

Sallie Ann went to the garden she tended so faithfully and pulled some fodder from the corn stalks, and some green pea vines. She then carried an armful to her new cow and calf. Nezzie lowed a soft sound as if she knew she had a new home and poor as it was, she had a kind owner and would become a member of the Dunn Family. Animals just seem to sense those things.

Charlie Dunn was a master at finding odd jobs around the Andersonville community. He and Grady had grown into two stout young fellows, but the ten years the family had spent at Andersonville found Teddie a frail eleven year old lad that tipped the scales at the depot at only 83 lbs.

The twentieth century had arrived. Trains passed Andersonville each hour. Passenger trains brought the mail and supplies for the men that the government sent to maintain the national cemetery. Northern people came to find and decorate the graves of their loved ones. All of this traffic gave the village of Andersonville a "shot in the arm" so to speak.

Few people in the north had not heard of the Andersonville National Cemetery. The locals quipped that the population of the town was 10,435; ten thousand of them dead and buried over behind the brick walls of the national cemetery. The town was dubbed "The city of the dead." On Yankee ""Decoration Day"," which came around in the month of May, the southern states had little to decorate or celebrate. The Civil War had drained Georgia and her sister states to a state of destitution.

The Central of Georgia Railroad and the town of Andersonville saw a few days of prosperity, those last few days of May when the Yankees came in droves to Andersonville, their pockets lined with "Yankee dollars."

There were few roads through the country, and people that went anywhere of any distance had few choices of modes of transportation except by passenger train or steam boats.

The victorious northern states lost many sons that were buried here at Andersonville. These people came to celebrate their victory and mourn their fallen soldiers that had sacrificed their young lives to hold the union together. The Central Railroad had built side or "spur" tracks there at Andersonville to park the special excursion trains, with their sleeper coaches, known as "Pullman cars." The very rich came in their own private railroad coaches or "palace cars." Few accommodations existed in the town for the visitors. The mourners would unload from their parked trains to find that the distance to the cemetery and prison park was quite some distance from the poor little town to the park that bore its name. There was some affluence ten miles away at Americus, Georgia.

The livery stable there would send over "surreys" and "buggies" and horses to pull them. They were for hire, along with a few rigs from the more prosperous land owners around Andersonville. Grooms and drivers were hired on the spot to tend the horses, and drive back and forth to the hallowed grounds.

Charlie Dunn had learned telegraphy and assisted the depot agent, Miss Maggie, to copy the many messages that came over the wires from all over the U.S., not to mention the many train orders to operate the special trains. He also "hired out" his younger brothers to Mr. Easterlin, owner of the local horse and buggies, as drivers to haul the "well heeled" northern ladies and gentlemen.

Sallie Ann Dunn would have Grady and little Teddie's white shirts starched and ironed, their hair trimmed and combed; even had them wear bow ties that Ida had bought in Americus.

Grady was talented to handle live stock and had Teddie hired out, along with himself as "plow hands" as soon as they could reach the handles of "plow shares." Teddie had a lot of "grit" that made up for his puny size. If Grady could get the mules "caught" and harnessed, Teddie could drive them. The lads looked good sitting in the driver's seats, although their pants were mended and they wore ten cent straw hats. The rich Yankee men would laugh at the "drivers," but they were generous with their tips. Teddie was one of their favorites and was much in demand as he loved the attention they gave him, and his pockets did jingle. He was so proud to bring his money to his mother and she saved it for him, as he was still and always would be her "baby."

Chapter 4

Lightning Slingers

Telegraph operators had a "handle" or nickname on the railroad. They were referred to as "lighting slingers." When Bill Dunn had been alive he saw to it that the older children gained employment on the railroad, as the pay was better than most jobs. He was also proud of his profession as a railroad track man, as his father had been back in Ireland.

Teddie's older brothers, "T", Claude, and Emmitt were gone from home by now. Claude had made a handsome young man. His wit was sharp and he kept everyone around him laughing. He was a telegrapher, and one of the best. Emmitt had not been heard from for two years now, as the West covered a lot of territory. Minnie had a good job on the Coastline. Ida seemed content with her store at Andersonville. Charlie, Grady, and lastly Teddie, were still living under Sallie Ann Dunn's roof. They seemed to be happy boys and helped their mother.

This would be a good place to tell of the Dunn children's schooling. Sumter County, Georgia, the county that Andersonville was located in, had a good or as good a school system as a poor tax base could afford. The one room frame white building was located on a hillside right in the village of Andersonville. It needed a paint job, but had a row of "double hung" window lights, no electricity, but a row of kerosene lamps along the outside walls. They were seldom lit, only for night occasions. There was a huge wood stove that vented through a long stovepipe, hung by haywire from the ceiling to a brick flue. On cold winter days the north wind would rattle the glass window panes. The cast iron stove would be red hot, as was a portion of the stove pipe.

Oak wood was racked outside by the town's people. Children were use to drafty buildings and were bundled in warm hand-me-down mended cloths. Most children wore hand-cobbled shoes. Money was scarce in those red clay hills, but oak trees thrived on the ridges, supplying good firewood.

The Andersonville school was fortunate to have a dedicated professor by the name of Clark, assisted by his daughter, Miss Polly.

He was a well-educated veteran of the Civil War. He was a no-nonsense man with a crippled hand that could hold a piece of chalk to write on the blackboard, but that was about all it was good for. He often told his students, "This is what a Yankee Minie ball did for me at the Battle of Bull Run." He seemed to know how to hold the attention of the rag-a-mag-tag scholars that walked the paths and red dusty roads to attend his classes. Teddie was one of his "star" students as was Charlie. Grady was the tallest, strongest lad in the class, but he seemed to have been blessed to use his large hands that seemed to know how to build anything. Tools just seemed to fit them. On cold days when the woodpile ran low, the professor would detail Grady Dunn to be excused from class, go down to Mr. Easterlin's mule lot, catch up a pair of mules, hitch them to his wagon and go to the oak ridge and cut a load of firewood. Teddie would slump down in his desk, not to be seen, but Professor Clark's stern voice would always tell him to take your little brother Teddie to help you. Grady was good to Teddie, but he worked the "stew" out of him. Charlie was quite a hand to delegate duties to his younger brothers, but he was a hustle around Miss Maggie's railroad depot down by the tracks. He quickly mastered the Morse Code. It was soon clear that he would avoid manual labor, and soon would become a "lightning slinger." He could send and receive messages almost as good as Miss Maggie. He loved to fish and hunt birds, which were welcomed to his mother's cook pots.

The local landowners were "strapped" for cash, although they lived a comfortable life that their land holding brought them. Soon after "T" had sent the milk cow and her calf to his mother, a kind gentleman, astride his fine saddle horse, stopped before the house that Sallie Ann Dunn made home. He was Mr. Pony Johnson, owner of many acres of farmland, and a fine pasture that joined the Dunn Farm. He tipped his hat and never dismounted the saddle horse. He made her welcome to let the boys bring the cow over to graze and be bred back by his bulls. Can you guess who took the cow to pasture and brought her back to be milked everyday? Yes, it was Teddie's chore. Old Nezzie loved to wonder into the ravines where the honeysuckle vines grew. The vines were evergreen and they seemed rich in protein. The cow had given more milk since she had good pasture. The cream was made into butter by Sallie Ann. The hen eggs she gathered brought her some cash as she sold them down at the store. She had about paid off her debt to Mr. Easterlin.

Grady never saw an idle moment. He had built a cow shed, pen, and a hen house, but his specialty was ox yolks he hewed from the oak and black gum logs that were rejected at the local sawmill. He would also borrow a well driller to bore water wells. He had castrated the red bull calf that had come with old Nezzie. He had grown into a strong young ox. Grady had traded varmint hides and fish with the superintendent over at the national cemetery for an axle and pair of spoked wagon wheels. The two-wheeled cart that Grady built from salvaged lumber was fitted with shaves and a driver's seat. The red bull had never run loose. His "operation" had gentled him as well as the constant attention of the boys that were growing to manhood. They had taught him to obey commands. Grady had "broke" Pete to the small yoke he had fashioned from Persimmon wood, one of the strongest materials that grew around Andersonville. The brothers often rode him bareback. Nezzie had a new calf by one of "Pony" Johnson's herd bulls now. The ox, as Pete now was, had bonded with the boys.

There was always a gathering of old men sitting on a long bench, or rather a board nailed to the hitching post under the shed over the sidewalk in the front of Easterlin's General Store. Captain Wertz statue dominated the town square. The buildings that existed were not elegant stone and masonry, just wood frame. The streets were not paved; even the sidewalks were of heart pine planks. They served the purpose of a solid place to walk, as the street was either mud or dust, depending on the weather. There was no snow in winter, but ice would cover the surface of the long water trough out by the ill-fated captain's statue. On cold winter days, the men that were too old or crippled to work would gather around the large wood heater inside the store. They were good old men, most of them veterans of the Civil War, now 45 years in the past as the year was 1905. Their ranks were growing thinner by the day by now.

Their hard earned wisdom and tales of the battles they had survived intrigued Teddie Dunn. He was now 15 years old and Sallie Ann had him in long pants, but they didn't have to be very long as he had not filled out much. Grady and Charlie were smoking and chewing tobacco, as they pictured themselves grown men. They didn't attend Professor Clark's school as they had all finished their fifth book and could read, write, and figure well enough. Charlie and Teddie were the scholars; Grady was the skilled workman and provider, along with his sister Ida, for their mother's home and well-being.

Chapter 5

W.T. Dunn, Jr. and His Brothers

When a problem arose that the home folks were having a problem, "T" Dunn would come in on the passenger train and walk to his mother's house, open the gate and stride to the porch and call "Ma." He had done well on the Central of Georgia, and had been promoted to a track foreman. He seemed to be a natural born civil engineer, and his father had taught him well the finer points of "track laying." Sallie Ann hungered to know the family he had started in Atlanta, but he was a busy man and times were hard. She would just have to wait a while. He assured his mother that he had a good wife named "Arch" and two fine sons.

His words to his younger brothers that seemed to stick in their minds for life were "when problems arise, just redouble your efforts and they will go away." He had not heard from Emmitt, somewhere in the west, but he knew, no news is good news.

"T" was a fair mixture of his mother and father. Like his mother, he was kind and responsible. He inherited h is father's work ethics, engineering abilities, but seemed to miss his dad's thirst for strong drink. The wheels of fortune got spinning around and no one knows where it will land. He always brought his family presents. This trip he had brought his mother a nightgown. Charlie was the proud new owner of a bird dog puppy. He brought Grady a "lock level" to survey terraces on hillside fields. Teddie was the proud new owner of a brand new single-shot .22 caliber rifle and a box of birdshot cartridges. Yes, "T's" visits to the home place of Andersonville were what kept Sallie Ann going. She still sang as she went about her household duties. Her favorite song was "December is as pleasant as May." She was graying now, and her short figure was a bit broader. She had never known anything but hard work and getting by on what she had. The neighbors often said that Sallie Ann Dunn could take a dull ax and chop a discarded crosstie into stove wood and never miss a "lick."

The Dunn boys came driving up to the store one morning in the two-wheeled ox cart that Grady had built over in the cemetery superintendent's shop. "Pete" was between the shaves, wearing the yoke that Grady had fashioned with a "draw knife." Teddie held the single line to lead the ox as he proudly sat in the driver's seat.

The old timers there at the store even stopped their checker game to see the contraption. Old Mr. Harden asked the ox's name. When he heard that he was named "Pete," he suggested that a noble creature like him should have a noble name, perhaps like, "General Sherman." They all laughed, but the name stuck in the form of "General."

Now that the Dunn brothers had transportation, slow as it was, they were on their path to success. Charlie made the "trades," Grady the strong one, so to speak, "laid his shoulders to the wheel," Teddie was right in the middle of any activity his older brothers tackled. They hauled shelled corn to Green's Mill to be ground into corn meal, grits, and chicken feed.

The "General" could be seen "snaking" crossties that Grady hewed to the "hill." At cane grinding time, the boys cut sugarcane and hauled cart loads to the grinders. They got paid off in syrup, which they took home to Sallie Ann.

Time marched on, the older boys were standing on the threshold of manhood, their happy days of roaming the hills and ravines around Andersonville setting bird traps, and bank poles along the creeks, and milking the cow. Why they even taught the "General" to do tricks like pushing the cart a head of him with his front feet in the cart bed. He became the most famous ox in those counties. When "Decoration Day" came around in May, Grady would put his "educated" ox through his paces to the delight of the Yankees, negroes and "carpetbaggers" that came by the trainload from all over the north with their pockets full of hard federal dollars.

Teddie had a talent for business enterprises. He would set him up a stand right by Captain Wertz's statue to sell the Yankee's lemonade, boiled peanuts, and syrup candy. He dressed in his best clothes, and wore his flat top straw hat. His signboard, above his stand read, "ICE COLD LEMONADE, made in the shade and stirred with a spade." It brought so many thirsty customers that he had to hire a black boy friend of his named "Jeb" to wash glasses in a washtub by his stand.

Among the crowd that came from a recently settled colony town named Fitzgerald that had sprung up, seemingly overnight over in the pine barrows, sixty miles southeast of Andersonville, was a Yankee girl. She was the granddaughter of a union veteran that had joined the colony of yanks that came from the windswept north to the sun kissed south to spend their last days. Teddie gave the curly headed young redhead a special smile and tipped his straw hat to her. Her friends saw the look in Teddie's eyes and the blush on the face of their friend they called "Tessie." Little did either care free youngster know that the wheel of fortune had paused there at a lemonade stand beside the railroad tracks at Andersonville, Georgia.

Teddie, since he left Professor Clark's schoolhouse spent time each day at the railroad depot helping the kindly Miss Maggie. Railroading was in his blood. He trimmed the wicks and filled the kerosene lamps that lighted the office and switch stands that were so vital to the movements of the Central's night train. In return, Miss Maggie taught him the "ins and outs" of telegraphy. It had become pretty clear that Teddie had much rather become a "lightning slinger" than a "clod buster" as farmers were known as.

One day as Teddie was sweeping the depot, the telegraph receiver started tapping out a call for Andersonville on the Western Union line. Miss Maggie announced that the call that was from Minnie Dunn at Pearson, Georgia. As Minnie sent the coded message, Miss Maggie copied the words on her typewriter. She called Teddie to her side as she pulled the short telegram from the typewriter. "This is for your mother, from your sister…go take it to her, quickly." Teddie tore out for home but he had learned to read Morse Code. He listened as the message was sent. He already knew what to tell his mother as she could not read very well. Sallie Ann held the message, typed on yellow paper with trembling work worn hands. Teddie blurted out that Minnie had sent for Charlie to catch the noon train for Albany and from there to transfer to the Coastline train that ran to Waycross, Georgia through Pearson where she was agent operator. Seems she had a job for Charlie at a nearby station named Kirkland, Georgia as agent operator. With tears in her eyes, a mixture of joy and sadness, she told Teddie to go quickly and find his brother Charlie and bring him to her side. Teddie found Charlie at the "peach packing" shed, building wooden crates to pack peaches in.

Charlie was almost a man and he was ready to leave Andersonville, as there was no opportunity of a good job there. Farming was a hard lot unless your family owned a lot of land and mules. Charlie caught the first thing "smoking" on the line to Albany. He had a change of clothes, a white shirt, and a black bow tie and a head full of knowledge of how to "run" a railroad. Teddie was the only one with a knack for saving his meager wages as a plow hand or his tips and fruits of his labor at his lemonade stand when the Yankees came on "Decoration Day". Charlie needed a few dollars for the trip and living expenses until his first railroad wages arrived on the Pay Train. Sallie Ann loaned Charlie ten dollars of the money she was holding for Teddie and pressed it into Charlie's hand as she kissed him goodbye and told him to be a "good boy." He ran all the way to the stationhouse, seldom if ever to return to his old "stomping grounds."

Once only 16 years ago there were ten in the Dunn Family, as they made a home in a crowded railroad company house so close to the tracks. Now there were only four, Sallie Ann and three of her children, Ida, Grady, and her "baby" Teddie. She had known all along that the same passenger train that had brought them to Andersonville, pulled by the sleek little steam engine with the "shrieking" whistle, would take them one by one away from her or bring them back to be buried in the graveyard by the little log church, perched on the side of that red clay hillside there at Andersonville, Georgia, sometimes called "The City of the Dead."

Time marched on and could you believe that 1906 had arrived? Teddie had passed his 17th birthday and had to stand on his tip toes to measure five feet tall. He would weigh himself on the warehouse scales at the depot. He could balance the 100 lb pee. Grady was two years older and a foot taller and weighed 40 pounds more with not an ounce of fat.

The carefree days of hunting and fishing and odd jobs came to an end one day for Grady Dunn. The telegraph instrument was clattering away down at the railroad depot. Miss Maggie copied a message to Sallie Ann Dunn. It was from W.T. Dunn in Atlanta. It read, "Have Grady Dunn packed and ready to catch the train to Atlanta. I have him a job as an apprentice on the bridge gang out of Macon. Once again tears ran down Sallie Ann's cheeks. Grady had been her "hands," there was just no job the gangling boy wouldn't tackle. He could read and write, but books were not his thing. On his cheek was a large black area that he had acquired when he overloaded the old muzzle loading, double barrel shotgun that his father had left hanging over the fireplace. It had exploded in his face. He had been lucky to not have lost the sight in his left eye. He always wore overalls and denim jackets. Charlie and Teddie were "dressers." I doubt if Grady ever wore a tie or shined his shoes that had left their prints in three counties.

What would the red ox that had grown into a giant, named "The General"do? Grady himself knew the day would come when he would have to go out into the world. He had a long talk with Teddie, telling him that he would have to be the "man of the house" and take his place to help his mother and Ida. Teddie was tired of the hard labor that Grady seemed to enjoy. Old Nezzie, the milk cow, and Teddie didn't have much love for each other and the ox was Grady's pride and joy.

Chapter 6

The Path

Sallie Ann Dunn dried her tears and waved goodbye to Grady as he strode down the red clay path with his pack on his back. She had seen her brood walk down that same path to seek their fortune in the world.

She had kept in touch with all of them, but Emmitt. He seemed to have been swallowed up somewhere in the West. She longed to see her grandchildren, but distance and daily duties posed a problem in those days. Ida never interfered with her brothers going on. Her mild nature and devotion to her mother kept her contented there at Andersonville. She was on the plain side and never had a "beau." She was her mother's heart as Grady has been her hands.

Teddie had his own mind, although it was often said that he was "tied to his mother's apron strings." Teddie had been quite a scholar in school, quick to learn; there was no doubt of that. He formed a close friendship with a neighbor boy by the name of Johnnie Harden. They both were interested in telegraphy. They learned at the knee of Miss Maggie, down at the railroad station. The boys had managed to obtain telegraph instruments and batteries. They twisted haywire together and strung it between their homes and sent messages to each other. Practice makes perfect, and before long they both had become "lightning slingers."

Teddie had enjoyed the .22 caliber rifle that "T" had brought him. He stalked the hedgerows to shoot birds. The larks, robins, brown thrasher and doves made delicious pies and gravy.

Chapter 7

Teddie's Accident

One day disaster struck. The kitchen room of the home place was not sealed and the poles that supported the wood shingle roof gave entry to all sorts of varmints and birds. That fateful morning Sallie Ann saw a rat snake coiled on a rafter pole over her dining table. It hissed and blew at her. She called for Teddie to get his rifle and come quickly to dispatch the intruder. Teddie came running, cocked his trusty gun and his unerring aim brought the large snake writhing to the well-worn wooden floor of the kitchen. Teddie disposed of the intruder and came back in the kitchen to assure his mother and sister Ida that he had things well under control. He picked up his trusty single shot rifle, loaded a scatter shot cartridge into the breach, leaned the barrel into his groin and slammed the bolt closed. The blast of the little gun sent a load of lead shot into Teddie's left leg below where it joined his frail body. Blood gushed from the wound with every beat of Teddie's heart. Ida plunged her finger in the hole that the charge had made in the boys leg. He lay on the kitchen floor, unconscious, his life ebbing away. Ida told her mother to run down the road to a neighbor's house and send them to the doctor's house, some distance away. When she returned, she saw the Ida was still by Teddie's side. A black woman that lived nearby had heard the commotion and was at Ida's side. The woman, known as Aunt Mollie, was a midwife and had delivered many babies; she knew a lot about bleeding and how to stop the flow. She told Ida to set a kettle of water on the cook stove. She "packed" the wound with rags that she had sterilized with the water that was boiling on the woodstove. Mollie then sent Ida to the barn to gather spider webs. Sallie Ann was no stranger to caring for sick and wounded people, as the Civil War had left many patients to be tended by the women folk. She prayed for Teddie's life; she had never lost a child, but now she knew that the "grim reaper" was nearby. Teddie still lay on the floor; his lights were out like a lamp that had been blown out.

By now several people had gathered in the yard. The animals that called Sallie Ann's house instinctly knew that death was in the air that hot June morning. The ox had a low bellow in his throat. Old Nezzie came up from Pony Johnson's Bermuda grass pasture with her new calf by her side. The yard chickens flew up in the old Mulberry tree. The birddog that Charlie had left behind strained at his chain, smelling the scent of blood, Teddie's blood, in the hot summer air.

Hoof beats were heard on the road. It was Dr. Grimes coming from Americus. Miss Maggie had sent a "wire" notifying the doctor of the accident. The sleek big mare that pulled the doctor's buggy the nine miles was lathered with sweat and red dust of the unpaved road. A neighbor caught the horse's bridle and held her while the doctor stepped to the ground, black bag in his hand. Ida met him at the door to the kitchen room. She took his coat and satchel as she led him to the patient that was still unconscious there on the kitchen floor. A quick examination revealed that the bleeding was under control. The doctor looked up as he arose from his patient. His first statement was, "Mollie, you have done a good job on Teddie's wound." She smiled a broad smile spreading across her broad black face. "Miss Ida knowed where his pressure points wuz." I just sterilized the wound and tied a boiled rag to make a tourniquet. I always use spider webs to stop the blood flow." Dr. Grimes instructed the group of onlookers to clear the kitchen table and carefully lift the frail boy to the table so he could sew the main artery and the gaping wound back together. He told Ida and Sallie Ann that he would make no effort to remove the load of lead shot from Teddie's leg as the bleeding would start again.

Mollie was well acquainted with Dr. Grimes as she had worked with him on several occasions. She boiled his surgical instruments and bathed Teddie's body. She lit the lamp over the dining table for added light and mopped the bloody floor.

The operation began on the unconscious lad that showed no response to the stitching of his wounds. What seemed to be an eternity to Teddie's mother and sister, the doctor straightened up and washed his hands in a bowl of hot water. He instructed Mollie and Sallie Ann to keep Teddie quiet and flat of his back, just as he lay, until he regained consciousness; keep him warm and quiet and pray that blood poison didn't set in as he had done all he could for the time being.

Teddie had lost a lot of blood, but was lucky that he received prompt and good care. Sallie Ann realized that the boy's recovery was now in her hands and it would be a long and painful trial for both she and Teddie. Dr. Grimes rolled his sleeves down and gathered his instruments into his black satchel. Ida helped him into his coat. She had a $5 gold piece that she pressed in the doctor's hand. He thanked her and gave her some pain pills and instructions for feeding the patient when he awoke. He also told Mollie that he would send some bottles of his special tonic that would help Teddie's "natures" to build his blood and give him appetite to speed his recovery. The doctor's horse had been watered and groomed by a neighbor and was chomping at her bit to return to her stall in Americus.

Teddie regained consciousness that night. He tried to arise, but was restrained by his mother who was sitting by his side. He remembered shooting the snake and then an explosion. A pain shot through his leg when he attempted to move it. He raised up to drink some chicken broth and to swallow some pain pills the doctor had left him. Mollie had gone home, but had assured Sallie Ann that she would be back at day break to change the bandage and move Teddie to his bunk in the shed room that now had only one occupant…Teddie, gave thanks to the good Lord that had spared his life. He seemed alert until the doctor's pills took affect. He went back to sleep.

The next morning his leg was swollen and his bandages were bloody but he smiled at Ida and his mother and assured them that he would be alright in a few days time. Little did he know that he would remain bedridden for six weeks. The men down at the store had heard the "news" as word of mouth spread quickly throughout a rural community. Even the superintendent over at the national cemetery came over to the widow Dunn's ten acres to offer any help she needed, as the Dunn boys had helped him in the upkeep of the cemetery on many occasions.

The ladies of the town brought covered dishes of food, and Mr. Pony Johnson rode up on his saddle horse to offer his condolences and help. Teddie was well known around the town and especially at the railroad depot. People helped one another in that day and time. Aunt Mollie walked over every morning to change Teddie's bandages, and watch for infection. Ida went back to her store. Johnnie Harden, Teddie's closest friend took care of the ox and Nezzie. Sallie Ann cooked and cleaned the house.

Teddie had begun to eat, but had to remain long days laying on his back. He could sit up to eat and read books that his friends brought him. He spent sleepless nights laying awake looking through a crack in the shingle roof of the shed room. There was a star that he looked for each night.

The big red ox "The General" would come up to stand under the Mulberry tree, just outside of Teddie's window. He could hear the animal as it "lowed" softly in the night. It missed Grady and seemed always to search for him to loop the plow line in the brass ring that Grady had put in his nose when they went to work. These things gave Teddie some solace.

There was not much formal religion in the Dunn family. Bill Dunn had none as the railroad kept him occupied and the struggle to feed and clothe a large family was always with him. Sunday mornings he read the Macon Telegraph newspapers as he sat on the company house's front porch in fair weather. He demanded peace and quiet from the younger children when he was around the house. Teddie and his father had some serious run ins over this subject. On one Sunday morning, Teddie persisted in playing a little toy fiddle that Santa Clause had brought him for Christmas. After several admonishings by his stern father to quiet the "racket," he snatched the little fiddle and played a tune on Teddie's behind, leaving the fiddle in splinters. Teddy, from that whipping on never again was close to his father.

Dr. Grimes dropped in about a month after the gun accident and gave Sallie Ann a good report on the now healed wound in the boy's groin. It was still sore when Teddie put his weight on it, but the "tonic" old doc gave him had his blood count up and he wasn't so pale and was as he had been, even before the accident.

Johnnie Harden kept the old men up to date down around the store, that Teddie was up and "raring to go," but needed a crutch. The next morning old man Jeb Smith stood knocking at Sallie Ann's front door. "Mrs. Dunn, I hear tell your son Teddie needed a crutch so he could stir about. I was crippled after the war and had several old crutches around the barn. I cut this set down to the boy's size and it would be a pleasure to loan them to him."

Teddie hobbled to the porch as he listened to the conversation. In a flash he grabbed the old crutches and with the help of Mr. Smith, he soon could swing his bad leg around and get about the yard. Teddie thanked the old veteran for the crutches. If Grady had still been around he could have fashioned him a set out of hickory wood that grew on the red clay hills, but Grady was long gone on the Central of Georgia Railroad.

A long, hot summer had baked the red clay hills around Andersonville. Camp Creek had dried down to pot holes of stagnant water. Sallie Ann Dunn missed the things for the cook pot that her boys had brought in. Even ""Decoration Day"" had not brought the usual throngs of Yankees to unload at the railroad depot for the procession up the hill to the national cemetery and the prison site. The peach crop had failed and cotton was short. Teddie hobbled about on his crutches. "T" visited his mother, and had along talk with Ida, "chirked" Teddie up telling him that he would have to be the "man of the house" as he would be 16 years old on the last day of August. "T" also suggested that Sallie Ann sell the ox, "General Sherman," for whatever she could get for him, as he was hard to manage since Grady had gone from home and Teddie showed little interest in livestock, which included old Nezzie, the milk cow. That old cow h ad been the one thing that had pulled the family through hard times after the untimely death of W.T. "Bill" Dunn. She had a new calf, a heifer, by her side, but she was losing her teeth from age as this was her 6th calf and it would make a good replacement for Nezzie by next summer.

Sallie Ann had taken good care of that old cow. On several occasions she had "snapped up" Teddie as he was bad to drop the bucket that he drew water from the well to water Nezzie. His mother never wanted "her cow" to drink muddy water, resulting from the splash of the dropped bucket.

Word spread quickly around Andersonville that Mrs. Dunn was considering selling the animals. Mr. Pony Johnson himself a dealer in livestock, an honest dealer he was, drew his saddle horse up under the Mulberry tree in the Dunn yard. Sallie Ann heard his horse neigh and his soft call, "Mrs. Dunn," out in her well swept yard. He had his dusty hat in his hand as he took a seat to read on the front steps. She greeted him with her usual cheery greeting as she dropped into her rocking chair that her son Grady had fashioned especially for his mother. Pony Johnson was showing his age these days, as Sallie Ann Dunn was. They had both weathered the hard times of "reconstruction" days that followed the defeat of the Confederate states.

Chapter 8

Hard Times, Claude's Death

The Rebels had a debt to pay, they lost their property, their money was worthless, and the slave labor that tended the cotton fields was freed. Those two that sat on the Dunn front porch were no stranger to hard times and disappointment. Sallie Ann had even lost her identity. She had found herself at the mercy of strangers and victors. She had no "bed of roses" as the child bride of Bill Dunn, himself an embittered young man that knew only hardship and hard labor. Perhaps he drank too much, and demanded too much of his children. Couldn't it have been that he was preparing them for the cruel world that awaited them as they grew up to take their places in the workplace, and society?

Mr. Johnson did business with a teamster that furnished oxen to loggers that used oxen to skid logs from the nearby Flint River swamp to the hill. He paid Sallie Ann for the ox, milk cow, and her last new calf. In the deal he would deliver her a younger milk cow from his herd. The gold money he paid her with would enable her to pay Mr. Easterlin down at the store the debt she owed him, Teddie's doctor bill, and still have a small "nest egg" to tuck away for a rainy day. Little did she know that day was not far in her future.

Before the new year arrived, Teddie, still on crutches, came swinging up the path with a sealed message that Miss Maggie had sent to his mother. It was from the undertaker at Rome, Georgia. With trembling hands, she opened the yellow envelope emblazoned with the words "Western Union." She did not cry out, as she read the first sentence, only tears formed in her eyes as she stumbled through the words, "It is with deep regret that I inform you that your son, Claude Dunn, died on the above date after a long illness with a venereal disease. His remains will be shipped to Andersonville for burial; copy to W.T. Dunn, Atlanta, Georgia."

Miss Maggie had copied the message and sent her porter, Sam, down the street to Ida's store for her to come down to the depot, as she had some bad news for her. Ida was a sensible young woman that knew the ways of the world. She felt responsible for her mother and young brother. She only sighed as Miss Maggie informed her of the death of Claude Dunn, just younger than her. She looked the operator in the eye and spoke, "I am not surprised, he was so handsome and full of devilment, and the crowd he ran with."

Ida sent a message to the undertaker in Americus to meet the passenger train at Andersonville and inter Claude's remains in the churchyard beside his father, Bill Dunn. Lastly she informed the undertaker that she would be responsible for the funeral bill. A preacher was found to say a few words before the grave that would soon be opened in the red clay to receive Claude's body.

The men at the store fell silent as the porter from the depot told that the train would unload down at the depot from the baggage coach that would ride just behind the engine of the evening passenger train from Atlanta.

Ida closed her store, locked the door, and hung a white bow of ribbon on the locked door knob. She hurried down the path to the yard gate that she had swung on as a child. She straightened her face as the worn out rusty ax head on a chain attached to a rusty chain pulled the gate closed behind her. She reminded herself of her brother "T's" words of wisdom to redouble her efforts in a time of trial.

Teddie had a roaring fire going in the fireplace as the day was cold. Ida burst in as she never knocked, "Where is Mama?" she blurted. Teddie asked Ida what was the problem to bring her home at this hour. She handed Teddie the telegram for him to read. He limped to the garden where his mother was gathering turnips, and told her to come to the house and talk to Ida. Sallie Ann braced herself for bad news. She never dreamed that Claude would be the first of her children to die; he was so young and handsome. The shock left her numb. She dropped the turnips and ran to her kitchen to console Ida and Teddie. She could be the strong one. She prepared herself for the sad occasion that lay ahead of her. She knew that the neighbors would be coming to give their condolences, and sit the night through to watch Claude's body till day break.

Aunt Mollie had been sent to "attend" Mrs. Dunn. She was to remain there until she was no longer needed, a good and faithful servant. The two women, one white, one black, had shared what little goods of this world that they might have had, through these hard times. You might say they were in the same old leaky boat. No longer was it master and slave, it was two older women that were simply friends in time of need.

The engineer that sat at the throttle of the passenger train knew that he had a corpse in a casket behind his "high-stepping" engine. He knew the Dunn family, tough old Bill, the section foreman in the years past, W.T., Jr. had climbed aboard the engine at Macon, as the train crews were changed.

He had told the old engine man, Wallace Scovill, that Claude Dunn's body was his passenger that morning, and please blow a mournful note on that engine's whistle when he reached for the whistle cord as he passed the station board before Andersonville Station. Out of respect he would blow for signals with his quieter air whistle. Wallace Scovill removed his cap, out of respect, removed his greasy leather glove, and extended his hand to shake "T's" hand. "It's a great honor to handle the boy's remains on my train. I have been on this run for many years. I remember when you were on your father's gang. He might have taught you well as you are a road master now. No disrespect, Mr. Dunn, but I was well acquainted with your brother. I well remember the time he and some of his friends pulled a prank on me. I was running late one day between Americus and Andersonville, and as I latched back on my engines throttle, coming out of Camp Creek Bottom, my driving wheels began to slip on the rails that had been well greased. I had to have my brakeman uncouple the engine after backing the train to the Creek Bottom. I then had to open my sand valve and sand the rails for traction. I lost thirty minutes off the train's schedule, and was put on report. I will always believe that it was one of Claude Dunn's pranks. I also heard tell that when he grew up he made one of the best "lightning slingers" on the line. He could send and receive messages and train orders faster than any other operator, and was headed to make a train dispatcher." "Yes," "T" replied, "He kept us all laughing with his practical jokes, and stories. Paw gave him several thrashings out behind the tool shed but he was out for fun and frolic. It must have caught up with him, sad as he was only 22.

Minnie Dunn had come from Pearson to attend Claude's funeral, but Charlie had to cover her agency at Pearson, as it was only two miles from Kirkland, Georgia. The whereabouts of Emmitt Dunn was known only to the good Lord above. Grady Dunn was off somewhere on the line of road on an "extra gang." Sallie Ann's neighbor brought cooked food to the home place that Minnie took charge of. She loved to cook and eat at the drop of a hat. Aunt Mollie had come over to the home place and had everything in order, the yard swept, the cow milked, eggs gathered, and beds made.

The walk from the graveyard was not long, but to Sallie Ann, it was a far piece. She remembered how she had carried Claude right up under her heart before he was born. She never told anyone that he was the most handsome of her boys, and he tugged at her heart strings when he went out into the world. She was made of a tough fabric and the thread of fortitude that ran through that fabric was the toughest. She dried her tears, thanked the good Lord that she had him for 22 years, and that he still was very much alive in her heart. "T" Dunn assured his mother that he would settle the funeral bill in Americus after he had a long talk with Teddie, still on crutches, that he would have to be the man of the house, as he was the last of the Dunn boys.

"T" walked down to the water tank along the railroad tracks, where the trains stopped to fill the locomotive's tenders with water, pumped from Sweetwater Creek. All the train crews knew the Dunn boys at Andersonville, as they were railroad folks.

"T" threw his grip up into the gangway of the squat powerful engine stopped at the water tank that was pulling a night local freight train. He greeted the engineer that was "oiling around" his engine with a long spout oil can, calling him by his first name. "How about hopping a ride to Macon with you fellows? It would be a pleasure Mr. Dunn; you just take that brakeman's seat ahead of the fireman, he can ride the back of the tank and 'cut' little chunks of coal to help the fireman as we do have a heavy train tonight."

The fireman was a busy man there at the water tank. He let the water spout up, slammed the water tank lid shut, climbed down along side the locomotive, opened the ash pan lever under the firebox, climbed back up the deck before the firebox doors, attached the steel shaker bar to the stirrups that rocked the firebox grates to expel the ashes and clinkers of the burnt coal that spent itself boiling the water in the boiler to generate steam, whose expansive pressure had powered the locomotives driving wheels. The ashes that were dumped there at the water tank between the rails were wet down with water to kill the heat left in them. Clouds of dirty steam arose that smelled of sulfuric acid that had an odor all of its own. Again the busy fireman dropped to the ground to close the ash pan lever. The engineer had sat in his seat rereading his train orders with his eye goggles pushed up on his cap. He was anxious to get on down the road, as he had a schedule to meet. He heard the ash pan lever click shut. He lowered his goggles to protect his eyes, folded his train orders written on green tissue paper, stuck them in is overall "bib" pocket, reached up for the engine's whistle and blew the signal loud and long to recall the rear end flagman. He leaned as far out of the cab window as he could to receive the "highball" signal from the conductor that rode in the caboose car coupled on the rear of the long freight train.

The kerosene lantern's light that was seen by the engineer was twirling around and around in a "highball" signal that gave him the authority to proceed. The conductor was the "captain of the cars" and as all captains were in command of their train, just as a captain of a ship on the high seas.

The engineer answered the "highball" with two whistle blasts, as recognition of signals, and the train was leaving Andersonville, Georgia and its cemeteries, both national and local with one more dead man interred into the red clay earth that surrounded the poor little village where the handful of living souls lived, far outnumbered by the dead.

There was a difference in this burial; it was the flesh and blood of Sallie Ann Dunn, the first of her brood, just in his prime. "T" Dunn's mind was wandering as he sat jostling along through the night, sitting in the cab of the Central of Georgia locomotive on the fireman's side of the boiler. His first thought was that he was glad that he had chosen to be a trackman on the railroad; at least he could labor in the fresh air and daylight, and sleep most nights in his own bed, with his family.

Each time the fireman stepped on the pneumatic pedal that swing the "butterfly" firebox doors open, the night sky was set aglow by the reflection of the roaring fire that was being stoked by the sweating fireman as his scoop swung back and fro between the tender car's coal pile and the gaping firebox door, adding "green" coal to the roaring inferno therein. The engineer's hand was upon the throttle and his eyes were upon the road as the engine labored over the steep grades and roared through the bottoms that would soon bring the train to the large town of Americus, Georgia.

"T" remembered the trips on the passenger train that his mother would make to Americus each spring with her eight children around her, to shop in the stores there for a better selection than she could find in the simple stores of Andersonville, or on the railroad company "Grab" coach. She would always buy the boys a new straw hat for the summer. On one trip, he remembered that his baby brother Teddie, in his excitement, had stuck his head on which his new straw hat was affixed, out the open coach window on the return trip and it had blown off and Teddie cried as it bounced along the tracks. That was a long time ago, but it had stuck in his mind. It was back in the days when Bill Dunn was alive and maintained that section of track. He came in the next day with the straw hat, somewhat worse for its wild tumble beside the passenger train, but all in one piece. "Is this the hat Teddie lost?" he asked. Teddie claimed his hat, only to hear his father's stern words, "I should give you a whipping young man, for being so careless." Sallie Ann took up for Teddie, but Teddie never forgot how quick-tempered and stern that his father was. "T" was stern but had the kind streak that he inherited from his mother.

Those days were long gone, as "T" Dunn was now the man of the Dunn household. He had placed his brothers, with the exception of Emmitt on good railroad jobs, and he would have to look around for Teddie a job. Teddie was too small to do the heavy labor of a trackman, perhaps Minnie could place him in a telegraph office, as he had shown talent as a "lighting slinger," but now he was crippled, but could get about without the crutches; he limped but was "game."

"T" knew there was no future there at Andersonville, unless you owned land or was a government worker at the national cemetery and those jobs were political, Northern Politics.

Teddie was left with his mother and Ida. He had nearly been taken by his gun accident, but had been spared. That wheel of fortune was still spinning around Teddie's head, that was chocked full of ideas and notions. Spring was not far away, and May would bring the annual crowd of northern people to their celebration of victory and emancipation of the slaves.

Chapter 9

Fitzgerald and the Yankees

Teddie had not forgotten the excursion train from the new colony town over at Fitzgerald that was "booming" as the new railroad, the Atlanta, Birmingham, and Atlantic was being extended to Atlanta and Brunswick on the Atlantic coast.

Fitzgerald had been designated as the center of operations and many jobs were being filled by railroad folks. That was not Teddie's main interest, it was that he had not forgotten the little red-headed Yankee girl, that her friends called Tessie. She was just a developing child, but her blue eyes were full grown, and had caused his heart to pound in his small chest and his face to flush. Would she return this ""Decoration Day"?" He would just have to wait and see.

Teddie had quit school, but stayed busy at any odd job he could find. He helped around the depot, swept the warehouse for Miss Maggie; in fact he was her right hand man if 17 years old made you a man. He wore long pants and chewed "Brown Mule" chewing tobacco, shaved a little fuzz from his chin every weekend with his father's old straight razor, shined his shoes, and sometimes wore a bowtie. He parted his black hair in the middle. He was quite a little man. The young girls around town thought he was cute and he was the "apple of his mother's eye" by no doubt, now that Claude lay sleeping beside his father down at the churchyard by the schoolhouse.

Mr. Easterlin had bought a dynamo to generate electricity that lighted his store until closing time which was well after dark most nights. Teddie went down to the store evenings to listen to the senior men talk politics and local gossip. The ranks of the old veterans of the Civil War grew thinner each spring as time was taking its' toll. On occasion, a "horseless carriage" as they were referred to, came putting into town from Oglethorpe or Ellaville or even Plains, Georgia through roads that were either nonexistent or in poor condition in those early days of the 20th Century.

Horses were afraid of the new-fangled automobile, mules and wagon buggies and oxcarts moved most freight to the railheads. The Standard Oil Company still delivered kerosene to Andersonville from Americus in a tanker wagon pulled by two of the largest mules in the county; Missouri mules, the old men at the store told Teddie. They also told him that the engraved letters on the mule's hooves, "J.D.R," stood for the initials of their owner, John D. Rockefeller, the richest man in the whole U.S.A.

That awoke something in young Teddie's mind that he would be rich some day, but believe me he had a long way to go before that day arrived. His mother was holding twenty dollars for him, but she had loaned most of his nest egg to his fast dealing brother Charlie, and he had not heard from him in quite some time.

Times were changing; sailing ships were a thing of the past. The era of steam was here. The old men at the store predicted that automobiles were just "Play pertties" of rich people and would soon be forgotten. Anyone would tell you that horsepower and mules would do the hard labor around the town and trains and steamboats would do all the cross country transportation. Some foolish people were even trying to fly, like birds do, what were things coming to?

"Decoration Day" came and went. Teddie set up his lemonade stand by the depot. His heart fluttered as the special train backed into it's spur track. The train from Fitzgerald, pulled by a jaunty "cabbage stack" wood burning engine emblazoned with the company logo, "Atlanta Birmingham & Atlantic," the new railroad based at Fitzgerald. They crossed the Central of Georgia Road at Oglethorpe, Georgia, only ten, miles to the east, as they continued on to Atlanta. Teddie should have made a note of those bold letters, AB&A, but his thoughts were of the young Yankee girl, with the kinky name of "Tessie." She was not among the young people that came from Fitzgerald, the only town in South Georgia populated by northern "pilgrims" as they were called by the people that lived at Andersonville. Where could she be? Had her folks failed and gone back north? Surely she hadn't married as she was but a slip of a girl. Death was unlikely. Should Teddie ask some of his lemonade customers where she was? But, he didn't even know her last name, only "Tessie." His day was ruined, but he was use to disappointment and went ahead with his lemonade business. If he was to become as rich as Mr. Rockefeller up in New York City and have his initials engraved in his mules hooves, "T.N.D.", he vowed he would never fall in love again.

Sallie Ann Dunn was a very resilient person. She had left her grief in the graveyard on the outskirts of town. She was a homemaker, her vegetable garden was a good place to shed her tears, and the hen house resounded with cackling hens that had just laid another egg. The petunia bed had to be watered with cool clear water drawn from the deep well that Grady had drilled before he left to seek his fortune. The ox was gone from under the Mulberry tree that he loved to lay under and chew his cud on hot summer days. The honeysuckle vines were once more clinging to the yard picket fence now that he was gone. Mocking birds and Joe Rees built nests in the gnarled half-dead limbs of the Mulberry tree that had seen the Yankee prisoners unload from the trains and march to the prison stockade to starve and die.

Sallie Ann never had an idle moment. She had done a days work by the time the sun was half way to its' median. The first streak of daylight found her lamp burning and a fire crackling in her cook stove in the kitchen room behind the main house with the "dog trot" hall that separated the front "setting room" with it's starched lace curtains and "settee" with it's velour cushions. The "ladder back" straight chairs and generous rocking chairs with split white oak bottoms, arranged before the big fireplace constructed of local stones chinked with red clay mortar. Behind that front room was the dining room with more straight chairs set around an unpainted oak table with two "let out" leaves to accommodate a large group of diners. The chair at the head of the table was like the others, but had "arm rests" and was reserved for the "head" of the family. There was a smaller dining table in the kitchen room that was used for every day use. On the other side of the "dog trot" were the bedrooms, only two, one for the father and mother, and the baby crib. The other bedroom was for the girl children. The boys had their bunks in a "shed room" behind the main house. "Slop jars" were in the bedrooms, and had to be emptied every morning. Women were proud of what little furniture they had poor as it may be. The front rooms had a wooden washstand, a porcelain washbowl and a pitcher of water sat on the top with a shelf below for homemade lye soap, towels, and wash rags. A "looking glass" hung on the wall, over the basin. There were no closets, clothes were hung in a shiffarobe or on wooden pegs driven in the wooden wall. Most people in those days took a bath in the kitchen, whether they needed one or not. Water was drawn from the well on the back porch, heated in a big cast iron kettle set on the cook stove to heat. The galvanized washtub was set on the well-worn kitchen floor that was scrubbed with a "corn shuck" mop most every day, so a little water splashing from the tub did little damage. A long handled "scrub brush" applied to the right spots lathered with the lye soap would leave the skin pink and clean.

Men folks sharpened their straight razors over a leather "strop" and shaved their whiskers standing before another looking glass. Clean underwear that had been boiled in the backyard and hung to dry on a clothes line, strung from the Mulberry tree to a high post at the cow lot. Sunshine on a sunny morning could bleach a lot of union suits hung on that clothes line.

Sallie Ann Dunn insisted on her children being clean and well groomed, even though they were poor. Minnie Dunn loved to cut hair. She was the barber in the family until she left home. Her father insisted on the girls not to cut their hair, but she "bobbed" hers off after Bill Dunn died. She cut her brothers hair monthly as they sat in a straight chair on the front porch. She had some hand clippers and scissors; she knew but one style, short and parted down the middle. The boys winced and moaned from under the cloth she had pinned around the necks with a big safety pin from Ida's store. After she left home, Sallie Ann did the best she could to groom the boys hair, but on those annual spring train trips to Americus, she would march the younger boys to the barber shop for a "professional trim." She had her "egg and butter" money to spend on the children. The haircuts cost only a quarter of a dollar each.

The house the Dunn's lived in, on the ten acres, was showing its age and was a bit dilapidated, now that Grady was away on the "extra gang," and living in a railroad "camp car" with a bunch of other "trackmen." The house had never been painted, but the flower beds and potted plants Sallie Ann tended with such loving care was what everyone looked at. She had her Petunias in the spring, Zinnias in the summer, Corn Flowers around the borders of the front porch, Dusty Miller for a background, a Dorothy Perkins rose rambled along the yard fence that bloomed in profusion with pink blossoms. There was a trellis at the end of the porch covered with Morning Glory vines that bloomed in the morning and closed with the noontime sun. The whir of ruby throated humming birds could be heard as they visited each blossom.

Sallie Ann put every old leaky cook pot filled with dirt from the hen house to grow Geraniums, red, pink and white, on the porches.

Nobody would even notice a loose weatherboard, or a rotting floorboard as there was no building inspector in Andersonville. This was the only home place she would ever own thanks to her firstborn son, W.T., Jr. It would make a home for her and Ida, for the years to come, even her baby Teddie would walk down the path as she knew he would, that ended at the railroad depot there along the busy tracks of the Central of Georgia Railroad.

Chapter 10

Teddie Goes to Pearson

Minnie sent for Teddie that summer. She wired her mother from Pearson, where she was agent on the Atlantic Coastline Railroad to put Teddie's clothes in his bag and send him on the train for Albany, change trains there for Pearson, and she would let him stay in the boarding house that she lived in. He could stay in the room with her as she was still single, and he could eat at the table that was "set" each day for the boarders.

Teddie's job would be to sweep out the depot and the platform where the trains stopped. There was a bicycle there at the depot which also was the Western Union Station, and Teddie could hold the position of "delivery boy." Along with the "official" bicycle, was a "pillbox" cap with a copper plate attached to the visor. It read, "Western Union." The recipient of the message customarily gave the delivery boy a 10 cent tip for the delivery. That would be his salary, besides his "board bill" which Minnie would pay each week.

Teddie could hardly wait to board the passenger train that would take him off into the world, the world that his brothers were seeking their fortune. He knew little about Pearson, Georgia down in the "flat" woods of South Georgia just north of the mysterious Okefenokee Swamp that covered thousands of acres of unexplored land although it was 1906.

The train from Macon, Georgia would arrive at Andersonville early in the afternoon and have him in Albany before dark. There he would have to wait for his "connection" to Pearson located on the "Coastline" that ran between Albany and Waycross. Sallie Ann was sitting on her front porch among her flowers as she told Teddie of this upcoming adventure. She had told him little of the world that lay beyond the national cemetery, the depot down by the tracks or the general store, his sister Ida's store on the square where Captain Wertz statue kept its vigil, chiseled in marble. She knew he had never been farther from Andersonville than Americus. There were many temptations out there in the world that had claimed the life of her beloved Claude.

Andersonville had gained a national reputation as being the burial ground for young men on their first adventure out in the world beyond their loved ones and fire side. A person had only to walk over the hill from the village along the railroad tracks to view now upon rows of headstones that marked the graves dug in the red clay soil of middle Georgia where they lay sleeping for eternity; a witness to the cruel realities of the world. All of those young men had arrived at Andersonville, who now lay sleeping over the hill on the same passenger train 42 years ago, that would take the baby she carried in her arms that cold winter night 16 years ago. She knew he had to leave one day, but he would take a bit of her heart with him to Pearson, Georgia. She still had Ida at home and they could get by, but that ramshackled old house that the Dunn's had called home would seem large and lonely with all her sons, Minnie and her husband gone.

Teddie himself had no fears for the paths unknown. He had about stopped limping on his gunshot leg that bore a lump where the bird shot abided. His small frame was a dynamo of energy just waiting to be set free. He had listened to the old men down at the store talk of life and love in very graphic terms. He knew the pitfalls of illicit love, the vices of strong drink, and heard cigarettes called "coffin tacks." He had never attended with any regularity, but knew right from wrong, taught at his mother's knee.

He ate the dinner Sallie Ann had set on the kitchen table for him. The menu was rather limited, but tasted good. There was fried side meat, black-eyed peas, fresh baked cornbread with plenty of cow butter and cane syrup, dipped from the keg on the back porch. There was a pitcher of buttermilk, left from the last butter-churning that had been lowered into the well shaft to cool, that he washed the plain food down with. She also had him a lunch packed for the trip on the train. It consisted of a cold baked sweet potato, a piece of the fried pork, and two well buttered biscuits left over from Sunday dinner, all packed in a half-gallon lard bucket, with the lid snapped shut.

Teddie dressed in his "Sunday best" outfit after a bath in the battered old tin washtub set on the kitchen floor. Sallie Ann laid out his best clothes, a white starched shirt and a black bowtie, a pair of knickers with a blue serge coat that matched. Teddie was very excited as he stepped into his union suit and a thrill went through his frail body, just to think he was leaving Andersonville and the old balky milk cow that would slap him in the face with her tail as he milked her by lantern light so early in the morning. As he buttoned his shirt and tied his black tie around his collar with a "fore-in-hand" knot, he felt a pang of pain go through his young heart at the thought of leaving his mother and sister, Ida. He consoled himself with the thought that they were both capable people and had somehow gotten along before he was born. He took the knickers from the chair back where they hung and stuck his stockinged feet into "fancy pants" that came to his stockinged tops just below his knees. With a twinkle in his eyes, he parted his black hair down the middle of his head, slipped his feet into his high top black shoes his mother had so carefully shined. He was ready to go, and I might say he looked quite "dapper."

There were three classes of people in southern towns in the early years of the twentieth century, the landowners, the poor, and the very poor. Railroad folks, if they had a job, fit somewhere in that middle group. Sallie Ann had Teddie's pasteboard, "please don't rain" suitcase packed with his meager belongings, two pairs of Carhart overalls, under drawers she had made for him on her old faithful "Singer" foot pedal sewing machine. She boiled and sun-bleached the empty twenty pound "Nampa's Best" flour sack and fashioned the soft cotton cloth into all sorts of clothes for her girls and boys, and herself. She included Bill Dunn's straight razor, lather mug, and strop, not so much as Teddie needed them but it would do much to make the boy feel that he was a man at last. The only Bible Sallie Ann owned was a large clothbound "family" Bible that Bill Dunn had bought from a "traveling"Bible salesman, soon after they were married up in the hill country of Tennessee. Bill Dunn had recorded the name, and date of birth of each of his children on the pages at the back of the large book. He had a fine style of penmanship that was as everything he did, was to perfection. He was not a religious man as he only opened the pages when Sallie Ann had a new baby. Teddie's name and date of birth was last on the list, Teddie Newton Dunn – August 31, 1891, on the page of that old book, which was by now timeworn with its corners "dog-eared." It sat on a stand in the front room gathering dust.

Teddie hugged Sallie Ann's neck, and promised to write often and would come home for Christmas. She blinked back her tears as she watched her baby walk down the same path that the others had taken to catch the passenger train that puffed to a stop down at the station that had been a second home to the Dunn children.

Miss Maggie Callen was still agent operator, sitting in her padded swivel chair before her desk that bore the telegraph instruments and levers that displayed the semiphor boards that signaled the trains from both directions. She well knew that Teddie would catch the train that day as she had copied the message on her "Royal" typewriter as Minnie Dunn had sent it from her office down at Pearson, Georgia in the "flat woods." She knitted sweaters there at her desk, between calls, but recognized Teddie's footsteps as he mounted the wooden steps of the station. She, herself felt pride as Teddie stood before her desk. He had been so anxious to learn the Morse Code and never shirked any chore she had asked of him. She would miss him. These thoughts ran through her mind as she wrote him a "dead-head" train ticket on "company stationery" that the bearer, Teddie Dunn, was on "company business" from Andersonville to Pearson, Georgia, "one way." The conductor on both the Central of Georgia and the Atlantic Coastline passenger trains would duly "punch" the "dead-head" ticket with the metal punch that they carried in their coat pocket, as he was loaded onto their train.

Teddie sat on the station platform's well-worn bench with his card board suitcase awaiting the wail of the steam whistle that heralded the approach of the train that would take him away from his mother's apron strings into the world of working men on the railroad. As was the custom in small towns, and villages, along the "line" loafers, unemployed workmen, and old men, would assemble at the train station to see who came and went on the "local" passenger train. They would note if the train was on schedule, set their watches by the "official clock" at the station, maybe even pick up a well read newspaper some passenger had left scattered on the waiting room bench. "Train Time" was the "event of the day" at Andersonville.

It was few men of all classes that didn't chew tobacco in public or women that didn't dip sweet snuff at home. Some men even chewed tobacco and smoked a pipe at the same time. No "gentleman" spit tobacco juice on the sidewalk or waiting room floor. Large brass spittoons were placed in waiting rooms for the convenience of passengers. Men were quite skilled in the art of spitting long distances to "ring" a spittoon, although misses did occur as witnessed by brown stains on the floor and walls, adjacent to the spittoons. Some of the larger stations had "restrooms" as the toilets were called for both men and women. These primitive toilets were seldom used, only in an emergency as they were seldom cleaned and were some distance out back.

Ice was a prized commodity in the countryside. Andersonville had no "ice plant" to manufacture ice, as the larger towns and cities had. The passenger trains were supplied with a large block of "ice plant" ice in Columbus or Macon that would in most cases, last for the "run" of trains. The block of ice was loaded into the baggage coach of the train. The crew men, known as the "baggage master" would kick-off a chunk of ice that he had chipped off with his ice pick to stations with an agent or work gangs along the line of road.

The station at Andersonville was better equipped than the ones at other small towns as it was often visited by northern veterans or survivors of the union prisoners that were buried over the red clay hill in the national cemetery. This station had a "porter," a black man named Pluck Jordan. He was a portly old fellow that was Miss Maggie's "Man Friday" around the depot. He helped the passengers with their luggage, swept the waiting rooms and kept the water cooler filled with spring water and ice when he had any. There was a rack fastened to the wall near the cooler which he kept supplied with cone-shaped paper cups. They were shaped in this manner so they had to be held and not set on a table at someone's home. Yes, a cup of ice water on a hot summer day in Middle Georgia could be as nice a "treat" as a fellow could have in that day and time.

Pluck tended the flower beds Miss Maggie insisted on having around the station grounds that would greet the "pilgrims" arriving from the north. Andersonville was not without a means of public transportation. There at the station, around "train time" sat a "surrey," a two-seated buggy with a driver's seat in the front. It had a canvas top and side curtains that could be taken down. It was as the sign announced, "for hire." The rig was owned and driven by an ancient colored man that had been a slave as a young man. He was known as Uncle Gabriel and he had taken the family name of his master, Johnson, as was the custom. The "Hack," as the vehicle was called, was powered by an iron gray mare mule that looked as old as the "Hack" and its owner. The three of them looked like they had arrived at Andersonville aboard Noah's Ark. The mule and its driver both would be napping in the shade of a giant Red Oak tree that grew before the station. The old mule's ears would droop, and he cocked one of his hind legs as he slept, standing in the shaves of the "Hack" where Uncle Gabe sat in the driver's seat sound asleep. Have no fear; they both would spring to life when they heard the station blow of the approaching passenger train. These trains were the only link rural communities had with the outside world. The general store was just a hop and skip from the railroad depot. The crowd of old men and loafers that assembled there to pass the time playing checkers or telling yarns of the past, and would lay the checker board or newspaper aside and amble over to stand on the station platform to witness the activities of "Train Time." Watches were set by the "Standard Clock" in Miss Maggie's office. Comments were made on how late the train might be today or purchase a bag of peanuts from the old peanut vendor that always showed up at train time. Without a doubt, the most important observation that the crowd of loafers made was who "came or went" on the Central's passenger trains, that not only brought passengers, but "express" shipments of perishable merchandise like fish that was salted in wooden barrels and baby chickens (bitties) in perforated cardboard crates.

The U.S. mail was in canvas bags locked with a "padlock." Patent medicine, quinine, Lidia E. Pinkham, Paregoric, Black Drought, Three C's, Caster oil, Epson Salts; you name it. Bundles of city newspapers, like "The Macon Telegraph," was most popular as it carried the local area news. What a boring place Andersonville would have been had no "train time" come twice a day, one from the west, the other from the east. The only difference in the usual course of events, under the August sun, was a departing penniless passenger with a lunch pail, his earthly belongings in a pasteboard suitcase. The thing that this passenger possessed made no visible showing as it was deep in his small body, was an indomitable will to succeed and amount to something more than a plow hand or cotton picker there in the red hills. This passenger was named Teddie Dunn. "Train Time" was nothing new to him as he, like the others, had done his share of meeting the train, but today he was to be a passenger on the train that would take him away from a life of simple drudgery there at Andersonville. The railroad had been his family's livelihood and Teddie went to ride not only to Pearson and his sister Minnie's depot, but to a better life somewhere out in the world. That wheel of fortune today would be the spinning drivers of that speeding locomotive, that was taking him away from the only home he had ever known, there beside the tracks at Andersonville.

The distant sound of the train whistle brought Teddie's mind back to earth. There was a pang of sorrow that went through him as he loved his mother and sister Ida, but their lives were cast here and they were happy to have a home and store, as many people had only the shirt on their backs, and lived from hand to mouth, they were the "very poor" and there were many of them around in the southern states that were still suffering from the loss of the Civil War even in 1905.

The "dead head" ticket in Teddie's pocket had been punched by the conductor of the passenger train that was now hollering "All Aboard" as he threw the coach's stepstool into the vestibule, climbed aboard himself and pulled the signal line cord that blew an air whistle behind the engineer's seat up in the locomotive cab. The engineer then answered the signal with two short whistle toots with his steam whistle, opened the engine's throttle that exhausted through its cylinder cocks beneath the cylinders. The exhausted steam hissed and raised the red dust of the main street of Andersonville. The black smoke that wafted back over the coaches and the station platform obscured the crowd of people and the depot from Teddie's view, but his sights were set on new visions far away from the track that his father and older brothers had tended. They were all gone and now it was his turn to leave home, poor as it may have been, but there had been much love from his mother, Sallie Ann Dunn.

Teddie wasn't the only one that felt a pang of sadness; Sallie Ann had heard the same train whistle as it took her baby away. She prayed to the good Lord to watch over him as he set out to seek his fortune in a wicked world.

Things would never be the same around the home place without Teddie. He had been her heart as Grady had been her hands. Hardships and childbearing had left its mark on Sallie Ann; she was nearly fifty, just a bit stouter, the wrinkles around her eyes and mouth were deeper, and her hair was no longer salt-and-pepper, it was salt gray. One thing was not on the wane, she still possessed a sunny disposition and a quick smile never failed her. She still had her daughter Ida to make a home for. Ida, nor her sister Minnie had shown any interest in marrying and starting a family. None of the Dunn children had shown any interest in farming the eroded hillside farms around Andersonville. Ida seemed content to live with her mother and tend her "notions" store on the square and take in sewing. She was just a homebody, plain and simple approaching thirty years old. The other Dunn children, including Minnie, were afflicted with a fever that had but one remedy, the rumble and roar of a heavy freight train as it struggled out of Camp Creek Bottom, the black smoke that drifted over the village or the shriek of the passenger train's whistles in the night, even the tinkle of the brass bells mounted on the locomotive boilers, seemed to bring a twinkle to their eyes. It seemed as though they would just wither away if they were not along the tracks or sitting in a depot, "slinging lightning" on a telegraph instrument, copying a train order or writing a switch list for some conductor on a midnight local freight train. It seemed as though crossties and cold steel rails, spiked to them, was the elixir of life to them.

Teddie had never been to Albany, Georgia; it was larger than Americus and had a depot that served both the Central Railroad and the Atlantic Coast Line, not to mention several "short line" railroads that served South Georgia towns that had sprung up in the flatwoods. He had to wait on the connection to Pearson, Georgia, Teddie opened his lunch pail and ate most of the lunch his mother had packed for him. There was a new drink on the market; it had a "catchy" name, "Coca Cola." The "fizzie" soda water was served in soda glasses at drug store fountains by young men called "soda jerks in special glass bottles shaped like an hourglass in stores that had a "drink box" packed with chipped ice. He would have splurged and invested a nickel in one, but he had no nickel to his name, as his brother Charlie had left on his nest egg and as yet, never paid him back.

The electric street lights came on at dusk and lit the sidewalks of Albany and the ACL passenger train from Montgomery, Alabama that would drop him off at Pearson, Georgia on its way to the junction town of Waycross, Georgia was late tonight. Darkness brought on a deluge of negative thoughts to a young man venturing from the only home he had ever known, a loving home that had sheltered him from the hard, cold facts of the outside world.

He stretched out on the waiting room bench, but sleep would not come to a homesick lad on his first night away from the home on the side of that red clay hillside. His mother and sister Ida had somehow held things together since his father was buried, in the churchyard back in Andersonville. There was a lot Teddie did not know about city life.

The thing he did know a lot about was how a railroad was built and operated as railroading had been the topic of conversation around the Dunn household, just as farming was around a farm family. He knew how to consult the train schedule board posted in the Albany station that he had never seen. He knew the train numbers. The ticket agent behind the iron grill-work window informed him that the "Coast Line" passenger train would arrive soon and he should go down to the train shed by the tracks and have his ticket in his hand to present to the train's conductor as there would be a rough crowd boarding that eastbound local passenger train that stopped at Pearson, Georgia, just before midnight.

The weather was fair and the stars shone in the night sky. He wondered which one he better "hitch his wagon to." The sky was now his limit as Andersonville had once been. The headlight of the eastbound train brought his mind back to reality as its beam stabbed the dark night with its yellowish carbide light even before the steam whistle and the tolling bell announced its arrival, 30 minutes late, at the Albany station.

Teddie grabbed his suitcase and looped his lunch bucket on his free arm that held his dead-head ticket. The earth trembled as the high wheeled "Pacific" type engine puffed past the waiting group of people that were departing Albany on the station platform. The black people were in one group, the white people in another as there were two "day coaches" one for the black folks, the other for the white folks. The white coach was known as the "First Class" coach, the black coach was known as the "Jim Crow" or the "Second Class" coach.

Teddie knew that people bound for Albany would be unloaded first, after the conductor and the train porter opened the coach vestibule and dropped his stepstool to the loading platform with a "clop." "Paying fares" as ticket holders were known would be first aboard to claim any vacant seats, the company "dead heads" or employees were loaded last and sat wherever they could find a seat or stand in the aisle. The conductor instructed the passengers that were boarding "his train" as he punched their tickets, to turn to the left if they were colored or to the right if they were white. That was just the social system as it was in the Deep South. Few, if any, passengers questioned the practice even though the south had lost the Civil War and the slaves were freed.

The train's coaches were crowded with passengers, all kinds of humanity, young people, old people, poor people, and in-between people.   Teddie clung to his suitcase as it held all his earthly belongings, the things that he would need in Pearson, if he ever got there. The first class passengers had a "step up" ticket that entitled them to ride the Pullman car that brought up the rear of the train. They enjoyed the privacy of the roomettes and make down seats with privacy curtains that were beds at night. There were no dead heads aboard the Pullman coach or "riff raff" as the step up fare was beyond poor folk's price range.

The conductor took pity on Teddie, as he looked so small and forlorn sitting on his suitcase, in the aisle of the day coach. He gave Teddie permission to pass through the 2nd Class coach to the baggage coach where the young fellow could stretch out on the packages and mail pouches. The baggage master would tell him when the train arrived at Pearson, and he as a railroad employee, as his pass ticket implied, could help the baggage master "work" Pearson, Teddie's new home.

The clatter of the old baggage coach's steel wheels on the steel rails interrupted by the clickety-clack of the rail joints soon lulled the tired boy to sleep there on the mail pouches. The train flew through the night, with the engine's whistle shrieking a warning to livestock on the track and road crossings. This train was a local train, one that stopped at all the regular stations and flag stops, if a passenger was destined there or "flagged" by a person desiring to become a passenger. The first regular stop was a small town named Sylvester. The baggage master opened the sliding side doors to unload "checked" baggage and mail pouches. Teddie jumped right in to help him, as he was not lazy, and always a willing worker. The conductor soon called "All Aboard" and the engineer whistled off.

Train rides were not new to Teddie as he had ridden them with his older brother to Americus on many occasions. They had gone there to see a Wild West show; Buffalo Bill's show had made an impression on his mind, the Indians, bareback riders, and trick shooters. Then there would be the circus, Ringling Brothers, Barnum & Bailey's. These "road shows" traveled all over the USA on special trains, known as "show trains." Local boys could earn a pass to the afternoon performance by helping raise the giant tents. Those days had passed, when his brothers had left home at Andersonville. Now it was Teddie's turn to leave the nest, ready or not.

The next stop on the Coast Line was Tifton, which was quite a town, with a large station. The train came to an abrupt stop that lasted for half an hour, loading and unloading people and goods under the electric flood lights that lit the station platform nearly like day. Teddie observed all the station activity, and felt that he was not merely a passenger, but a part of the scene, that would provide his "bread and butter." He vowed that someday he would be a station master and handle the railroad company business, come hell or high water. He remembered the cold March days he had plowed a mule hopping from one cold clay clot to another. He hated that clay that would stick to the plow like cement and resist his every effort to remove it, man, that was the dangedest clay in the whole wide world there at Andersonville away back there, somewhere back there in the darkness of the night.

The baggage master called the names of the flag stops along the way east to Pearson, Brookfield, Enigma, Gladys, Alapaha, just villages along the line.

Teddie could tell by the exhaust of the engine that the land was flat, and the grades there were not as steep as they were around Andersonville. The night was dark and the moon was just a sliver in the star studded sky, but the gloom of the giant longleaf pine trees towered into the sky at times it seemed as though the train was going through a tunnel, the trees closed in so close.

Where were the farms, the big cotton fields, the ravines, the big farmhouses? He could see sawmills by the yellow light of the burning sawdust piles behind them and the piles of giant pine logs, waiting to be sawed into rough lumber that was so in demand to build the great cities of the north. At each of the stops along the line, he could hear the croaking of a thousand bullfrogs that populated the flat lily pad ponds that punctuated the virgin pine forest.

Willacoochee was the next station, the baggage man informed the wide awake boy. Teddie tried to pronounce the Indian name that he had never heard of before tonight. It did have a rather exotic sound to a fellow from upstate Georgia. The only Indians Teddie had ever seen were members of Buffalo Bill's Wild West Show that could ride horses with such abandon. This area of Georgia had been Indian Territory until Andrew Jackson had driven the last of the Creek and Seminole Nation into the depths of the Okefenokee Swamp and across the southern border of Georgia into Spanish Florida, only eight years ago. There were many Indian names that remained on the creeks and rivers that drained the flatwoods. The river, with a strange Indian sounding name that formed the northern boundary of the true flatwoods, was the sluggish, black water, Alapaha River.

Teddie noted that the train slowed down, and he knew by the hollow sound of the train that they were crossing a long trestle. He asked the baggage man what river the train was crossing. He called out "Alapaha." The soil was of a different nature, beyond that river, what hills, or ridges that existed were sand, the bottoms, or "bays" as they were called where deep black muck formed over the ages by rotting leaves and logs. The red clay hills that Teddie had known in Central Georgia now lay far behind.

Chapter 11

South Georgia Flatwoods

The people that inhabited South Georgia were different, although they were of British extraction. They spoke the same language as he did, but with more of a drawl. The people that met the night train as it chugged to a stop at the station there at Willacoochee were "flatlanders" only one generation away from the original settlers that had pushed westward from the Atlantic coastal settlement of Savannah or Brunswick. These hardy people whose forefathers had been flavored strongly with Scotch-Irish blood. They had been the survivors of bloody Indian wars, Yellow and Malaria Fever, carried by the swarm of mosquitoes, and black bears that raided their crops and livestock.

There was danger at all points, Cottonmouth Moccasins and huge Diamondback and Cane-Break Rattlesnakes lurked in the wiregrass pine forest and the black water rivers and the creeks that fed them. Alligators lay sunning on the mud banks, and bellowed their mating call at night. Panther's screams were often heard in the remote bays. These people took these hazards in their stride, as they knew little of the outside world. They, as the Indians before them, had become hunter-gathers; barter was common among these "swampers." They were proud folks, pledged allegiance to very little, other than family and friends, which were few and far between, and liked to be known as "Georgia Crackers," but don't confuse them with "Florida Crackers." The name, "Cracker" had been bestowed on them by outsiders as they drove their ox teams along the sand rut roads. They relied on the platted cowhide whips, ten feet long that they carried coiled on their shoulders, to get the attention of their beast of burden or any varmint that crossed their trail. The crack of those whips could be heard long before they arrived as they popped the whips with a report much like a gunshot. Their aim was legendary, as they could pop a fly off a critter's back at some distance.

This area of Georgia had hardly known that the Civil War had occurred as the Yankee invasion of General Sherman's forces had passed them by as it marched through Georgia leaving a trail of devastation from Atlanta to Savannah. There were no spoils of war to be taken by the north, no cotton, no fine mansions to burn, no slaves to free, no cities or towns to plunder and they knew of the fears and dangers that lurked in what was known as "The Pine barriers" of Coastal Georgia.

Teddie had heard the old men around the potbelly stove at the store talk of this area when he was a boy at Andersonville. In fact, he had heard Sallie Ann, his mother, wonder why his sister, Minnie, had ventured into this wild frontier area. Why hadn't she gone to Macon, Columbus or even Albany, which were civilized. Now her baby was following Minnie down there into the boondocks.

Times were hard enough, there in Middle Georgia, but civilization had brought some degree of safety and order to people. Sallie Ann shrugged and went ahead with her chores with a song on her lips and a smile on her face, there in Andersonville, that's left from one memorial day to the next one in the year to come. She received letters from her older sons, all but Emmitt, somewhere in the west, unknown to any of the other Dunns. Charlie Dunn had married a saw mill owner's daughter, Lillie Tillman, from Kirkland, Georgia down in the flatwoods. Sallie Ann was glad that Charlie had married well, as he was a bit wild, and she hoped that this Lillie could settle the boy down a bit.

Don't think for one minute that Charlie Dunn wasn't a go-getter. He was good at what he did, was a good telegrapher, loved the hunting and fishing that he found in South Georgia. There were few fences to cross, quail abounded in the longleaf pine wiregrass ecosystem, and after all, Mr. Tillman, his father-in-law, owned several thousand acres of pineland, along the Alapaha river drainage. Teddie didn't care much if he hadn't seen Charlie at Kirkland Station where he was an agent. The lights were out, and the station was closed at the small village of Kirkland between Willacoochee and the larger town of Pearson, the county seat of Atkinson County and the destination of the wide-eyed young man from Andersonville.

Minnie Dunn loved her baby brother, Teddie, who was now standing on the threshold of manhood. Minnie had inherited her mother's sunny nature to the point that she was somewhat of a "gusher." Pearson Station was open and Minnie stood in the depot door, framed by the yellow lights of several kerosene lamps turned up to just before they started to smoke their glass chimneys, Pearson was not yet wired for electricity. The Atlantic Coastline Railroad had brought civilization to the sprawling sawmill and turpentine industry that was nurtured by the vast pine forest that seemed inexhaustible to the ax and crosscut saws of the native woodmen, not only a raw civilization, but jobs to a new class of people.

Minnie Dunn had a good job, and she was paid hard cash every month. She had a nice room at Mrs. O'Hara's Boarding House across the wide sandy street from the railroad depot where she was agent operator for the Coastline Railroad and the Western Union telegraph lines.

She spotted Teddie, as he swung from the train's baggage coach, to the station's wooden platform. He bade the kindly baggage master goodnight as he grabbed his suitcase from the open door of the coach. Minnie had business to attend to as she performed her duties that would soon be shared with Teddie. He was rather rumpled, and smutty from the long ride behind the coal burning engine that was now quenching its thirst at the tall water tank beside the track. Both Minnie and the station there at Pearson were larger than he had expected them to be. She had thrived on those bountiful tables Mrs. O'Hara set three times a day. Teddie hoped his sister would not hug and kiss him there in her office door, in front of all those grown men, but she did. She laughed a lot and commented on the knickers he was wearing, as they just wouldn't do, here in Pearson, and how she remembered when Claude had worn them on the streets of Americus, back in the "Old Country" as the flatlanders referred to Middle Georgia.

Teddie had long since eaten the last of the lunch his mother had packed for him in the lard can that now lay empty somewhere along the tracks that he had just come along. He was hungry, dirty, and tired from the long train ride and the many stations that it had stopped at. Minnie told him to scoot across the street to the boarding house, a large unpainted two-story wood frame building, built of the native heart pine lumber that was known world-wide.

Teddie had walked in sand before, but never none as deep and shifting under foot as this street that was churned by wagon wheels and draft animals hooves. He could vaguely see the piles of animal manure that shown darker than the white sand. There was a rough board sidewalk in front of the boarding house where a lamp was burning brightly in the front window, framed by lace curtains. He wiped his feet on the high steps to the wide front porch and its empty cane back rocking chairs, fashioned from white oak, by a local craftsman. He reached for the doorbell mounted on the massive front door that a person had to twist the key by hand to make a prolonged ring that the lady of the house could hear, clear to the big kitchen down the wide hall with its oversized "wood range" as a cook stove in those days was known. These old ranges were equipped with a warming oven on the smoke pipe, and a hot water reservoir on the side of the firebox.

Mrs. O'Hara answered her door bell, as train time usually brought travelers to her door for rooms and meals. She welcomed all comers, at all hours, as long as they were sober, had some cash on their hip, and were white. Teddie was welcomed, although he had no cash on his hip, but was on Minnie Dunn's "ticket" and would be white after a good scrubbing with octagon soap and hot water from the wood range's hot water tank.

Mrs. O'Hara had judged many people over her lifetime, and she seldom made a mistake, even at first glance. Teddie seemed to pass the landlady's inspection at a glance, "Come right in son," she said. "Minnie told me to expect you. Come right on back to the kitchen and wash up a bit, as I have you a plate of food in the warming oven. I fixed it just for you at suppertime." She also informed him that she intended to fatten him up a bit, during his stay in Pearson. She had what was known as a "bull pen," a sleeping porch across the back of the house, just for single, working men and boys.

The bathroom facilities were rather primitive; with a pump over a lavatory. Water was pumped to a tank on a high steel frame tower by a windmill on top of the water tank. The ladies and "first class" boarders could use the wet-flush toilets at the end of the halls. The men usually went to the barber shop, down the street for a hot-water tub bath located in the back of the barber shop where they got a shave and a haircut every Saturday night.

There were black women that washed clothes for the public, for a fee, and delivered them back to the owners in a basket, balanced on their heads. Such was the every day life of single people in Pearson, Georgia. The food was good, and Teddie ate hardily. He looked like a plow line with a knot jerked in it, when he pushed away from the large wooden table covered with an oil cloth cover. He drank two glasses of a drink that was new to him, he liked it very much. Mrs. O'Hara informed him that it was sweetened ice tea, as there was an ice man that came every morning in a mule-drawn wagon to pack her ice box on the back porch with factory made ice, supplied by the O'Neal Ice Company in Jacksonville, Florida, shipped on the northbound Atlantic Coastline train that originated there in Jacksonville.

Teddie slept like the dead for the rest of the night, although the cot he slept on there on the boarding house sleeping porch left much to be desired. Other men came and went throughout the night, but Teddie was dead to the world. He awoke with a stark in the strange surroundings, and smells of breakfast cooking in the nearby kitchen. Suddenly a large black woman with an arm full of split pine firewood was standing over him. A broad smile spread over her face. "Young man," she said. 'You sho ben a sleepy head. Yo sista Minnie setten at da table wid dem udda white folks. She tole me to roust you outta dat bed and wash yo face in da wash basin by the back door and present yoself in the dining room."

Teddie knew he had a friend in the woman that was known as Aunt Pet, the main cook at Mrs. O'Hara's Boarding House. Minnie Dunn rose from the long dining table that was stacked high with platters of scrambled hen eggs, cured ham, sliced bacon, fried crisp, bowls of red-eye gravy and steaming corn grits, white as driven snow. One of Aunt Pet's helpers was coming through the swinging door to the kitchen with a large tray of soda biscuits, right out of the wooden range's oven. On the "dumb-waiter" in the center of the table were pitchers of cane syrup and, moulds of fresh-churched cow butter. Minnie greeted her brother warmly, as she pulled out a straight chair next to hers, there at the dining table. After a hug that came close to lifting Teddie off of the floor, they sat down, side by side. Minnie had worked late at the station and most of the other boarders had gone to their daily labors, leaving them to their selves, there at the table. Minnie had already helped her plate and was on her second cup of steaming hot coffee. She started in on Teddie, after their greeting. She asked him how his leg healed after the gun accident; how their mother and sister Ida were getting along, back in Andersonville. She continued on as she shoveled in the contents of her breakfast platter. She did ninety percent of the talking. Teddie answered his sister's questions as best he could, but he wished she wouldn't have mentioned how small he was and that she intended to "put some meat on his bones." He remained silent as he thought how successful his sister had been putting on quite a bit of meat on her bones since she had left home, four years ago. Why, Minnie must be in her mid-twenties nowadays, and still single.

Teddie had not dressed in his knickers, but in a pair of khaki long pants out of his pasteboard suitcase, his white shirt and celluloid collar and bowtie. He passed Minnie's inspection. The two of them crossed the sandy street and railroad tracks to the depot. Street scenes here at Pearson were very different from the streets of Andersonville. Not only the streets, but the people were different also.

This country, in deep South Georgia, and the surrounding counties still were "open range," meaning that livestock was free to roam as they pleased through the woods and swamps, not to mention the unpaved streets of Pearson. A herd of shaggy "briar goats" had passed the night, after the train had run, on the station platform. Minnie "shooed" them off the platform, but they left their droppings to be swept off.

There was a "hog wallow" in the ditch occupied by a razorback sow and her litter of little spotted pigs, having their breakfast. The sow's ears had been notched by her owner with his "mark," but she was free to roam and make her living off the land. She was very protective of her pigs, and could show her temper if disturbed while nursing her brood. Teddie could see a small herd of spotted cows and calves down by the Railroad water tank where the locomotive had dumped its ashes. Minnie told her brother that the cows scratched through the ashes for salt and minerals, when the ashes cooled. Teddie had never seen such cattle, they were not milk cows. They were stock that the settlers had found here, wild cows that had escaped or had been abandoned by the Spanish people in North Florida, a hundred years ago. Their horns were long and their hip bones were prominent. They would make their living year round in the bays and burnt over wiregrass range, which stretched for miles and miles to the south.

The men would build traps and bait the cows or go on horseback, "cow hunting" to coral the wild cows and "mark" their unbranded stock with their "brand" burnt into their hide with red-hot "branding irons," then turned loose again. If a fellow could catch a cow or calf without a brand, he could burn his brand on it, and it was legally his property, as his brand was registered at the courthouse, there at Pearson, Georgia. Minnie explained that if you had property you valued, it was best that you build a fence around it to keep the stock out. Woe be to anyone that bothered branded or marked livestock.

The people on the streets were lean and gaunt; many were red-haired and freckled-faced. Few were clean shaved, many were barefooted. The men wore wide-brimmed, high-crowned black felt hats that had little shape left in them. Overalls were in all stages of disrepair. The older men wore homemade cotton shirts and heavy britches held up by strong yellow gallowses, and high cowhide boots that had never been polished. They originated from a dozen families that had wandered into the heartland of Georgia from the coast. Some Indian blood also coursed their veins from away back, before records were kept. They seldom "hired out" at public work, and were self-reliant and tightlipped. The women folk were plain; I mean plain! They went barefoot also, never wore makeup, nor cut their hair. They balled their long hair up in buns and wore cloth bonnets made of checkered gingham or feed sack material. Both long skirts and blouses or long dresses were worn, with the ever present bullwhips coiled on their shoulders, to drive livestock out of their way. Snuff was used by most grown women, as was chewing tobacco by the men folk, and best an outsider had better not get clever with either sex.

The climate was milder here than it was north of the "fall line" of Georgia. The buildings were seldom built of brick or stone, native wood, logs or rough pine lumber, some hand hewn right on the building site by the builders. Neighbors helped each other "raise" houses and barns, long before the railroad came through, life had gone on.

There were a few upper-class citizens, merchants, lawyers, landowners, and doctors that dressed better and lived in substantial houses, drove buggies or rode fine saddle horses, they dressed as people did in cities or large towns, but they were few and far between. The big steam powered saw mills were owned by rich folks in far away places.

Chapter 12

Pearson and Minnie's Depot

Minnie Dunn showed Teddie around the Railroad station, the Western Union bicycle, and the official cap with "Western Union" written in bold letters across the front. She told him that most of the telegrams that she copied were destined for the bank just down the main street, or for the Suwannee Manufacturing Company, a large sawmill, just outside of town. The reputation of the Western Union Company was the prompt delivery of messages, and a signed receipt by the recipient to confirm the time of delivery, rain or shine. When there were no messages Teddie was to sweep the platform and freight warehouse, every morning, fill the depot lamps, switch stand targets lamps with kerosene and trim the wicks.

There had been a saloon in Andersonville. Whiskey was sold by the drink at a wooden bar; by the drink, or bottle, with a few exceptions to law abiding, responsible white citizens. The black people had their own "joints" or bought liquor from "bootleggers." Pearson was more on the style of a Wild West town, board sidewalks, open saloons abounded Dance halls, with "Taxi dancers," women that danced with anyone for a fee, to piano and fiddle music. These women were not local women; they had been brought in on the passenger trains by "hustlers" from the cities like Jacksonville, Florida or Columbus, Georgia. They knew their "trade," and could "fleece" a half-drunken cracker man and convince him that he was having fun and a great dancer all the while. Things were relatively quiet on the street of Pearson through the week. Come Saturday night, the town was filled with people from all over the area that had come to town, to "trade" and let off a little steam and Pearson was the place to do it. They came with their families and alone, from the backwoods, work camps, railroad work groups, preachers, loggers, blacksmiths, cow traders, card sharks, bible salesmen, fur traders, dirt farmers, and a few plain hell raisers.

The law men kind of took a vacation on Saturday nights; sins of the flesh were overlooked, as Pearson needed the cash flow. The bright lights, loud music, painted women, dealers in beer and whiskey, were wide open for business and the saloon doors swung both ways, in and out, and when a fellow's money ran out the bouncers would give the poor befuddled fun seeker the old heave-ho, out into the sandy street. Bar tenders and floozy women, seldom drank while on duty, as they needed all their wits to plying their trades, as theirs was a profession, the oldest.

Transportation in that day and time was primitive; distances were far between settlements in the pine barrens of South Georgia. The rural people came to town in mule drawn wagons and two-wheeled carts, loaded with their families and trade items, be it ax handles or fur pelts. The poor people came in ox carts pulled by plodding oxen that had "snaked" logs, or "broke" land in the springtime. Others came on horseback or on foot. Some of the more affluent, flagged the passenger train along the new lines that were penetrating even the most remote regions of the area. The freight trains were bringing the splendid pine and red-heart cypress logs to the steam sawmills that sawed them into the lumber that was so in demand, worldwide.

In the Pre-Civil War days, cotton had been king in the red clay hills of middle and north Georgia. Large plantations and small farms grew cotton for the world market. Cotton and its culture here in South Georgia took a back seat to lumber pine tar, the turpentine and rosin it produced when distilled. What farming that existed in South Georgia was known as "patch farming," just a man and his family clearing a few sandy acres on an upland cut over ridge. These people found the moist sandy land, well suited to grow tobacco, and corn to feed the mules, horses, chickens and pigs. Some farmers would set a copper still up in the bays where there was a creek to furnish cool water to distill corn liquor, on the sly of the law. Some was sold to bootleggers to be hauled away to cities in Georgia and Florida. Some was consumed right there on the farm by the men folks.

Tobacco, pine gum, and corn liquor, were the cash crops that paid the bills at the store for the flour, salt, coffee, baking soda, tea, spices, lye, harnesses and horse collars for the mules and horses. Calico cloth, buttons, pots and pans, plow points, gun powder, dynamite, fish hooks, shot gun shells, cartridges, bullets, kerosene for the lamps, and possibly a sack of peppermint candy for the children or a sack or two of sweet feed for a pet saddle horse.

The creeks and rivers furnished fish for the catching by any means convenient, hook and line on a cane pole, cut from a cane break along the creek where a fellow was going to fish. Bait, earth worms, was dug from where the slops and dishwater was flowing out of the kitchen door. When the water was low, seines were used to furnish fish fried on the creek bank in hog lard along with corn meal "hush puppies" and washed down with iced tea. These fish fries were sort of a social occasion as several families would gather to eat a bait of branch fish.

Hunting was another important source of food for the table. It was not so much of a sport as it was something for the cook pot to fill the bellies of lots of hungry children. Game was plentiful in the forest, bays and hammocks of the flatwoods, varmints abounded, and none were spared for "table fare." Rabbits and squirrels were favorites in the winter, quail was trapped and shot in the open cut over woods and around the field hedge rows. Morning doves flocked to corn patches that hogs and cows had been turned into. "Dove shoots" were a fall occasion for neighbors and friends to gather, doctors and lawyers from the towns, like Pearson, were invited and doves by the one-horse wagon load were shot. The women folks cleaned and fried them, served with hot grits and flour gravy, soda biscuits and butter were hard to beat on a cold November night. Most evenings, leftover cornbread, crumbled in a bowl of sweet milk or buttermilk, was the table fare of the crackers.

While we are on the subject of hunting, let's not forget the hound dogs, and bird dogs that every farmstead owned. Why, they were members of every rural family, and they thrived on table scraps. They were used to drive deer to hunters stationed along the swamp edges, at deer stands, to be shot with buckshot. Wild turkeys moved in droves, but were very wary, a noble bird that was most impossible to stalk. A patient hunter would locate a large tree where the birds flew up to roost at dusk for the night. The hunter would station himself in a "blind" of bushes and leaves before dawn near the roost tree. The turkeys would be scattered upon lighting on the forest floor, and would gobble and cluck to regroup for the day's forage. The skilled hunter would "yelp" them up, with a homemade caller, made from a block of seasoned cedar wood, hollowed out to form a small narrow box he could hold in the palm of his hand. With his other hand he held a strip of slate, that when drug over the thin edges of the cedar box would imitate the cluck or yelp of the confused birds, which would run to the sound they thought was one of their drove. A quick shot and the noble bird would find himself roasted in the woodstove oven and gracing the table of a flatwood family for Thanksgiving or Christmas dinner surrounded with cornmeal dressing, homemade sausage, and sweet potatoes, scratched from a "tater hill," where they had been banked after digging in late summer. The taters were put on beds of fresh gathered pine straw, covered with dirt, capped with an old tin washtub to keep the bed dry. They kept well through the winter in these "tater hills."

Collards or turnips from the fall garden were boiled with fat salt pork. The holiday feast was topped off by blueberry, huckleberry, and blackberry or gooseberry pie. The berries and wild grapes had been gathered by the children and womenfolk back in the springtime, and canned in glass fruit jars, boiled in the wash pots out in the yard. About the only thing that was store bought on the table was the salt and pepper, the flatwoods and the fields were their larder, and they seldom went hungry unless they were lazy or just drunk on their own home brew.

Night hunting with the dogs was enjoyed by both old and young men. The hound dogs were of several breeds, red bone, blue tick, black and tan, or a mixture of breeds, known as a pot licker hound. Varmints of the night were pursued by the dogs and their owners, some on horseback, some on foot, some with rifles, but always with kerosene lanterns, a sharp ax and a burlap sack.

Moonlight nights were preferred but any night that was cold enough to keep the rattlesnakes and cottonmouths in their holes, would do. Opossum and raccoons were the most sought after. These varmints often ended up in the cook stove or cook pot hung over the huge fireplaces in the cabins that were called home. The main object of the night hunt was for fur hides or pelts. Raccoon hides were good as cash money when scraped and stretched on barn walls to cure in the cold winter wind. Opossum hides were of less value. Bobcat, fox, and other hides brought a premium price, if well cured. The hunters would build a fire and listen for the hounds to jump a varmint then the race, and finally a change in the tone of baying of the dogs, announcing that the critter had been "treed," or run into a hollow. The dogs could make the woods ring with the music of their tongues.

Alligators abounded in the swamps and rivers that drained to both the Atlantic Ocean, as the Satilla River does. A ridge of pineland divided the drainage of the Alapaha River to the Suwannee River that meanders through North Florida's west coast along the Gulf of Mexico.

These denizens of the dismal swampland around Pearson were valued for their hides and "gator tail meat." The belly hide was in demand for ladies purses and shoes in the fashion centers of the world. The muscular tail meat tasted like a cross between chicken and pork, and when boiled with rice and hot peppers, could fill many a youngun's belly. These critters were hunted by men in boats by torch light. The gators eyes would shine like live coals in the blackness of the night. They were wary critters, and could be dangerous when cornered, but would be gigged, shot and roped by the hunters.

The owner could always recognize his hound from the others of the pack. Many tales of past hunts, jokes, political opinions, or just plain gossip was aired around those firesides that furnished light and warmth, away from the prying ears of the womenfolk there in the solitude of the backwoods of far South Georgia.

Life was far from perfect here, but people seemed to enjoy their freedom, and surviving on what the land had to offer, and their "wits." Most everyone had a touch of Malaria Fever, which they controlled with quinine powder measured and taken on a pocketknife blade. Women often died young in childbirth as doctors were few and far between. The roads and trails were impassable in wet weather, mules were slow and oxen were slower. Midwives delivered most younguns, and they were in a survival of the fittest situation.

About the time that Teddie Dunn made the scene at Pearson, the railroad was bringing a great awakening to the area that had slept for so long. The rattling trains mounted on the steel rails pulled by fire breathing, smoke belching, steam powered locomotives were bringing in not only people and products, but the twentieth century with all its new fangled inventions, and luxuries.

From the cities of America, towns were springing up where only the sighing of the wind in the needles of the virgin pine trees that swept endless to the blue Gulf of Mexico on the southwest and the stormy Atlantic Ocean to the east. A way of life was changing. Where once a five hundred acre tract of virgin timber could be bought for a muzzle-loading shot gun or just by staking a claim; now it had a cash value.

The chants of the sweating Irish and Negro rail gangs could be heard as the graders and track layers were opening avenues through the wiregrass flatwoods. Seldom would a person be out of hearing of axes chopping or the swish of cross saws that brought the monarchs of the forest, the towering pine and cypress trees, crashing to the ground or splashing into the shallow black water sloughs known as simply, "the round about," "the feather bed" or "knee knocker swamps," half moon lake" or perhaps "sand sink". There were no red clay hills in the flatwoods as there were around Andersonville, the city of the dead, along the tracks of Central of Georgia Railroad that was well established before the Civil War.

Chapter 13

Railroads & Industries of South Georgia

The railroads that were crisscrossing South Georgia were built along the ridges of land that the animals and Indians had trodden, long before the white settlers had arrived with their axes, guns, steel traps, tools and whiskey. Some were just "tram" roads that connected with the state chartered lines that hauled people and finished products such as lumber, crossties, rosin, and turpentine, termed "forest products." Some of them bore the names of the saw mill owners that the tram roads supplied with giant logs. Names like Suwannee Manufacturing Co., Lee Tidewater Cypress Co.., Herbord Lumber Co, Twin River Lumber Co., Valdosta and Ocilla Railroad.

The public service chartered lines were the Ocilla, Valdosta Southern, the Georgia and Florida, the Waycross Southern, the Brunswick and Birmingham, and the new line that was being constructed at the time of Teddie Dunn's arrival at Pearson, was the consolidation of several tram lines.

The Atlantic Birmingham and Atlantic, the AB&A road would play a large role on the life and love of the unbeknown young man that was sweeping goat pills ("manure") off the rough board platform of the railroad depot that his older sister was agent telegrapher operator, a lightning slinger, at Pearson, Georgia.

Please, dear reader, don't for one moment think the wheel of fortune had stopped turning for the boy with a slight limp, that stood on the threshold of manhood in a land that was standing on a threshold, only it was not manhood, but development and it is not for me to judge whether the changes that would come were good or bad.

Minnie sat her brother down on a waiting room bench and told him the nature and ways of these cracker people. She advised him to steer clear of the element that made home around the saloons and Honky Tonks that preyed on innocent young fellows with a few dollars in their jeans. She asked of his progress with the Morse Code and the telegraph instruments that were clacking away in her office. Teddie assured her that he knew the Morse Code dots and dashes that represented every letter of the alphabet. He would be required to both send and receive messages and train orders sent to stations along the line by dispatchers that could send codes over the wires like lightning, thus the nickname, "Lightning Slingers," and as everyone knew, lightning was about the fastest moving thing around, unless it was women folk spreading gossip or a "card shark" slipping an ace out of his sleeve.

Train dispatchers, at their headquarters, seldom if ever repeated a "send." The operator had to repeat the "send" back to the dispatcher with style and speed, or he would never be called a "Lightning Slinger." That was more a title than a slang nickname; it had to be earned and it didn't come overnight or at a college, stated on a diploma. Practice was the key and Minnie would see to it that he would earn that title as he was too small and weak to ever make it on the track gang as Grady or W.T. Dunn had.

Teddie had his cap set to better himself and break out of subsistence farming or hard labor that was the lot of so many people in America. He had no family resources to send him to college, or offer him a position in a family business. The only thing that the Dunn family had to offer was a hard scrabble living with a pick and shovel that had put bread on the table, and calluses in their hands.

Pearson had little to offer a young man; it was just the county seat of a rural South Georgia county that had the good fortune to be located on a mainline railroad that afforded a means of transportation for the only resource Pearson had been blessed with, the seemingly endless pine forest that stretched southward through Atkinson and Clinch county to the Florida state line. The forest had brought jobs other than farming and stock herding to South Georgia. A strong lad, black or white, could find work at the steam sawmills, turning logs on a sawmill carriage as it flew back and forth to meet the teeth of a giant circular saw filed to razor sharpness that chewed its way through the pine logs that had been sawed into square cants of heart yellow pine that gave off, one by one, the prime lumber that brought top prices on the world market. That money didn't end up in the tar smeared overall pockets of the men that labored from the time the sawmill whistle shrieked at the first crack of dawn until it sounded at dusk dark just as the night hawks called for their mates and the frogs in the mill ponds started their nightly serenade and the water moccasins slid from their dens to feast on them.

The lumber companies did furnish their mill hands with shotgun houses, long and straight like the barrel of a shot gun, constructed of their own product, pine lumber, and a brick chimney for a cook stove and fireplace fueled with pine "slabs," the waste sapwood and bark saved from the logs to square them into "cants." These minimal houses were on mill property and grouped in what was known as "sawmill quarters." A strong back and a weak mind was the only qualification to gain employment at the mill. The mill owners and the lumber brokers up north pocketed the real money that the lumber brought on the world market. Little was wasted at the saw mills, the sawdust that was "tickled" from under the high speed saws that sang its high pitched song to accompany the chugging of the steam engine that kept the big flywheel spinning that was "belted" to the saw husk, the pulley that transmitted power to the saw blade.

The highest paid employees of the mill, other than the manager and the bookkeeper, was the sawyer, a man that "gauged" the saw from his station above the log carriage, where he had a clear view of the log that was the next candidate to be milled into lumber. He had a lever on a notched gear that he could adjust the saw position to saw the most lumber from the cant. He was skilled at his profession and was, with few exceptions, a white man wearing a pearl gray Stetson felt hat and khaki pants and shirt and collar and bowtie.

The sawdust that accumulated on his hat brim as he controlled the powerful saw was the badge of his profession. These gentlemen were usually iterant and stayed at the best boarding house in Pearson. The other important positions at the sawmill were the millwright, that kept the mill in adjustment and repair. He was talented as a mechanic, tinkerer and could fashion with the help of a blacksmith, replacement parts for the mill, usually a white man that drew good wages and lived in a nice house on a quiet side street in Pearson.

Next was a lumber yard foreman, that sorted and graded the rough lumber for drying in carefully racked stacks for air drying on the yard before being moved to the planning mill for finishing and onto the dry kiln, a large brick oven, heated by steam piped from the mill boiler, for a final drying that the buyers demanded before it was loaded by black laborers into boxcars of the Atlantic Coastline Railroad sidetrack that "spurred" into the mainline track that would whisk the lumber to Savannah, Brunswick or Jacksonville to be loaded into ships bound for far away markets.

The waste wood, slabs, sawdust, and planer shavings would be used by the black fireman to fire the mill boilers to furnish the steam that powered the mill. Sawdust and shavings were so abundant that they found many uses around Pearson, they were free for the hauling as they accumulated around the mill yard in great piles and when set afire, they would create a blue smoky haze around the mill and nearby town that did discourage mosquitoes that plagued the area in the summertime.

The fresh milled sawdust was spread on much used floors of barrooms as many men just spit tobacco juice on the floor. The barkeepers would sweep the whole mess into the sandy streets out front of their establishments where the horses and oxen would trod the mess into the sand.

Tents would be raised on vacant lots around town to shelter religious revivals that drew large crowds of people that were drawn to the piano music and lusty singing of town people that were moved by the hellfire and damnation sermons of evangelists and preachers that did their dead level best to save the souls of sinners and saints alike.

Can you guess what was spread ankle deep on the weeds of the vacant lot that found itself the floor of the tent? Why it was fresh sawdust hauled from the sawmill. Many sinners were saved from the fiery pits of hell as they trod down the sawdust aisles of the "tent meeting" to kneel before the makeshift alters constructed of scrap lumber from the same mill the sawdust came from. That was not all the mill furnished; where do you think those saved souls owners were baptized on the next Sunday? You were right if you guessed the nearby sawmill pond, rimmed by lily pads that were blooming with their yellow and white blossoms among round green leaves that floated on long stems that went to the bottom of the black water.

There was power in that swamp water beneath the moss hung age old Cypress trees anchored in that same muck of the ponds edges. These trees, lilies and the frogs, snakes and stump knocker perch fish that made their home in those same waters had seen the Creek Indian squaws fill their water jugs, was now being used to quench the thirst of the sawmill boilers, and wash away the sins of Georgia cracker people that had survived the hardships of a wild land.

The pine trees were the backbone of the Industrial Revolution that was awakening in this backwoods country. The railroads were paying hard cash for wood crossties to mount their steel rails on. The little "cabbage head" engines that pulled the log trains were so named for their bulbous smokestacks, belching smoke and exhausting steam, depended on fuel cut from the forest by wood cutters and crosstie hewers. There was no coal to be mined here, so the fire boxes of the little "puffer bellies" burnt wood cut to fit their fire boxes.

British explorers in their wooden sailing ships of old were the first to realize that the southern pine trees were superior to the northern species. They grew tall and straight, clear of limbs or knots for perhaps fifty feet strong and smooth. These virgin stems were ideal for ship's masts.

The sap of the pine trees was impervious to water and weather, even the salt water of the Atlantic Coast of Georgia. This pine sap or tar, as they termed it was superior to any coating for ship hulls, sails, and ropes. This thick, sticky sap of the southern pine ran freely when the bark at the base of the tree was hacked away and a box was hewn into the wood trunk, below the wound delivered by a tool named a gum hack. This was applied by a strong hand of a woodsman. The pine sap would run freely down the sloping wound to collect in the box that had been hewn in the tree. After a week or so the wound or streak, as it was called, would heal, and the woodsman would lay another streak to the bark opposite the first streak, with his sharp hack. The resulting "face" above the box would in a couple of years resemble a house cat's whiskers, and were called by woodmen "cat faces." Other workers carrying metal dip buckets would go from faced tree to the next, dipping the amber gum with a shaped wooden paddle from the boxes which were filled with pine gum, which they smeared into the two gallon dip bucket with a handle for carrying.

Wagon trails had been cleared through the wiregrass, gallberry, and palmetto undergrowth so a wagon or cart that hauled a white oak gun barrel that held 55 gallons of the thick dip, the life blood of the pine trees. The mule or ox that pulled the "dip wagon" through the stately pine forest was trained to stand and wait on the command that the dip crew would call to it, to stop or go, as usually there was no one to drive the intelligent draft animal through the crop of boxes which could number 10,000 boxed pine trees.

Pearson was located in the center of this industry, which was known as "naval stores." The woodsmen that were employed in working the trees worked on shares with the big land owners that furnished the men who were with few exception, black men that specialized in their trade and would seldom associate with other black men. The "man" furnished his hands with barrels, the dip wagon, and the animal to pull it, and transportation to the crop, a shotgun board house, staked them throughout the winter months out of his commissary located in the vicinity of the "quarters." They were paid on the basis of the "points" of pine gum, by the barrel they brought for the dock in the quarters or the turpentine still. These stills around Pearson were big business. The gum was dumped into a large vat, boiled until the volatile steam coursed through the copper coils which were submersed in cool water that was circulated from a pond or deep well to condense the "spirits of turpentine," a clear liquid that dripped from the spigot at the end of the coil. The turpentine was very aromatic as it dripped into jugs or cans, perfuming the area with its fresh pine aroma.

Turpentine found a ready market worldwide as a superior vehicle for paint, a solvent that had many uses in industry and medicine. The sediment left in the vat was pine rosin, which when cooled, crystallized and was used as a base for varnish and coatings, soap and even dressed fiddle bows at the saloon and dance hall down the street in Pearson, or on fine violins up north in Carnegie Hall, which came out of the flatwoods of South Georgia in box cars or tank cars loaded along the stations of the Atlantic Coat Line Railroad.

Teddie Dunn's eyes had been wide open for the last few days since his arrival at Pearson. He had seen another lifestyle that was very different from around Andersonville, back in the "old country." Pearson was experiencing growing pains, as all the other towns that had sprung up since the railroad had connected the populace cities of the coast and the interior. People had come to find work in the forest industry, and the prolific railroads. As always, there is an element of society that follows the honest workers. They have no intention of working for a living or promoting a high standard of morals or stable homes. They intend to prey on the weakness of others, that one seeking their fortunes through avenues of honest endeavor, live by the Ten Commandments, build churches and school houses. These shysters, both men and women, pick the weakest characters to beguile, with their false promise of fun pleasure, and quick riches. They could care less if their victims fall by the wayside, sick, addicted to strong drink, and bad habits. The card sharks, prostitutes, bootleggers and con men would only pick their pockets, take their watch, even knock out their gold teeth, and then seek another "pigeon" or "John" to fleece as sheep to be shorn.

The passenger train from Jacksonville, Florida would always bring another fortune seeker to set his feet on the station platform that Teddie kept swept so clean, at Pearson, Georgia. Could we call these new arrivals "babes in the woods?" Among the crowd there to meet the arriving train was always members of the bad element, spotters and pimps that had an eye for innocent suckers. They were proficient at their trade as a blacksmith or turpentine worker that laid the streaks on the pine trees, to tap their sap.

Minnie Dunn was a good, kind woman, as was Mrs. O'Hara, Teddie's landlady. They were well acquainted with shysters and kept their young "ward" from Andersonville under their wings. Don't for a minute think there weren't respectful, Christian citizens of Pearson; there were churches of all faiths, mostly Baptist, both primitive and missionary that were well attended on Sunday. Schools that taught reading, writing, and arithmetic, and how to mind your manners or get a good paddling out behind the wood shed, and another one when the scholar arrived home. The good people had their neighborhood, and let the evil one stay in their well defined dens of iniquity over on the back streets.

Chapter 14

Pioneer People of the Flatwoods

The law was in a bind, so to stay, as they were not there to eradicate evil, just control it. As this was free country, and besides, the lawmen had to make a living themselves and a sheriff or constable could barely make both ends meet on the pittance that the city fathers paid them. It seemed that the shysters knew how to play the law, and it was easy for a policeman to look the other way, as long as his pockets were being "lined" with ill begotten dollar bills. Sins of the flesh could be winked at. Capital crimes, like murder, kidnapping, and rape were a different matter. Justice could be swift in the backwoods; the sheriff could save face and let the night riders do his dirty work. Juries were slow and could be embarrassing to prominent families. Behind the courthouse there was a jailhouse equipped with a gallows, but the county could be saved a lot of expense that influenced votes at election time, if a rope could be strung over a good, straight limb by a crowd of night riders. The culprit was left dangling at the end of that rope, at the scene of the crime in the backwoods, as a reminder to any poor soul that was tempted to commit a dastardly crime.

The devil seemed to go about his duty of tempting good people in the flatwoods, just as he did in the cities. Late on a Saturday night, a good church going fellow, even a deacon, could be seen "bellied" up to the bar at a saloon or tavern, toppling a few shots of whiskey as he enjoyed the company of a painted woman in a short skirt with long dangling earrings, peering over his shoulder as he enjoyed a few hands of cards in a friendly game of poker, as she "tipped" her friend across the table as to what kind of cards our good deacon was holding. There at the dance hall, back on the backstreet, a good father was dancing with a "taxi dancer" to a victrola machine's squeaky music, while his good wife was home nursing a sick child. I am sure the devil was smiling. He didn't confine himself to the "red light" district of Pearson late Saturday night. He attended churches there in the "wildwood." A good family man and his attractive wife, with her children by her side, for all appearances a fine lady in her Sunday best bonnet and long skirt exposed a well turned ankle to a neighbor gentleman, across the aisle, while all heads were bowed, as the "sin killer" preacher, was praying for lost souls. Could that have been a faint smile on her face behind that bonnet as she passed the potato salad to the handsome neighbor as all the church goers enjoyed dinner on the grounds of the churchyard. Didn't the devil hear what the preacher had to say about him? Could it be that he had beguiled this good neighbor and his fellow deacon's wife? No way, they both had good farms, and well marked stock on the open range. Only a dark bay separated the farm, and seldom did a person go into its dense gum and "gallberry bushes". Even the stock avoided it.

Friday was sale day at the livestock auction in Pearson. The wife knew her husband had gathered some of his goats and pigs, and that he and his older boys were driving the animals to market Friday. She prepared a good breakfast for her men folks and wished them well at the market. She got her youngest children and her girls off to school, banked the fire in the cook stove, took her apron off, hung it on a peg, and strolled out across the field.

Her steps quickened as she skirted the bay that separated the farms. She could see the handsome neighbor plowing his oxen on the other side of the bay, where the devil had taken up residence.

As good neighbor passed the edge of the bay behind his plodding oxen, our sanctified wife and mother was sitting on a stump with her skirts array and her knees pulled up in a most unladylike posture.

Our neighbor's plowman seemed to forget his marriage vows, and unhitched his oxen to graze, and left his plow in the furrow it had just plowed. The smile on his face was as wicked as the devil himself as he watched with pleasure.

The two sinners fell into each other's arms in an embrace that could lead to only one end. What took place there in the green wiregrass of the bay, only the devil and a wise old owl on a limb above that kept hooting…who, who, who, knew what took place.

The next day, the temptress's husband asked his good wife why her foot prints led to the bay through the fresh plowed field. She managed a smile, assisted by the devil and informed her good husband that she had gone to hunt the milk cow's calf that had strayed to the bay. She could not hide her lying eyes, and as sure as the next spring came around, there was a killing over across the bay and a hanging down at the jailhouse.

There are two fresh graves down in the same churchyard in the flatwoods now; one man with a load of buckshot in his chest, the other with a rope burn on his neck. Only the wise old owl that only keeps repeating…who, who, who, and Satan with that evil grin on his face.

The wise old preacher had prayed that his flock would listen to him when he warned that "the wages of sin is death." Oh yes, there is another sinner, claimed by the devil, a woman with a burdened mind that sits by the open fireplace on dark cold nights listening to the wind as it sights through the pines. She has perhaps a greater punishment to bear in her heart for years to come. The good book says, "Vengeance is mine," but the mills of the Gods grind slowly but exceedingly, fine.

Teddie knew right from wrong. He remembered how his brother Claude has come to a bad end, so young. His biggest problem was riding that high-wheeled bicycle through the sand beds on the road to the sawmill. He pushed it as much as he rode it, but he never went out on the route without it and the pillbox hat with Western Union, written in bold letters across the front. He was by nature a neat, clean boy and passed both Mrs. O'Hara's and Minnie's daily inspection.

He practiced telegraphy on the key that Minnie had set up for him on the Western Union wire out in the freight warehouse. The Western Union wasn't as busy as the railroad company wire. He had managed a short message to Miss Maggie Callen at Andersonville in Morse Code. She returned the message, stating that his mother and sister Ida would be glad to know that he was settled in and was on the job. Minnie just beamed as he tapped out the message slowly, but surely.

Chapter 15

The AB&C Railroad at Fitzgerald

One day, Charlie Dunn and his bride, Lillie drove up from Kirkland to visit Minnie and Teddie. They were driving Lillie's Papa's horse and buggy. This was the first sight Teddie had of Lillie. She was a slender young woman, neat and quick spoken, and only a couple of years older than Teddie.

Charlie would have been a tall man if only he would have stood up straight and gotten the hump out of his back. He, like Teddie, never went without a collar and tie, usually black. His hair was long and dark, clipped short, but a shank would not behave and along straight lock hung on his forehead. Perhaps the Dunn brothers always wore their collar and tie was because they wanted to appear as professional men, "lightning slingers," not laborers on a railroad work gang, or was it an Irish custom?

While Lillie and Teddie were getting acquainted, Charlie was in deep conversation with his older sister. He told her that the new railroad out of Waycross, the Atlantic, Birmingham and Atlantic, had their sights on building a track north to Atlanta, Georgia, and was now well beyond Fitzgerald, approaching Manchester, Georgia.

The company was advertising for agent operators and he thought he would apply for the agency at Fitzgerald, Georgia, as it was growing by leaps and bounds. People had come from the north and seems as though what was just a shack town was going to be headquarters for the struggling company.

The city fathers had offered free land in the heart of the town for two new depots, one a passenger, the other a freight house. Not only that, but a 500-acre tract for a mechanical repair shop a round house for its locomotives, a ten track switch track, an ice plant, scale track, and a coal chute.

This complex would be a terminal for train crews and the large two-story passenger station would house the dispatcher's office, and superintendent's office upstairs. The yard and shops would be located a mile or so north of town and would be named, Westwood.

Prospects were good for high paying railroad jobs, including "lightning slingers," as new stations were springing up along the line that would connect South Georgia with the populous cities of North Georgia.

The Colony City of Fitzgerald would be the center of the operation. Charlie was "chomping at his bits" to move Lillie and himself to the Yank-Reb boomtown that only a decade ago had no railroad, only a turpentine still, and a commissary surrounded by the quarters of the black woodsmen that bled and collected the "pine gum" that oozed from the "cat faces" they hacked in the tree trunks that dominated the rolling hills, just a hop and a skip from the Ocmulgee River.

Steamboat whistles could be heard as the river steamers plied the swift red torrent, stained brick red, as it surged through the red clay hills of Central Georgia. Macon had been the head of navigation on the river even before the Civil War. The Ocmulgee joined its sister river, the Oconee, just down river from Lumber City at "the forks," as it was known.

The first English settlers and traders pushed and paddled their flat bottomed pole boats from the Atlantic Coast of the original English Colony of Georgia, the southernmost colony, bordering with Spanish Florida and its capital city of Saint Augustine, the oldest city in what is now the United States of America.

The two red rivers mentioned before, the Ocmulgee and the Oconee, formed the mighty Altamaha river that emptied its muddy red waters into the blue Atlantic Ocean between Savannah and Brunswick, Georgia at the Altamaha's mouth. The port town of Darien would accommodate the shallow draft sailing vessels of that day and time, which were shallow draft and could negotiate the mud bar of the river's delta.

Mary Musgrove established one of the first trading post and settlement. She was a very enterprising woman, half Native American, half English that seemed to be able to trod the narrow path between the red and white race. She and her white husband, who was a close friend of General James Oglethorpe, the English king's right hand man in his new colony of Georgia.

She served as a "go between" and could speak the language of the Creek Indians that were being disposed of their time honored hunting and fishing lands. Mary seemed to be talented at spreading oil on the troubled waters of the Altamaha River that drained the pinelands of South Central Georgia. Her trading post at "the forks," where the Ocmulgee River joined the Oconee River, to form the Altamaha River, branched to the west and was the jumping off place into the unchartered wilderness of South Central Georgia.

The guns, powder-lead s hot and rye whiskey she had traded for the Indians cows, deer hides, and fur had fortified the Creek warriors beyond the west bank of the big bend of the Ocmulgee River, which had never been ceded to the British crown.

The Creek Indians were slow to adopt the ways of the British settlers that were never satisfied in their westward push beyond the "big bend" area of the Ocmulgee River that bellied deep into the pine and cypress lowland, below Georgia's "fall line," where the foothills of the Appalachian had been settled by British colonists long before.

The Creek Indian nation held title to the lands that Pearson and the Colony City of Fitzgerald that had sprung up on until the year 1820. The Creek Indians were driven from their last stand by Andrew Jackson and the Georgia Militia.

The Indians had fought a losing battle against the white settlers and only after many settlers scalps were taken, as many Indian people were killed, and the pine barons opened to legal settlement. The overriding factor was that the proud Indians were decimated by the white man's diseases they contracted, as they had no immunity to these old world plagues. The Ocmulgee River had been the mode of transportation from this heartland to the Atlantic Coast at Darien. Countless virgin pine logs had been rafted downstream to the saw mills there. Pole boats had breasted the river's current, powered by the glistening black muscles of sweating, Negro slaves laboring under the merciless Georgia sun.

The steamboats that brought relief to the raft men and pole men had brought the first movement of civilization to the settlements along the river banks.

Late in the 19th Century the melodious tones of the riverboat's steam whistles were being heard less and less. The death toll of the river steamers was heard around the turn of the century. The railroad had taken the cotton traffic that once went to market on the coastal Port of Savannah, and Brunswick that could accommodate the deep draft, ocean-going steamers. The Altamaha River went back to the slumber it had known before the settlers had used it as their main avenue to Georgia's interior.

Steam power was now powering the noisy steam engines with their shrill whistles and bells clanging along the ridges of South Georgia. No longer did the whistles announce "steam boat around the bend," to the sleepy towns along the rivers.

Nowadays the whistles announced "train time" to thriving towns and villages that had sprung up along the railroad tracks that ran through the forest and swamps of South Georgia to the center of commerce and industry. Transportation seemed to be the life blood of civilization and industry, and those shining steel rails were the veins that carried the blood, and the throbbing steam engines were the heart that circulated it to the financial centers of America.

Railroads needed communication to operate trains in opposite directions, hence the need for "lightning slingers" to send messages ahead of the train over wires charged with electricity, that had to be "slung" by a human hand, even the small hand of Teddie Dunn, that didn't seem to fit too well on a plow handles pick or a shovel.

The conversation between Charlie Dunn and his older sister, Minnie was private. Teddie was getting acquainted with his new sister-in-law, Lillie Dunn and didn't hear his older brother and sister's voices some distance down the platform, there at Pearson. Little did he realize that his future was at stake, on the wheel of fortune; his fortune.

Minnie confided to her brother that when June came around she would become the bride of George O'Neil. He had been coming to the towns along the Waycross-Albany line of the Atlantic Coastline Railroad to drum up his ice business. He was the son of the owner of O'Niel Ice and Coal Company of Jacksonville, Florida. He was a handsome man in his thirties, a dapper dresser, a city fellow, not a country bumpkin or Georgia Cracker. He wore shined shoes and a tailored suit of clothes over a collar and tie.

He had stopped at Mrs. O'Hara's Boarding House on several occasions and Minnie had caught the through train to Jacksonville last Christmas to meet the O'Niel family at their fine home at Eagle Bay on the St. John's River. George had asked Minnie for her hand in marriage and she had planned to accept his proposal and engagement ring, come Christmas. Charlie Dunn was pleased to here this news, as he had often said that it was just as easy to love a rich man as it was to love a poor man. He laughed at his own joke, but Minnie gave him a swift kick on his shin. Charlie agreed that when he got a job on the new line over at Fitzgerald he would catch the train over to Alapaha, Georgia and journey over to Fitzgerald on the Ocilla Southern Railroad which connected with the AB&C railroad at Fitzgerald, and place his application for a station master, hopefully at Fitzgerald. If everything worked out and he would take Teddie as his helper, as he was Minnie's helper at Pearson.

Teddie loved his brother Charlie, but he was disappointed that he said nothing of the twenty dollars that their mother had loaned to him some years ago when he left Andersonville. Charlie seemed to have forgotten that loan of money. It was Teddie's money he had earned hauling Yankees over to the prison park that overshadowed the village.

What was it about the name Fitzgerald that somehow rang a bell in his mind? He liked Lillie; she had class, although she hailed from the flatwoods. She dressed well and didn't have a bullwhip coiled on her shoulders. She wore no bonnet to shade her face from the sun, but she wore shoes, nice shoes. She needed no bullwhip as her tongue was rather sharp and she could whip Charlie Dunn in line, shortly, and he seemed to know when her eyes flashed, she meant business.

The trains came and went. Freight trains stopped at Pearson, switching boxcars for rosin loading at the turpentine still. Lumber was loaded at the sawmill on flatcars and boxcars.

Carload lots of twenty mules arrived in stockcars with slats on the sides for ventilation, "spotted" at the stock pen chute for unloading. The mules had been shipped from Tennessee. They were big fine mules, larger than the little ones raised on vines or carpet grass.

Crossties were stacked high, awaiting the railroad timber inspector before being loaded in ragged old company gondola cars.

Watermelons were grown on the sandy new ground fields that were being cleared on the ridge land around Pearson. The mild climate allowed the melons to ripen just before the 4th of July market up north. The farmers would bring the melons in by the wagon load to be loaded in ventilator cars that the Atlantic Coastline Railroad had designed for the Florida produce farmers and citrus groves that had developed there in the last few years.

Pearson's streets were busy these days, people had money in their pockets; banks had opened. Telegrams arrived from all over the United States, and were delivered by Teddie Dunn, on his high wheeled bicycle, despite the sand beds and the dogs that took great sport in chasing a fellow with a tacky pillbox hat on his head.

The twentieth century came to South Georgia on the railroads, not dirt roads. There were paved streets and roads in cities and towns like Macon and Atlanta and up north. Oxen and mules could struggle along with sleds and high wheeled log carts. Horses could pull lightweight buggies and carriages over the rutted trails. Bridges were built of wood timbers and plank floors that rattled and banged as the beast of burden plodded them. These primitive structures were few and far between.

Shallow creeks were forded in most cases even when the animals had to swim to the far bank. The major rivers like the Ocmulgee, Satilla, and Altamaha were crossed on ferries, flat-bottomed barges that were pulled across the deep, swift water, guided by steel cables anchored on either bank. These cables could be lowered to let a steamboat pass by the ferryman when he heard the boat whistle for passage. Road maintenance was hit and miss. Each county was responsible for improvement, repair of bridges, and washouts. Once a year each tax payer of his county was required to join his fellow tax payers, or hire a "hand" to represent him to spend a period of time on "road duty."

Automobiles were the "play pretties" of well to do people. Rich men's sons roared around the cities on pavement, but autos were useless on the back roads of rural Georgia, especially in wet weather. They were expensive and undependable.

The railroad system was expanding, nationwide, moving passengers, mail, express packages, bulk freight shipments of fertilizer, logs, lumber, coal, crossties, steel, rosin, livestock, bricks, even sand, to the cities of America, and the new towns and villages that sprung up along the tracks.

In case a town was bypassed it soon was only a name, and was soon forgotten. Speed was the password these days, and the railroads were fast and dependable, almost all weather service at a price people could live with.

Bullwhips still cracked around the streets and byways of Pearson and Atkinson County. Razorback hogs still wallowed in the mud holes, sheep and goats seemed to like the protection they found around town. Street dogs slept in the sunshine, after a midnight coon hunt. Longhorn cows, known as "piney woods scrub" stock wandered around town, looking for salt or the lush weeds that grew on vacant lots. They bore their owner's brand burnt in their hide and would lay down right in the street. Traffic and pedestrians simply went around them. They have roamed the wiregrass woods and prairies of South Georgia and North Florida since the Spanish brought them over to furnish hides and meat for their armies and missions, three hundred years ago.

The railroads were a blessing to the cows. In cold wet weather, the banks and fills afforded the only dry ground for miles. The fertilizer and wood ashes that trickled from the wood burning engines and leaky boxcars resulted in lush grass that was more tender than rank wiregrass and bush browse that the flatwoods afforded. These native cows had become familiar to the steam whistles that would sound in a rapid session of toots known as stock blows. They seemed to know just when to move off the tracks and avoided being sent flying into the bush by the locomotives. "Cow Catcher," a strong steel frame that was mounted ahead of the engines pilot wheels would keep any obstacle from going under and derailing the train. The free ranging stock served a purpose to the railroads as they kept the company's right of way grazed down and open. Few cows were killed, but on occasion the train would arrive at Pearson with the carcass of a cow or mule draped across the front of the engine. Buzzards and opossums delighted on the remains of slow cows or uneducated calves.

Teddie Dunn had learned a lot about South Georgia in the time he had been Minnie's right-hand man. Today at train time he was about to witness a scene not in the backwoods but right at the railroad station in downtown Pearson, Georgia. He had learned a lot about life and a little about love. Today he would witness firsthand, an act of swift southern justice, on a makeshift stage, the platform of the railroad station, that he kept swept. That day, as was the custom, people sat in their wagons or buggies to pick up friends or family that were expected to arrive on the noon train. Teddie thought nothing of the two redheaded men sitting in a buggy with a lap robe over their knees, as there was a chill in the autumn air. The fine pair of matched horses stood at rest, dozing in the weak sunlight. The men and the horses stirred as the train sailed into the house track of the station. The conductor opened the vestibule door of the passenger coach, and dropped his step stool to the wooden platform. The first passenger to unload was a well dressed city fellow. He was wearing a jaunty costume, a tweed suit, collar and tie and wore a black hat and shined shoes. No sooner had his foot touched the stepstool than the redheaded men threw their lap robes aside and before his other foot landed on the platform a hail of well aimed bullets hit the traveler. The revolvers the men held were still smoking as the team leaped into their harness, and the buggy vanished into a cloud of dust, and the fancy dude lay crumpled on the station platform, his eyes wide open, and his black derby hat floating in a pool of red blood, his blood.

A crowd came running at the sound of the gunshots, which were not common at noontime. The sheriff and his deputy came riding their saddle horses to the scene of the crime. Minnie came out of her office with her pad of accident reports and to authorize the train to leave Pearson. The train crew seemed rather unconcerned as they hauled all kinds of people and tried not to involve themselves in family feuds and lovers quarrels. The sheriff sent his deputy after the coroner and the undertaker. He identified the victim's body as a man that the Smith brothers had put on the train and told never to return to Atkinson County, or he would leave in a coffin.

The sheriff ruled the killing "justified homicide," as he had deflowered their sister. The undertaker was given the name of his kin by the sheriff, as he knew the victim. The black hearse was loaded into the black horse drawn vehicle, by some bystanders. It left with its black curtains pulled, stirring the same dust that had settled after the getaway of the Smith brothers.

The next day, the lover's remains, wearing a shroud and laying in a pine coffin, his arms folded over his chest riddled with bullet holes, only his eyes were closed. Teddie helped load the remains into the train's baggage coach the next day at noon.

Minnie talked to Teddie one evening as they sat in the telegraph office. She confided in him that a relief lightning slinger would relive her of her station duties as she planned to go to Jacksonville, Florida for the Christmas Holidays, only a few days away. She hoped that he would assist the relief operator just as he had her. She told him that she was well pleased with his efforts to learn telegraphy and agency work.

She hoped he could catch the message wire open and wire his mother and sister Ida a Christmas telegram, in care of the agent at Andersonville, as Miss Maggie Callen had retired and moved to Americus, Georgia.

Teddie's landlady was a large woman in many ways. Mrs. Dora O'Hara was a cracker woman, raised in the flatwoods of Atkinson County. Her father had been a logger and teamster with a quick Irish wit. Her mother bore thirteen children that she raised on rations that the woods and swamps provided. Dora married well. Mr. Dudley O'Hara was a lumber inspector with the Suwannee Manufacturing Company there at Pearson. He was from Savannah, Georgia, well educated and from a prominent family. Soon after he married Dora, a Yellow Fever epidemic swept through the flatwoods and Dudley O'Hara was among those poor souls that lay at rest out at Spring Hill Church. Dora O'Hara was a handsome widow, with a large insurance check in hand in the year Teddie was born, 1891. She was weary of the ways of her childhood. She had lived in two different worlds, one as a cracker girl, the other as an uptown cultured woman and she could play either hand. She bought the large two-story white house across the railroad tracks from the yellow train station in Pearson, and remodeled it into a boarding house for ladies and gentlemen. A home away from home to accommodate travelers, school teachers, traveling salesmen, known as "drummers," and last but not least, railroad telegraphers, known as "Lightning Slingers," and a young Western Union delivery person, an aspiring "Lightning Slinger" from the old country by the name of Teddie Dunn. Teddie had much respect for wise older women and an eye for the young girls.

He never left in the mornings that he was not given an inspection by Mrs. O'Hara, or the black woman named Hattie that had taken him under her wing. She would come out of the big kitchen out back of the house with a big wooden stirring spoon waving in her big black hand, and a worn out pair of bedroom slippers on her wide feet. She was a wonderful cook and could put flesh on a hidebound runt, be it man or beast. She had lived around white folks so long that her sharp eyes could evaluate a person of either race, at a glance. Mrs. O'Hara needed no bouncer around the place as Hattie and her big wooden spoon could have put the worst of the crowd around Pearson out the door into the sandy streets to wallow with the hogs, where, by her decree, they belonged.

On the other hand, no hungry tramp, hobo or cracker that found himself broke and disgusted, couldn't ask for a meal, but mind you they ate on the back steps of "her" kitchen. It was a "rule of the road" that these unfortunates would spend an hour splitting firewood to size from the slab pile (woodpile) that she and her helpers fired her cook stove with, or they would leave with a knot on the side of their head, raised by that big wooden spoon she armed herself with.

The street dogs around town all knew the path to Hattie's back kitchen door. They were smart enough to open the back gate of the picket fence that surrounded the well swept yard with its pink and blue petunia beds and ancient gardenia shrubs with their delicate white blossoms that perfumed the air with their sweet aroma. The gate was hinged to open out and was weighted with a worn out ax head as a weight to keep it closed so the livestock could not enter. The dogs knew how to "jimmie" the gate with their snouts and await the hambones Hattie would throw out her door to them.

She was a kindly woman, with a big heart, but hated "sorryness" with a vengeance. Her parting words to Teddie would always be, "Me and Ole Miss," referring to Mrs. O'Hara, "don't have no white trash lain round dis place." Those words, "white trash," made a lifelong impression on Teddie's young mind. Her biscuits, sausage, and buttered grits had put some flesh on his bony frame at last.

Mrs. O'Hara's business abilities impressed Teddie. She never failed to collect the 25 cents Minnie left to pay for his noonday meal at the boarding house, which Mrs. O'Hara held out her hand for. She sat at the head of the "star" or resident boards table, the other iterant diners, cattle traders, and goat men, sawmill workers, all white men ate at the other table. No sad stories or floozy women were welcomed; it was cash on the barrel head. The black people ate in Hattie's kitchen with the black help where she collected the money, and put it in a coffee can, on a high shelf. Mrs. O'Hara had no cash register to ring up sales. She had a long leather purse that she kept in her bosom close to her heart between her generous breasts. She had a deft movement that could bring forth her money purse to make change or deposit the collections.

Teddie wondered how much money could be stored in that "no man's land" between those mounds of flesh, as white as the cotton grown around Andersonville, Georgia.

Minnie Dunn seldom invited her brother to visit in her comfortable quarters at the O'Hara House. There was a big fireplace with an overstuffed sofa before it and starched lace curtains hung at the long double hung windows. An ornate lamp set on a side table, another hung on a pull down chain from the ceiling. There was a wash stand and a full length mirror hung on a clothes closet door. The large poster bed dated before the Civil War sat in one corer with a mosquito net pulled aside. A hand crocheted bedspread draped over a billowing feather mattress with feather pillows covered with embroidered slips. Luxury did exist in the flatwoods, if a person had the money. Railroads paid good wages to their white collar workers, as well as the ones that wore blue collars. Minnie enjoyed these good wages to the hilt.

Women seemed to guide the destiny of young Teddie, as they would for the rest of his days. First it was his mother, Sallie Ann. She sheltered him as a child because he was her last baby and was sickly and not as strong as her other children. She taught him many traits that would prove invaluable. Honesty, pride, hard work, make the best of what comes your way and never come home empty-handed, was instilled in Teddy.

He owed his very life to his sister Ida, as he surely would have bled to death on the kitchen floor when he shot himself. The snake he shot died, but he survived after a long recuperation at his mother's hand.

Maggie Callen, back in Andersonville, always welcomed him to her railroad depot. She was a patient woman that could see the boy's dexterity to avail himself to tackle any duty or problem that lay before him. Never would he shirk a duty or complain and was very adjustable to any situation. When his sister Minnie sent for him she and Mrs. O'Hara opened a whole new world to him. These women, and don't forget the black woman named Hattie, that taught him how to spot "white trash," and to scrape his feet before he entered the O'Hara house. She hated sand or animal manure off the streets and paths of Pearson, Georgia that was in much abundance. Who would step off the wheel of fortune to shape the young man's future? Minnie was leaving Pearson to marry George O'Niel and be a member of his prominent family way down in the city of Jacksonville, Florida.

The Irish are a "happy-go-lucky" clan that believes their lives are guided by saints, Patrick for one, spirits of those gone before, leprechauns, the wee ones, luck, guardian angels and destiny. How, dear reader, do you think a true son of the old sod could be left stranded in the gloomy depot of the piney flatwoods of South Georgia? Could it be the bride of Charlie Dunn? Lillie Tillman Dunn would step forward to be Teddie's guiding star.

Spring came to Pearson, sure as a "guns are iron." Birds sang, bees hummed, flowers bloomed, alligators bellowed for a mate, and the perch fish were fanning beds in the sandy pond bottoms. Winter had retreated to the north. Teddie had started to mix and mingle with some of the local young people of good families. They had invited him to join their church group, to attend the cane grindings, peanut boiling, hay rides, barn dances, known as "frolics," or square dances. All were chaperoned by the old folk, and no sparking was allowed between the sexes. Some promenading was allowed beyond the prying eyes of the elders. Prom partners were selected from the group by an empty bottle being spun on the sandy ground beside a bonfire. A fellow's next prom would be the maiden that the bottle pointed to, be she fair or plain. Teddie had a high opinion of himself, he always dressed neat and had a quick smile. Where did he find that small narrow-brimmed black derby hat he could cock at a jaunty angle on his head when in the company of the fair sex?

Professor Clark, his honored school master had set him at the head of his class, back in that ramshackle one room school house perched on the side of a red clay ravine up in the old country of Middle Georgia at Andersonville, Georgia, "The City of the Dead."

The learned professor had crammed a lot of book learning in his young head in the five years he attended classes. His education was broadened by the old timers that sat on the well worn wooden bench under the rusty tin shed in front of Easterlin's General Store down by the statue of Captain Wertz, hung because he obeyed his commands.

Teddie's older brothers, Grady and Charlie, had drug him along on their daily hunting and fishing expeditions till he had a belly full of that sport. Grady had taught him the lesson of hard labor the hot July day they drilled a water well on the Pennington Farm, or the cold March days he spent plowing a mule in the cotton fields of Pony Johnson. That stubborn wet clay he had to kick off the cold steel plow points with his bare heel, did more to make him study the Morse Code, and how to tap it over the charged wires, to one day become a railroad lightning slinger than to be a clod hopper on a pore washed away Georgia farm.

The changing of the seasons brought a new course of events to the flatlands around Pearson. It was a busy time on the farms. Syrup had been boiled and bottled, the smokehouse was full of cured hams and bacon, and the salt boxes had a good supply of salt meat, and sow belly for boiling the fresh vegetables that were sprouting in the garden patches. All the winter chores were finished, hog killing, tobacco plant beds built, land turning for corn planting, hides cured, baled and sold.

Now the tobacco fields were set with loving care by the farmers and their families. Corn was knee high and needed side dressing with nitrate of soda, a soda water bottle cap to the hill, thrown by barefoot children and plowed under by a plowman shouting, "Gee and Haw" to guide a mule along the rows around the stumps and snags that still bore witness to the majestic pine trees that had been recently cut and their trunks drug by straining oxen yoked together, to the tram railroad "heads" to be shipped to the steam sawmills.

Busy times on the farms and forest did not stop the social life of the flatlanders. Sunday was a day of rest. All day meetings with dinner on the ground, or rather board tables out in the churchyard, were enjoyed by all, babies were shown off, ice tea was enjoyed as was fried chicken, banana pudding, potato salad, and chicken and dumplings were enjoyed by everyone.

Some congregations had no church building. They just built a brush arbor and enjoyed the fresh air of summer and the singing and fellowship after a morning of preaching the gospel. Teddie had no way to travel except on the company bicycle, or on the passenger train. He would have stuck out like a sore thumb at such gatherings of flatlanders. He did enjoy gathering at one of his friends homes in a good section of town and joined in singing popular songs and hymns around the piano. He spent most of his limited income on clothes and soda fountain treats such as Coca Cola, Cherry Cola and ice cream.

Teddie had his bait of countrified things. He often stated that he was from the country. He had his wagon hitched to not a star, but a railroad and never ventured far from the rails.

Minnie Dunn packed her belongings in a big steamer trunk, paid Mrs. O'Hara a month's room and board for Teddie. She turned her depot duties over to a relief agent operator, signed out with the train dispatcher and ended her railroad career. She loved Teddie, but it was time for a change. She had a long talk with Teddie while they waited on the train bound for Jacksonville, Florida where she would change her name to Mrs. George O'Niel. She told Teddie that she had wired their oldest brother, W.T. Dunn of her intentions and would he please place Teddie on some kind of railroad job until he was old enough to hire on as a telegrapher.

W.T. had become general road master of the Central of Georgia Railroad and assured Minnie that Teddie would be placed as a water boy-messenger on an extra work gang that was relaying rails between

Columbus and Macon, Georgia. He would be living on the line of road with the gang of immigrant Irish track men and would report to a foreman July 1, 1907, only three weeks away at Macon, Georgia.

The relief agent operator was a young man, single and only a few years older than Teddie. He asked Teddie to stay on and help him with his new assignment and deliver the Western Union messages until he could find a fellow to replace him. The agent operator jobs were awarded to the qualified senior employee that bidded on a vacancy, as the job was put up to bid. This relief operator was just an extra board man that didn't have enough service time or "whiskers" as seniority was termed on the railroad, to stand for the Pearson position, as it was a choice station, and the pay per hour was good.

Teddie knew all these things so he understood that his "whiskers" would have to grow for a couple of more years before he could be hired out as a lightning slinger. In fact, he needed to grow more than whiskers, he needed to grow in statue, and experience as there was much responsibility involved in operation of trains on a busy line by train order and time table. Passengers and crewmen's lives depended on train orders sent over the wires all hours of the day and night. There was no room for error as two trains were speeding toward each other on a single track. One mistake could result in a tangled mass of twisted steel and broken lives.

Charlie Dunn had a talent at finding work on the railroad. His serious approach to duty impressed superiors. He dressed well, clean shaven; and articulate manner set him aside from other applicants. Behind most outstanding men there is usually a strong willed woman to prop her man up when he falters.

Without a doubt, Charlie had wooed and won a jewel of a girl when he married the gentile old timber baron's daughter, Lillie Tillman. She was a determined, intelligent young woman, wise for her years, a no-nonsense person, and she looked well enough.

The officials of the Atlantic Birmingham and Atlantic Railroad had decided to locate their headquarters at the Colony City of Fitzgerald. The generous land grants offered by the town's city fathers could not be rejected. Its location in the center of South Georgia that was only a few years ago virgin pine forest, was now a virtual boomtown. Those Yankee veterans attacked town buildings with the same vigor General Sherman had shown in his march to the sea. Through Middle Georgia that brought the south to its knees.

The first time Charlie Dunn had stepped off a two coach passenger train, pulled by a "cabbage head" wood burning engine off the Waycross Northern Railroad onto a wooden platform of a wood frame station, about like the one at Pearson, he could not believe his eyes. No longer did it live up to its nick name of "shack town." The blue smoke of burning piles of stumps and pine slash hung like a veil over the tents and clapboard buildings that three thousand northern immigrants, mostly from the Midwestern states, some Georgia crackers, negro laborers, and the usual crowed of "camp followers," were calling home.

Charlie Dunn was not the only man that had taken an interest in Fitzgerald, named for the Indiana Civil War Veteran, Mr. Phlander Fitzgerald that organized the colony company, bought and surveyed the land that lay on the uplands a few miles west of the Ocmulgee River, twenty-two miles south of the well established river port town of Abbeville. The sleepy county seat of Wilcox County that now boasted a through railroad linking Albany with Savannah on the Georgia coast, named the Seaboard Airline. That road was scrambling to build a branch line down to serve Fitzgerald as a link to the north from the south, a rail line was extended from the county seat of Irwin County, Ocilla, northward for the ten miles to Fitzgerald by the Ocilla Southern Railroad. That line would connect Fitzgerald with the Atlantic Coastline Railroad at Alapaha and on to Valdosta, near the Georgia-Florida border.

Chapter 16

Fitzgerald

Fitzgerald was now served by three railroads, linking it directly to Atlanta to the north and Waycross the south. Mr. Raud, a visionary railroad builder, took the AB&A Railroad under his wing. He had family connections in New York that had their eyes on the potential of South Florida as a vacation land for the northern tourists traffic.

A branch line ran from Fitzgerald, eighty-two miles southwest to the popular tourist town of Thomasville in the far corner of Southwest Georgia's Plantation Resorts. This era was the heyday of American railroads with its' Pullmans sleeping cars, private cars of the very rich. The specialized freight cars were transporting anything from pig iron to circus and Wild West shows that were now rumbling and roaring through only vast stretches of seemingly endless pine forests and brooding cypress swamps. These iron horses seemed determined to awaken the Deep South.

The sandy trails that had only heard the hoof beats of animals or the padding of moccasined feet of Indian tribesmen, or the cracking whips of the ox drovers had faded into the past.

Now the steam whistles echoed across the land. The click-clack of the steel wheels of railcars as they passed over the bolted joints of the steel rails that had been laid through the wiregrass and palmetto breaks, had replaced the call of the Ivory Billed Woodpecker or the gobble of the noble wild turkey gobbler as he gathers his hens that only answered "put-put-put."

How could the infant town of Fitzgerald fail with all its rail connections, high land just above the flatwoods and below the red clay hills of Middle Georgia?

The recently completed station at Fitzgerald seemed to Charlie Dunn to have stepped out of a Spanish storybook. It was built of formed concrete, two-story with wide timbered shelters on both sides. The orange-red "knee tile" roof had been shipped in from Cuba. The Spanish architecture gave the elegant building an exotic style that would have felt quite at home in St. Augustine, Florida. It contrasted with the Yankee architecture of the houses around the town's broad streets.

The Office of the Trainman and Division Superintendent was on the second floor of the new station. Charlie's polished shoes made the wooden risers of the double staircase rattle as he ran upstairs to mount the long hallway. He passed the train master's office door as he intended to introduce himself to the superintendent. There it was, a closed door with a sign hung above proclaiming that he had found the office of the head operating officer of the AB&A Railroad.

Charlie straightened his bowtie, cleared his throat and knocked on the oak door. The slight gray-haired lady that opened the door said only one word, "yes." Charlie asked if he might speak to the superintendent. She asked if Mr. Huddelson was expecting him. "Well, no ma'am," he stammered. She asked his name. "Charlie Dunn," he replied. A large man in a suit of clothes, collar and tie entered the reception room and sized Charlie up and down. "I am Harry Huddleson. Did I hear you say you were named Dunn?" he asked. Charlie had an easy nature about him, and was hard to rattle. "Yes, I am Charlie Dunn." The superintendent removed his coat and hung it on the hall tree where his hat hung. He took his pocket knife from his pants pocket; he opened the box of cigars on his desk and offered Charlie a cigar which he accepted. The two men lit the King Edward cigars. The room clouded with blue cigar smoke as the men began to talk.

"I once knew a man up on the Central of Georgia Railroad when I was a train master on the Central up in Atlanta. I worked with a gentleman by the name of W.T. Dunn. He was general road master for the Central of Georgia Railroad and was a pleasure to work with and was a natural born civil engineer, and had the respect of the men he supervised."

"Yes sir, Mr. Huddleson," Charlie replied, has he dumped his cigar ashes in the large ash tray on the superintendent's desk. "I am acquainted with Mr. Dunn," Charlie replied. "He is my older brother, and all of us brothers and one sister were taught railroading by our father, Bill Dunn, a track man all his life. We were raised in section houses down in Mobile, Alabama when he was section foreman on the Louisville and Nashville Railroad, then at Andersonville on the Central. I am a telegrapher and quite good at agency work. I know how to route freight shipments, handle collections, figure reports to the demurrage bureau; agency work is my favorite duty. I have been working on the Coastline for several years, but I would like to work for your line, right here in Fitzgerald."

Mr. Huddleson rose from behind his desk, extended his hand, "Glad to have you aboard young fellow, a route and rate man is hard to come by this side of Atlanta. Your office will be down at the freight depot down on Main Street, one block south of this building. I will notify the supervisor of the agency that you will soon report for duty."

Charlie was stunned at his good fortune but didn't let it show. He stuck his cigar in his mouth and his long legs had him back down the hall, down the stairs to the concrete platform and into the waiting room to where Lillie was waiting.

She sprang off the bench when she saw him coming. She could tell from the smile on his face and the strides he was stepping that the interview had gone well, but she would have to wait to hear just how well. With all his talent and abilities, he had a fault that he was never able to overcome. He was a poor hand to handle money.

Minnie and Charlie Dunn had gone their own ways. Minnie settled down with her husband in a well furnished apartment located in a good neighborhood, down in Jacksonville, Florida. Charlie and Lillie rented an apartment a few blocks from the depot where he spent long hours in a small office calculating freight bills and routing freight shipments to points over the entire U.S.A.

As usual, Charlie had trouble raising the rent money for the nice little house on Fitzgerald's Central Avenue. Old Mrs. Werner, their landlady, wanted her rent money up front. Charlie fumbled around in his pockets, but seemed to be a bit short of cash. Lillie came to his rescue as she knew why he couldn't find the money. She had gone through those same pockets the night before and put it in her purse to pay their bills, or Charlie would have bought a birddog or gotten into a poker game down at the poolroom. Lillie would hold the purse strings through the years to come. She had found herself pregnant, and knew they would need a home in Fitzgerald and there would be bills to pay.

A big chance had come into Teddie Dunn's life. For the first time in his life, he was not under the protective wing of a loving woman. He had said goodbye to Mrs. O'Hara and Hattie down at Pearson. His stay there in the flatwoods of South Georgia had given him maturity and self-confidence. Minnie had been a patient good teacher and spent much time to teach him the ins and outs of railroading, and how to relate with the public, and demanding railroad officials. She taught him how to dress, use good manners and principles of good behavior. She just seemed to love the little scamp, but she was gone now. Teddie would never forget the flatlanders, the livestock that enjoyed their freedom to range free in the pine forest, sandy streets and even those stubborn old goats that still spent their nights on the station platform. The wild Saturday nights when the streets and saloons were crowded with cracker people that had come to town to let off a little steam.

Teddie must have gotten a little bit of that South Georgia sand between his toes, although he always wore his shoes. He knew that he would return to the land of the sighing pines and the chirping frogs in the black swamp water ponds. The all day sings, the swift southern justice that awaited people that couldn't live by the rules enforced not by jury, but by pistols, shotguns, or night riders wearing bed sheets, mounted on swift Spanish mustangs that could see their way on dark nights.

Chapter 17

Teddie and the "Steel Gang"

Teddie had once again packed his meager belongings into his pasteboard suitcase and caught the passenger train. He had no ticket for the conductor to punch, just a message from the General Road Master of the Central of Georgia Railroad to allow Teddie Dunn passage to Macon, signed W.T. Dunn, G.R.M. That message was all Teddie possessed between the rock and the hard place.

Once again, "T" had stepped out to offer him support. This time he would have a real job on the railroad. He could line up with the other employees to hear his name called by the paymaster and be handed a brown envelope with his name and payroll number printed on the outside and hard money on the inside, his money.

As the train steamed toward Macon through the darkness, Teddie tried to sleep on the hard cushion of the seat. Sleep did not come as his mind was so loaded with thoughts of his mother and Ida back at Andersonville. He hoped to have some time off to go visit them and tell them about Pearson and the people and things he had seen there. He wondered if his brother Grady had finished his apprenticeship and was a section foreman. Grady was only two years older than he was and that was too young to be married and have a family. "T" would know, and tell him all the family news when he saw him on the line of road.

Teddie tried to look out the window of the coach into the darkness, as the train sped on through the night. He thought of all the animals of the forest that were on their nightly venture to find food and breed with others of their kind. His thoughts had turned to Charlie and Lillie; had he found a job at Fitzgerald? What was it that was ringing a bell in his mind that he couldn't bring forward? Suddenly, with a stak, he knew what it was that was bothering him about that name, "Fitzgerald." It was an odd name for a town and from what he had heard said about its beginning was even odder. Now he had it solved.

That was the Yankee town that the excursion train had come to Andersonville on Decoration Day with their band and baskets of flowers to lay on the graves of the Union soldiers that had died of deprivation, starvation, diseases, and at the hands of their own comrades. That special train was from Fitzgerald, not the northern states.

He had pitched his lemonade stand down at the depot along the side tracks to refresh the thirsty Yankees that talked so funny. That was all well and good, but it was the young Yankee girl with the wavy red hair that was haunting Teddie's restless mind.

That was all long ago and far away now. She may be married to some Yankee boy there at Fitzgerald.

Teddie had drifted off to sleep and dreamed of the girl's haunting eyes and rosebud lips, that only told him her name was Tessie Barwick, moved to Fitzgerald from Pennsylvania, way up north. Teddie was jolted awake as the train braked for the stop at the city of Macon, Georgia in the red clay hills of Central Georgia, the head of navigation on the Ocmulgee River.

There was a switch engine working the yard at Macon's terminal railroad station. Teddie approached one of the switchmen to orient himself. The gruff, but kindly man told him to go climb up on the switch engine and it would soon return to the switchyard office.

The office was a busy place as everyone seemed busy writing switch lists to build trains that would depart to other points on the line of road. A young man with a suitcase was ignored.

Teddie could hear a telegraph instrument tapping out a message over in a corner of the busy office. The sound comforted him, as he could read the message that was being sent. Railroad folks look out for each other; in fact, they were like a large extended family. They may shout and swear at each other under stressful situations, but when the chips are down, they are all brothers under the skin.

Teddie knew better than to interrupt an operator when he was busy, so he sat his suitcase down and waited until the baldheaded old operator with a green celluloid eye shade pushed his swivel chair back and stretched. He smiled and greeted Teddie with, "Well, well…boys look what the cats have drug up, would you?"

Teddie tried to stand tall and smiled at the men that he hoped would help him find a way to the out lying point where the work train was relaying rail. He knew that if a railroad man joked or made fun of you, he liked you. He retorted with his own crack, "No, it wasn't a cat that drug me in, it was that midnight local passenger train pulled by some extra board hogger that threw the passengers out of their seats and into the aisles every time he applied the air brakes. I probably would look better if a cat had drug me here.

Teddie knew the lingo of railroad men and recognized that it was no atmosphere for a sensitive, thin-skinned individual. What would have been taken as an insult by a flatland farmer down in Pearson, was a friendly greeting at a railroad switchyard in the cities of Northern Georgia.

The old lightning slinger that was welcoming the bedraggled boy that was trying to become a man, in a world of men, had found a friend.

The kindly operator cracked again, "Fellow, you look like you have one long gut, and it is empty." "My wife", he continued, "packed me a lunch that would have fed a plow hand. Reach up there on the wall where the lunch pails are hung and reach in and get you a sausage and biscuit to tide you over."

Teddie pulled the well worn message from his coat pocket and handed it to the operator that had introduced himself as Sam Triplett. Sam grunted satisfaction as he folded the yellow paper and handed it back to Teddie. I am well acquainted with Mr. Dunn and copy and send his messages most everyday. "Did I hear right that you are Teddie Dunn? There aren't that many Dunns around this neck of the woods, or should I say rails."

"Could it be that you fellows are kin?" "Yes, Mr. Triplett, I am his youngest brother," as he washed down the last mouthful of the shared lunch with a gulp of water from the office water cooler over in the corner.

Once again fortune had led Teddie to a kindly person that was to make the rocky road to success a little smoother. Sam told Teddie that he had just given a section foreman a "lineup" on the movement of trains on his section that extended to Lizella, Georgia, where the work gang was relaying rail and had their camp cars parked on a side track.

Teddie grabbed his suitcase and with a hurried thank you, ran to the nearby tool house where the foreman, Henry Stovall and his hands were waiting for a freight train to clear the mainline to Lizella. Henry Stovall glared at Teddie with the suitcase clutched in his hand. "I don't haul hobos on my push car, and you sure look like one."

Mr. Stovall changed his tune when he read the message Teddie handed him. "Welcome aboard fellow, I would not dare offend W.T.

Dunn, my big boss man, or he would put me to walking the right of way, with a suitcase in my hand."

Teddie climbed on top of the push car that was loaded with new crossties. This scene of the section hands straining at the pump handles that powered the small car along the rails, silently pulling the small push car loaded with crossties, track tools, Teddie, and his pasteboard suitcase perched atop the load.

They clipped along on the levels and flew down the hills. Uphill was another story, all hands, but the foreman and crank hands, would have to jump off and push with all their might to crest a steep hill on the rails that led to Lizella, Georgia. Teddie pitched in with the straining laborers on the hills, to the satisfaction of Mr. Stovall, who was surprised at the strength that Teddie displayed that morning on the long hauls. His body, small as it was, was a dynamo of energy or was it mostly willpower?

Lizella wasn't much more of a town than Andersonville, just the usual country stores, hitching post, water trough and those everlasting red clay streets. There was a telegraph office and depot, and the yellow section houses facing the tracks, not the road. There was the work train loaded with steel rails fresh from the rolling mills at Pittsburgh, Pennsylvania. There, laboring in the sun was some fifty white men all dressed alike speaking in a lilting tongue.

They were all Irish trackmen that went around the world laying railroad track. They were proud of their trade, and had their own head men. They were not employees of the railroad that contracted their services. They were a hardy gang of men from a land even poorer than South Georgia. Hardship and manual labor was their bill of fare. They chanted and sang age old songs that Teddie had never heard. They lived in the camp cars, ate in dining cars, and ate food prepared in kitchen cars by their own cooks.

These cars were specialized equipment designed for employees to live in weeks or even months on end at a time. The foreman had a private camp car to live and dine in. No toilet facilities were included; men just had to run to the bushes, and bathe in creeks or ponds. This string of camp cars were parked in a side track just beyond the town, and would be Teddie's home for some time to come. He had long known of camp cars, as his father had spent his last days living in one. The food was good, discipline was enforced by the foreman, and weekends were free time, no women were allowed aboard the camp cars.

Teddie was to be "water boy" and assist the company foreman and his straw boss, with the records that were to be kept, how many kegs of bolts, spikes, tie plates, were used along with a rail count. The pay was three times what he had earned as a plowman. His food was charged out to him, and deducted from his pay. The Irish gang was glad to have a water boy, as they consumed copious amounts of cool water dipped from a large tin bucket carried along with them as they worked.

Teddie noted as he walked toward the foreman's car that there was a small crank car turned off the track at a road crossing. This crank car was powered by one strong black man known as "Crank Hand." He alone could handle the three wheeled vehicle with only one cushioned seat for the road master to sit on. The crank hand sat on a board and powered a geared crank handle that could send the light car speeding along the track.

Teddie knew that the foreman was being visited in his camp car by the road master. He mounted the footboard that was a step up to the screen door on the side of the car where he could hear men talking.

The knock he made on the screen door was answered by a firm voice that Teddie thought he had heard before. He swung his suitcase up into the car and mounted the threshold to stand before two well dressed men that welcomed him to enter. He was left speechless to find himself standing before his handsome brother, W.T. Dunn.

"T" Dunn extended his hand to Teddie and spoke, "Could this be the boy I last saw laying on mama's kitchen table, more dead than alive?" "Yes," Teddie answered, "Thanks to our sister Ida, and mama's nursing, here I stand.

"T" introduced his brother to the extra, or rather steel gang foreman as they were laying rail. His name was Willis Hudson, a large man that was beginning to show his years by having to work in the hot sun and cold winter wind. He rose from his seat at the desk where the two men had been pouring over maps and papers.

Willis welcomed Teddie to the work camp. His face softened when he smiled and there was a twinkle in his blue eyes with the crow foot wrinkles in the corners.

"T" suggested that they move to the next camp car that was the foreman's dining car reserved for the foreman, his assistants, and guests. "T" seemed right at home aboard the camp cars. There were doors cut in the ends of the cars so men could pass from car to car, but they would have to step over the couplings or "draw heads" as they were called, to enter the next car.

A long single table, with a white linen cloth spread over the rough boards, ran the length of the car. Straight chairs with arm rests, upholstered with black leather were set on either side. A larger one was at the head of the table. It was reserved for the foreman. The kitchen car was next in the lineup.

Willis Hudson called for "Pat" the cook; Patrick Hogan was his full name. He was a small man with a little round stomach and a bald head. He was a jolly gent dressed in white pants, his under shirt and with a white apron tied around his waist that went to his polished black shoes.

"Morning Captain," he said with a low bow, "and what will it be? There's still coffee in the pot, hot as Hades and a pan of my finest biscuits that the lads didn't see, a bit of bacon, crisp and brown." The foreman scowled at the cook. "How many times do I have to tell you not to enter my diner in your underwear without your cook's bonnet? We have important guests and you are not the cook on a garbage scow."

"T" looked amused as the cook retreated to his kitchen car. Teddie was flattered, as he had never before been referred to as "important," even though he knew the foreman was referring to Mr. W.T. Dunn.

After some time, the cook, Pat, entered the private dining car, which had once been only a Central of Georgia boxcar hauling cotton seed to feed mills up north. Pat had taken reprimands to heart. This entry was as it should have been when the general road master was aboard. He wore a fresh white jacket, buttoned to the starched collar, and on his bald head was a tall cook's bonnet that was the badge of his trade, might I say a "chef?"

Willis Hudson drained his coffee cup, pushed his padded chair back, and excused himself as he had reports and payrolls to send in to the paymaster in Atlanta. "T" rose also and wished Mr. Hudson good day.

The Dunn brothers had a lot of catching up to do, and there was no better place to do it than at the table on the private diner parked at Lizella, Georgia. This was probably the first time "T" and Teddie had sat down alone. There was a span of many years between the Dunn brothers, one was Sallie Ann's oldest, the other her youngest. Their father's untimely death had thrust "T" into the position of head of the Dunn family at an age most young men weren't dry behind their ears, and Teddie was still in knee pants.

Andersonville offered no opportunity for a young man that owned no land or livestock. It was just "Johnny get your gun" on the railroads that were seeing their "hay day" from coast to coast. They all, girls included, had grown up early and now all but Ida, had ventured into the world.

The twentieth century had brought new rules to the railroads of America. The age limit for a man in train service, which included telegraph operators had to have reached their majority at twenty-one years. Clerks, apprentice helpers, and such could be employed at age eighteen and Teddie would be "legal" in a few weeks, August the 31st 1909.

"T" told Teddie that Mr. Hudson would "wink" at those few weeks and put him to work tomorrow, as a water boy. He didn't think much of his title, but "T" had reminded him that railroad jobs didn't grow on trees and that he himself had once held that title and that only hard work, long hours, and responsibility to duty would bestow a more lofty title in the years to come.

The conversation turned to family news. "T" had kept in touch with all of them. He himself had a good wife named Arch, she had bore him several children. Some were in school and doing well in a town just south of Atlanta named Jonesboro, Georgia, that he called home.

"T" continued to update Teddie. He informed him that Grady was still single and would soon be awarded a section when one came open. He was a hard worker and the strongest of the brothers, but had little ambition to be an official and aspired only to be a section foreman, as his father had been.

Charlie Dunn needed no advice; he was smart and hard working but needed just the wife he had married to keep him in the middle of the road. Also, our brother Emmitt, you know as much as I do, he has vanished.

Teddie, I have had reports on you from Andersonville and Pearson. Miss Maggie Callen informed me that you were resourceful and could copy a message years ago. Our mother said you gave her no problems as to behavior but you did not aspire to be a farmer or spend your life in rural areas, those bright lights and sidewalks beckoned to you. Not only that, but you had a turn for business deals and legal matters and you had a good record at Professor Clark's Schoolhouse.

Minnie wrote me that you had a good aptitude to duty and had no bad habits other than tobacco.

"T" advised Teddie to stay close to the steel foreman, Mr. Hudson so as to gain experience not only of track building, but how to manage work crews and keep records. Practice on the typewriter, your day will come, and I will always be near you. Oh yes, Teddie, stay on the good side of that Irish cook, Pat, and never underestimate the Irish workmen, and their clever ways. Ole Pat is a fine cook and he will fatten you up for sure.

Life on the camp cars was no bed of roses. Teddie soon found out that the title "water boy" was the lesser one of his duties. He had to rinse off the chunks of ice that the trains kicked off to him, get water from local wells or springs for the drinking water of the workers, rinse the water bucket and the dipper they all drank from.

Pat, the camp cook, had a jug of chlorine and gave Teddie a small bottle of the smelly chemical that only a few drops would purify a bucket of drinking water. Sanitation was of the utmost importance as a plague could wreak havoc among a work gang. Teddie well knew this to be a fact, as his father had died of Typhoid Fever off with a work gang just like this one.

These Irish lads worked like fighting fire. Each one well knew his duty, just as teammates on a ball team. This gang was divided into two groups; the lead group was dismantling the rails. The lead men and bolters were busy with their long handle wrenches, unbolting the angle bars that connected the steel rails.

They were followed by unskilled laborers that gathered the angle bars and stacked them beside the track in neat piles. The bolts and nuts, or "taps" as the Irish called them were put in buckets and set aside to be used by the following gang.

Next were the spike pullers, with their "crowfoot bars" pulling spikes that freed the rails from the steel tie –plates which were left in place for the new rails to be mounted on.

Then the six-man team of rail totters with their "rail tongs" lifted the worn rails aside to be later loaded on flat cars on the ever present "work trains" that supplied and salvaged track materials to the laborers.

Mind you that the mainline had to be kept open for train traffic although it was slowed or delayed by the "relay project." The flow of traffic, the work trains, and materials was the responsibility of the extra gang foreman, employed by the Central of Georgia Railroad and his clerks and helpers, of which Teddie Dunn was one, finally.

The relay gang was close behind with the same skilled men, with the exception of the spike drivers, the elite of the trade. They were the most experienced men, usually older and better dressed. Many wore black derby felt hats. They worked in pars, one on either side of the spike to be driven that would anchor the new rail to the crossties. These spike drivers had a chant to time their blows with their special spike hammers delivered with a sounding ring as the metal met metal. They squatted on bent knees and swung the hammers in a circular motion timed to miss the blows of his partner, or "mate" as they spoke. They would chant, "Bow down Mattie" and another spike was driven home.

Teddie had to run from one gang to the other. The August sun bore down on the sweating Irishmen that were eternally calling for cool clear water. They got breaks as the trains would creep through the work zone. They would light up their white clay pipes and puff away and lament their lot laboring on tracks they would never ride on, except on the camp cars. They would tell Teddie of the green valleys of Ireland, and the cool breezes of the Irish sea, and how they longed to return with a bit of cash in their "pokes." "T" Dunn was correct, Teddie learned much railroad love, track building, and labor relations.

To his delight the foreman had a portable telegraph instrument that could be clamped to the telegraph wires strung along the tracks and connected to the train dispatcher in Macon. Some train conductors or foremen could tap out a short message to get a traffic lineup or send a trouble message. Teddie was delighted to inform Mr. Hudson, his foreman, that he was a "Lightning Slinger" of sorts, and would be glad to be of any assistance, while some of the other "hands" could fill the camp cars kerosene lamps with kerosene oil, and trim the wicks, chop firewood for the cook stove or even may tote water to slack the unquenchable thirst of the Irish "Blokes" that had little "truck" with Yanks or Crackers.

Teddie spent evenings talking to Mr. Hudson at the foreman's car discussing railroad gangs. He was told that it was the best policy not to mix the races, either have a black man gang, a Chinese gang, or as the one at Lizella, an Irish immigrant gang.

The foods they ate were their typical traditional food, Irish mutton stew and boiled potatoes. The brand and names of tools were unique, their attitudes and incentives were very different. They were all good trackmen, but never mix the white, black or yellow races. There would be grumbling, arguments, misunderstandings while the work at hand went undone.

Teddie had a bunk in the end of one of the sleeping cars. The bunks were three levels high and each man had the responsibility to keep his covers clean, to sweep the floors, and light the lamps at dawn and douse them at "lights out." Teddie was finally accepted as he was of Irish descent.

The men were a hardy lot. They took great pride in their profession as trackmen, be it ever so humble. Thirty men could be slept in a bunk car which was higher and longer than a standard box car. They were clean, as conditions would permit. Hot weather would find the men sleeping in bed rolls under the stars. They seemed to get by on little sleep. In the winter they would build a bonfire in an open space behind the track using discarded crossties.

There was a fiddle, pipes, and a kettle drum among the men. They would string up the fiddle, rosin up the bow, and the festivities would commence. They loved to dance by the light of the fire or the moon if there was one. The lack of female dancing partners posed no problem. They would just assign a group of the "gandy dancers", as they were known far and wide, to fill in for women partners. To designate the men that were to be women they would pin a white handkerchief to their coat lapels, and the Irish fling would commence. Quartets were formed and the pipes would wail their mournful melodies and tenor voices would ring through the Georgia forest and fields as the fellows would sing the ballads as old as Ireland itself. They sang of their true loves, mothers, and sisters far across the Emerald Sea.

The Irish gandy dances had a dark side as well. Their sport seemed to be fighting, as they relished a free for all. Fists would fly, oaths were heard, hats were trampled in the dust, teeth were loosened, and eyes were blackened.

From what Teddie could overhear, the main problem was whether you were an orange man or a green man, Catholic or Protestant. This was an ongoing problem that never seemed to be settled. One minute they would be dancing, and then the fur would fly. The poor devils would fall out of the bunks at the captain's (straw boss) call the next morning with scrapes, swollen knuckles, black eyes, and knots on their heads; the more battered they were, the prouder they were.

Breakfast, hot tea and biscuits, was served in the dining cars, as was the evening meal. The noon meal was the main meal of the day. The cook and his helpers would load huge pots of stew, and mutton if it could be found, onto the small railcars called push cars that could be pulled by pump cars. The light weight cars could be "turned" off the track to clear the main line for train traffic. Away ole Pat, the cook, would fly down the rails until he overtook the workers at the worksite. The men would give a cheer when the "push car" was seen coming toward them. Tools were dropped, and the cars were turned off the track. Each man had his bowl in his kit, and a line was formed and the men marched past the steaming pots of stew. Pat, the cook, ladled each man's bowl, as he passed, onto the loaves of fresh baked rye bread.

Teddie had been with the gang all morning dipping water for the men, in his capacity of "water boy." He heard those two words constantly. He had never eaten any mutton stew before he "signed on" with the extra gang. The very smell of the course meat being cooked, took his appetite, but Pat cooked the foreman and his crew things more to their taste, and would always have a lunch for Teddie, even banana pudding, on occasions. These work gangs were a man's world. His brother "T" was wise to place him in the environment.

The lessons he learned on the "steel gang" would dwell in his mind for the remainder of his days. When life dealt him a rough deal, he would fortify his mind with the Irish's will to survive and to redouble his efforts, and to take pride in his work.

Buzzards circled in the blue Georgia sky, their sharp eyes searching the ground below for easy pickings to feast on, dead animals that would give them no resistance. The human race had its vultures, in the form of gamblers, pimps, and prostitutes that feasted on the failings of others. These people slept under rocks until payday arrived for the Irish trackmen.

These human vultures seemed to have a sixth sense to know when payday arrived along the rail line. Money would awake them, and they would catch the first train smoking, to a light with the tools of the trade, a deck of marked cards, loaded dice, tents to raise a short distance from the camp cars even some with a red lantern lit before a pink tent, for the privacy of the fallen angels to play their oldest profession known to mankind. The wicks Teddie trimmed in the camp cars were not the only wicks that got trimmed.

The track men had little to show for their hard labor on the tracks, their hard earned money had flown away with the camp followers that had spread their wings and flown back to their roosts to await the next payday.

The Central of Georgia Railroad had new rails laid, and as sure as the sun rose, the ring of the spike hammers, and the Irish chants could be heard at the work site. Teddie realized that few, if any, trackmen got rich on the wages of a trackman. He had heard the foreman quote the old adage of the railroad company, "Kill a mule, buy another, kill a man, hire another."

Lots of trackmen died young, and were just buried along the right-away by their fellow workers, with a few words read from the good book and an old Irish hymn sang in a tenor note. Few ever returned to Ireland, it was only a dream in their stout hearts.

Summer turned into Fall, Winter passed, the camp cars were moved by the work trains. Pat, the cook, was always a dither when a move was made. He would swear at the train crew that would couple to the string of camp cars. They would always knock down his stovepipe, spill his stew, or cause his bread to fall; but curses fell off the train men's backs like water off ducks backs, and away the camp cars would rattle, leaving a cloud of black smoke over the cotton fields of Central Georgia, as they followed the progressive re-rail work.

August found the work completed and the extra gang was disbanded and the camp cars were parked at the Columbus, Georgia yards of the Central of Georgia Railroad to await their next assignment.

Teddie Dunn was no longer a boy, he was still small for his years, but the year on the camp cars and the kindness of the railroad foreman and the old camp cook, Pat, had given him an education in the school of hard licks. Where would he go from here? He knew his fortune was not at the end of a pick or shovel handle. He now knew that he was worth a dollar a day from his ears down, and unlimited wealth from his ears up.

The Irishmen had liked Teddie and gave him good wishes and their blessings, whatever they were worth. What he really needed was a job. He had saved himself a small nest egg, enough to buy him a ticket to Andersonville on the through-passenger train.

He had bought himself a new suitcase without one shred of pasteboard on it. He had a new pair of patten leather slippers that shined like a fresh polished stove pipe.

Andersonville had changed little. The statue of Old Captain Wurtz was there in the square. He strolled down the sidewalk to his sister Ida's store. She was not there to greet him, only a young colored girl was busy at a foot powered Singer sewing machine. She stood as Teddie entered the store. She was wide eyed, then blurted "Lordy, Lordy, I knows you. You Miss Ida's brother, Mr. Teddie. She left me to mind her store while she go to see bout her mama. Miss **Sallie Ann** be a bit under da weather."

Chapter 18

A Visit to Sallie Ann

Teddie thanked her and hurried up the road past the church and the graveyard where his father and brother Claude were buried. The red clay road up to his mother's house had not changed. The red dust that stained everything a dull red had already dulled the shine on his new shoes and the new leather suitcase. His steps quickened as he drew near the house that held so many memories of his boyhood, and his brothers that had walked away from. He had only a few more steps to the gate that was standing open, and had no more than stepped on the first step to the front porch than Ida ran to meet him.

She was so overcome at the sight of the well dressed young Teddie that she burst into tears as she threw her arms about him. "Oh Teddie, why didn't you wire us and I would have met you at the station. You have made a handsome young man. Mama will be tickled to see you. She is resting well, after a bout with the fever that had her down. Come on down to her room, and I will get her up and tidy the room"

Teddie was shocked to see Sallie Ann, her hair was white as snow, and the lines in her face were deeper. She was sitting in her rocker awaiting the special guest. Ida had told her that Teddie had come in on the train. As Ida ushered Teddie into the room, Sallie Ann burst into life. "My baby, my baby," she cried. "You have given me new life. Ida had told me that you were fine, and I would be proud of you. Please sit down by my side and tell me all about yourself. Your leg is healed, even though it is shorter, and you did grow some more. I am so glad to see you. You will never know how many prayers I have said for you."

Sallie Ann was proud to see that Teddie had developed into a well-rounded young man. He was quite handsome with his black wavy hair that he combed back with a part in the middle of his head. His teeth were strong and even; he was well proportioned, although the gun accident had left the wounded leg an inch shorter than the other. He had to have a buildup on the heel of his shoe, so he didn't limp as he had.

He dressed neat, and was clean shaven. His smile reflected his self-confidence.

She did note that he had no interest in agriculture, livestock, guns, bird dogs, hunting or fishing. In fact, he stated to his mother that he had a belly full of those things as a boy. He would catch his fish with a silver hook, let police and soldiers do all the shooting and dogs and cats could fend for themselves.

Why, she wondered, did he have to set that black derby hat at that cockeyed angle on his head, and stick that white clay pipe between h is teeth, and have a cud of chewing tobacco in his cheek.

She knew he had stayed around those Irish gandy dancers that only knew railroad cars for a home. She could smell no strong drink on his breath, but he thought he was "cock of the walk" and had kissed the "Blarney stone," for sure, as all the Dunn men had, not to mention Minnie Dunn O'Niel.

Sallie Ann seemed to display her sunny personality from the moment she cast her eyes on Teddie. Ida suggested that they sit on the front porch and enjoy the cool breeze while she prepared supper. She set it on the same kitchen table that Teddie had laid on that dreadful day he shot the snake that threatened his mother.

The food was plain and simple of fried fritters sopped in sugar cane syrup with sweet milk to drink.

They reminisced until the stars shown brightly into the cool night sky. It had been a big day for the three. Where would Teddie like to sleep? The guest room was made up for a guest, but Teddie told them that he would like to once more sleep in the shed room, just like he did when he was a boy.

With a lamp in her hand, Ida led the way down the hall and lit another lamp in her bedroom that she shared with her mother. Sallie Ann told Teddie that it was so good to have him back home and hoped that he would stay for a spell. Teddie laughed as he told her that he never intended to plow another contrary mule and that he had his sights set on a telegrapher job over on the new rail line that ran from Waycross to Atlanta where Charlie had a job at the Yankee colony town of Fitzgerald, where that road had it's headquarters.

Ida told her brother that he would have to depend on Charlie to help him get a job as "T" was not in good health, and was under a doctor's care in Atlanta. The last time he visited in Andersonville, he was pale and gaunt; just tired and over worked, he had assured her, but she was worried about the hacking cough that he had.

Ida spread up Teddie's old bunk and filled his pitcher on the stand with well water. The yellow light of the kerosene lamp cast shadows on the rough pine board walls of the shed room as Ida moved around the room with a broom knocking down cobwebs that the spiders had spun.

Teddie set his suitcase on a bench and undressed. He carefully hung his new store bought clothes and hat on the wooden pegs in the wall, where he and his two brothers had hung their overalls long ago. He opened the shutter so he could be awakened by the rising sun. The quilt felt good as a fresh night breeze heralded the coming of winter.

There was long standing stories that Andersonville was haunted by the ghosts of the Union soldiers that had died in the prison camp and were buried just over the hill in the national cemetery.

Moans could be heard, angels had been seen fluttering among the rows of marble headstones. Sobs and wailing awakened dogs that howled and run under porches to hide. The glow of ghostly fires could be seen in the thickets around Providence Spring.

Was it only the fires of night hunters or was it the camp fires of Union Prisoners ghosts huddled together, planning an escape? No doubt, the place could cast a spell on a body.

Teddie had a lot on his mind; he tossed and tumbled through the long dark night. He dreamed of bygone days and people; the Rooks brothers, Mr. Bill Easterlin, and Pony Johnson that had been so kind and generous to his widowed mother. He lived in the real world, ghosts and spirits were for dreamers and soothsayers with their crystal balls that allowed them to gaze into the half world of witches and hobgoblins that had no place in his life.

He did think that he heard the red ox named General Sherman, lowing under the old mulberry tree that had finally died of old age. He remembered the story that his father had told him as a child of the stormy night he was walking the track of his section in the rain. There was an old graveyard along the right of way. Bill Dunn, like his son Teddie, did not "hold with haints" as the black folks put it. But the desperate sounds that came from that graveyard were real.

Was some poor soul trying to climb from his grave? The hard breathing was plain to hear, emitting from the caved in grave with a toppled headstone. The lantern that Bill carried to light his way and the shovel he carried on his back gave him comfort to approach the grave to satisfy his mind as to the source of the struggle that was in progress below the surface of the old cemetery.

Most people would have run in terror to report a "haint" that was climbing out of its grave, but not Bill Dunn, as he would have faced the devil himself. He crept silently through the graves holding his oil kerosene lantern before him until he could peer down in the recess of the old grave. He laughed aloud as the yellow light of his lantern revealed a tired old white billy goat that had fallen into and was trapped in the bottom of the deep caved-in grave. Among the splinters of a rotten pine wood casket and a few rags and bones of some long dead settler. Bill Dunn peered down the steep end of the grave and the white form of the goat leaped out and vanished into the darkness.

Chapter 19

The Trip to Fitzgerald

Teddie once more turned his back on Andersonville. He loved his mother with all his heart, but the home place was not the same. It lay behind him just as his boyhood did. The sun would never set on him again in the city of the dead.

He was determined to make his mark in this world, and Fitzgerald seemed to be the place for him to begin. Some unseen hand was guiding him back to South Georgia.

He could have caught the northbound AB&A Train and gone to Atlanta, which was the city of choice for young people to seek their fortune. Instead he boarded the southbound passenger train that September day in 1909 at Oglethorpe, Georgia, the junction point of the AB&A and the Central of Georgia Railroad. This was the first time Teddie had seen an AB&A passenger train with its second-hand coaches. The coaches were second-handed. The locomotive was something out of the past, a "dinky" bought off some bankrupt log railroad. It had only four driving wheels, two pony wheels, and no engine truck wheels and had been converted from a wood burner to coal fired, but it could rattle right along with its combination baggage second class passenger coach and the first-class passenger coach.

They were both constructed of wood and supported by truss rods. The engine and coaches were equipped with air brakes, although the engine had no power reverse and the engineer had to "throw" a lever as long as he was, called a "Johnson Bar" to put the ancient engine in reverse. Was this the railroad that Teddie Dunn was boarding to take him the 60 odd miles south to Fitzgerald, Georgia and his place in the sun?

The new leather suitcase Teddie was living out of was "checked" to Fitzgerald and would ride in the baggage coach. The AB&H was not a first-class railroad as was the Atlantic Coastline or the Central of Georgia's were. He had seen such trains as he was now boarding. The Ocilla Southern Railroad at Alapaha, Georgia, down near Pearson had a train like this one, with like rolling stock that terminated in Fitzgerald, the Yankee Colony that was the talk of South Georgia. Oh well, mighty oaks grow from tiny acorns, Teddie was musing, as he sat in the old coach in the "smoker section" where the people that smoked were required to ride as they enjoyed smoking and chewing tobacco that might offend ladies and children. Ladies of that day seldom smoked, and never chewed, at least in public.

The old coaches creaked and groaned as they clipped along through the towns and villages of Central Georgia, ever southward. The little engine seemed as anxious as Teddie to get back to the sand ridges and flat pine woods of South Georgia. After crossing the Flint River at Montezuma, Turkey Creek, Hog Crawl and Pennie Hatchee Creeks, the red hills were no more. "Could Fitzgerald be far", Teddie asked the train conductor?" The bewhiskered conductor pulled his gold watch from the vest pocket of his well worn uniform by the long gold chain that was draped across his chest; glanced at the big watch held in the palm of his hand, pushed his pullbox hat back on his head, and dutifully announced that his train was on time.

Time seemed to be the most important thing on a railroad. The little steam engine got down to a hard pull on a long steady grade as the rails led south of Cordele. Dense clouds of black smoke drifted past the coach windows to settle among the tall pine trees in place of the cotton fields of Dooly County.

Teddie talked to the men in the "smoker," As the train picked up momentum once more.

The train's crew member, known as the flagman, also in an excuse for a uniform was a talkative fellow. He told Teddie that many Yankee folks rode this train to Fitzgerald; seems there was no end to them. They were all bound for Fitzgerald, and were all good people of some means and called themselves Colonists. Teddie told the flagman that he, as a boy, had become well acquainted with northern people, as they had come by the trainload to his hometown of Andersonville, on Decoration Day to lay baskets of flowers at the graves of the Union soldiers that had perished at the prison camp there during the last year of the Civil War. The young men agreed that they were different in many ways from southern people, but seemed to have money.

It seemed that the train's engineer was using all the steam the fireman could generate to blow the whistle that seemed to echo more in the flatwoods. The flagman reminded Teddie that the livestock were roaming on open range, here in the southern counties, and they seemed to spend most of their time on the tracks of the AB&A railroad than they did on the wiregrass range.

Teddie was told that the engineer on the throttle of the engine #32 that was hauling the train to Fitzgerald today was Omar Fairfield, a dandy engine man that usually brought his train in on time. Teddie did not know it at the time, but that name would become part of his destiny.

A stop was made at the water tank just north of the village of Rebecca, Georgia for engine water pumped from the swampy waters of Double-Run Creek. While the train was stopped, Teddie stretched his legs as the train wheels cooled from the hard run from Cordele.

He could hear the whine of a sawmill that put him in mind of Pearson, Georgia. Would Fitzgerald be like Pearson with its sandy streets and sleeping livestock and the briar goat's sleeping on the station platform? Would Fitzgerald sleep through the week, and come to rollicking life on Saturday night? All these questions flashed through his mind, there at the water tank at Double-Run Creek.

Omar Fairfield sounded the #32's whistle long and loud for the flagman to return to Teddie's passenger train from the position he had taken some distance back down the track, to protect the train from any train movement behind.

The train that was filling its tender with water to generate steam to power the engine's tall driving wheels, that with every revolution would bring Teddie and all his worldly belongings, packed in that leather suitcase up in the baggage coach, that much closer to Fitzgerald, "The Soldier's Tribune Colony," whatever that might mean. He only hoped they would have an opening for a "Lightning Slinger" in the train dispatcher's office in the big new station that was the talk of the "railroad folks."

Sims Burns, Teddie had learned, was the talkative flagman's name. He was out of breath as he ran to climb aboard the rear coach. The high-ball signal he gave Fairfield at the throttle of the #32 brought two quick whistle blasts that echoed up and down the creek bottom. The drivers of the light engine slipped on the shining steel rails for a couple of revolutions, but then held the rails that led to Fitzgerald. Flagman Burns rolled up his red flag on the short wooden handle, stamped the dust off his shoes and sat down next to Teddie.

Their conversation was railroad talk, as the two young men were like all railroad men, never tired of tales of the rails. He informed

Teddie that after the next station stop at Rebecca, they would cross the Alapaha River and be on their last lap of the journey to Fitzgerald, where the trains changed crews and engines for the trip to the lines terminal in Waycross, Georgia.

Teddie told Sims Burns that he well knew of the Alapaha River and its course near Pearson, where he had spent a year, as messenger boy. The hollow sound the train made as it rumbled across the river trestle would be the last of the fields and villages unless you counted the flag stops of Arp and Abba.

The train seemed to sense that it was on the last leg of its long journey from the hills and rills of North Georgia. Engineer Fairfield poured the steam to the #32 and she strutted her stuff, the telegraph poles beside the track flew by, like fence posts.

Travel on the railroad was a smoky, dusty trip. Teddie went into the toilet at the end of the coach to freshen up. The toilet commode was dry. To flush the contraption you simply stepped on a pedal that opened a hopper dumping whatever was contained in the bowl directly onto the track beneath the coach as it sped along, not the most sanitary arrangement, but who would know the difference, as there were thousands of acres of pine forests outside, and besides no one was supposed to be on a railroad track.

A lavatory with running water was there for the passengers' convenience. The sign over the lavatory warned that the dingy water was "wash water," and not safe to drink. The water would flow only when the passenger would activate a hand pump mounted on the wash stand. Soap was not supplied, although there was a roll of paper towels.

Common people rode the coaches in the Georgia backwoods and a little grime and dust of the road was to be expected. Wood burning engines had been smoky, but "Man Alive!" these coal burners belched clouds of black smoke and hot cinders that smelled like tar and left a coat of smut on everything and everybody.

The Teddie Dunn that stepped onto the concrete platform of the station at Fitzgerald was a confident, well-dressed young man ready to make his mark in the world. He and the palatial station of the Atlantic Birmingham and Atlantic had much in common. The station had drained the coffers of the railroad, just as the new suit of clothes he had left with just some small change to jingle in his new pockets. He and the new railroad had bet their last penny on Fitzgerald, and it too was struggling to stay afloat financially.

Chapter 20

Teddie's Last Move

"Around and around she goes and where she lands, no one knows," the gambler shouted as he spun the roulette wheel at the saloon. Teddie had landed amidst a crowd of strange looking people.

Train time was the event of the day. Many people just came to see who arrived, how they looked and what they had, or even to hear what language they spoke. No town in Georgia had just sprung up seemingly over night in the towering pine forest carpeted with wiregrass. There were thousands of northern settlers determined to build a city where only yesterday there was no railroad, telegraph lines, and few roads to speak of. It was ten miles to the Ocmulgee River and the steam boats that had been the link to the Atlantic Coast and Macon, the largest city south of Atlanta.

Nothing of this magnitude had ever happened in the pine barrens as this area had been termed. Many despairing words had been spoken by the local people that had just eked a poor living out of the land that seemed to grow only pine trees and wiregrass. Pine tar, saw logs, scrub cows, sheep, and goats had been the cash crops.

Now here came this second invasion of Yankees. They did possess a work ethic seldom seen in southern people. They seemed to be better organized and many were, shall we say, well heeled. They brought their big fine saddle horses, Belgian work horses, well-bred milk cows, beef cattle, and their substantial architectural styles. They were industrious and better educated than the pioneer people, the Crackers.

The crowds of immigrant workmen that the city's ambitious projects attracted swelled the throng. It seemed that everyone was busy going or coming. They all had to be fed, housed and entertained.

Teddie pushed through the crowd to the baggage room of the station to claim his suitcase. He then stepped to the ticket office where he heard a telegraph instrument clattering away. The nearby train register book was being signed by the arriving train crew.

Sims Burns, the flagman, that had befriended Teddie, stepped forward and introduced him to Omar Fairfield, the locomotive engineer that had just signed the register. He was quite handsome, a Yank from the state of Indiana. His face was rather black from the smoke of the engine. The only white skin was around his eyes where the eye goggles had protected his eyes from the smoke and cinders that showered back into the cab where h e had put the little engine through its paces. Those goggles, that were pushed up over the brim of his cap, the red bandana under his collar, the gold watch and chain in the bib of his starched overalls, the oily leather gloves, the timetable in his hip pocket, and his shined shoes, were the badge of his occupation of a locomotive engineer.

He struck quite a good figure that would turn the eye of the finest lady, or floozy at the saloons and dance halls down on East Pine Street, the Mecca of the camp followers and settlers craving a little sport and entertainment after a hard day's labor.

Fairfield shook Teddie's hand. Little did either man know that fate had laid its hand on their shoulders, one a Yank, the other a Rebel.

Teddie desperately needed to locate his brother Charlie. The "Lightning Slinger" on duty in the ticket office informed him that he well knew Charlie Dunn. He no longer was an operator up in the dispatcher's office upstairs, but had been promoted to supervisor of the Freight Agency, located two blocks south of the passenger station, along the tracks.

The train crew invited Teddie to join them at the Colony House Hotel down Central Avenue, run by Mrs. Hall.

She catered to railroad men and set a most delicious table. He had the 25 cents that the meal would cost and was some kind of hungry. This was Teddie's day to meet people, good honest people that would give him the support he would need.

There were two other young men that had arrived in Fitzgerald on the same passenger train that had just left the station for Waycross, Georgia and its connections for Savannah, Georgia, and Jacksonville, Florida.

The two men noted that Teddie, in his suit of store bought clothes, collar and tie, and black derby hat, was someone to watch and get acquainted with. One of the fellow travelers introduced himself as P.G. White, a native son of Georgia, the other a Greek boy, named Nicolas Pope, a native of far away Greece. He knew a smattering of English, and intended to open a café in Fitzgerald. These three young men would put down roots, in his own way, in the booming Colony City of Fitzgerald.

Teddie was quick to catch the carnival spirit of the street people that were as busy as a swarm of honey bees zooming about the business of the day. The town which was only fifteen years old had paved sidewalks. The only livestock in the streets were horses and they too were busy hauling people and goods. This town was so different from Pearson or Andersonville, which seemed to slumber until "train time." The ring of hammers and the whir of handsaws could be heard in every direction as the carpenters were raising new buildings that had replaced the shacks of the first arrivals in their covered wagons and aboard the churning steamboats that plied the Altamaha and its main tributary, the Ocmulgee River.

Teddie found his brother Charlie at the large wooden building with its raised platform to give easy access to the string of boxcars that were parked alongside.

There were a dozen or so black men transferring boxes and bundles of merchandise that was destined to be delivered by "dray men" driving their delivery drays (wagons) to the stores and warehouses about Fitzgerald.

Teddie was directed by a white warehouse man about his age, named W.A. Troupe, a native southern country boy, come to town. He directed Teddie to the spacious office of the freight depot where he found Charlie Dunn pouring over a stack of way-bills and correspondence, that kept the railroad traffic flowing. He was tall, in his mid-twenties, but was beginning to stoop a bit, and could never keep a lock of his black hair from falling across his forehead. He always wore his white shirt and collar that sported the ever present black bow tie that seemed to be the badge of authority on the railroad. He was the agent and supervisor of the clerks and porters that reported to him. Not only that, he had to meet the public, and collect the payment of the freight bills. Charlie had to handle a lot of money, for the railroad company and the carload shipment that arrived and departed, each day. He was a busy man. He had in the office a telegraph operator that kept him informed as to train movements and connected his office here at Fitzgerald with the other stations of the AB&A Railroad that now lived up to it's name, Atlanta, Birmingham and Atlantic, not to mention the branch lines to Waycross and

Thomasville. It hadn't obtained the status of a first-class railroad, but it served a lot of towns and had great connections with first-class railroads. Fitzgerald was the nerve center, so to speak, of the far flung instant line.

Charlie Dunn needed help, and he was no person to overlook anyone who could help him, or finance him. Teddie was "it" as he was still too young to be employed as a telegraph operator, copying and delivering train orders, but he could send and receive the messages that seemed to come into the office at Fitzgerald. Lillie Dunn, Charlie's wife from Kirkland, was the "spark plug" that kept Charlie clicking, but she was homebound now, with a baby boy named Will Dunn, for his grandfather, the old hard bit section foreman, William T. Dunn.

Charlie rose to his feet to greet Teddie. He extended his hand to Teddie's and made an effort to push his hair off his forehead. His words had an urgency in them, "Where in thunderation have you been keeping yourself boy? I have not heard from you since brother "T" told me he had placed you on the Central's extra steel gang. You still look like a boy in men's clothes." Teddie had become used to being referred to as a runt, and it shed right off his narrow shoulders. What he didn't shed off was the fact that Charlie had seemingly forgotten the twenty dollars that their mother had loaned Charlie three years past. That was Teddie's hard earned money she had been holding for him.

Teddie smiled, and told his older brother that their brother "T" Dunn had helped him get a start on the railroad, but he had heard much talk of Fitzgerald and the opportunities it offered a man that was ready to roll up his sleeves and get down to "brass tacks," and he was that man. A "Lightning Slinger" didn't have to be a giant, the lightning (electricity) did all the hard work of sending messages. Charlie laughed and told him he could help him with the agency duties until an operator's job came open and he was twenty-one years old, as the rule of the road required. Charlie told Teddie that Lillie would fix him a room, and he was welcome to put his feet under his dining table. Lillie would cook for him, and see to his clothes, but pocket money would be up to him to "moonlight." He then told Teddie that he was sorry that "T" was in failing health lately. Poor boy was only a shade of his old self and those cigarettes were causing him to hack and cough continually.

Minnie was settled in Jacksonville, and had made Charlie some small loans to tide him over. George O'Niel had done well in the ice and coal business, as Florida was coming into its own since Henry Flagler had built his Florida East Coast Rail line opening South Florida to development. The Atlantic Coastline was serving Central Florida and the old port city of Tampa, on the Gulf Coast to a flood of northern tourists, or "snow birds" as the southern people termed them.

Chapter 21

Fitzgerald in 1910

Fitzgerald had been one of the first towns to ignite the movement of northern people to the land of sun and sandy beaches of Florida. Railroads were the magic carpet that whisked the tourist from the frigid blast of the north wind that brought only ice, snow, and misery. The northern tourists had money that was burning their pockets and would not be long before the poor blacks and white laborers would follow them to build hotels, cities, roads and homes.

There was no better way to get through than on the passenger trains.

This was the heyday of the budding rail system of the rural south that was only yesterday chugging through the flatwoods to bring logs to the mills and cotton to the north. Railroads were coming to full bloom!

One of these railroads was the Seaboard Airline, and it also was Florida bound. The very wealthy came in their private cars, and rolling palaces. There were solid trains of the sleek varnished coaches with stained glass window decorations.

The same little converted wood burning steam engines were pressed into duty on the AB&C Railroad that passed through Fitzgerald with solid trains of private cars, and Pullman coaches bound for Thomasville, Georgia down on the Georgia/Florida border, during the winter months.

The money these tourists spent trickled down to the carpenters, brick layers, cross tie hewers (cutters), and even "Lightning Slingers," tapping out messages and train orders that kept the trains on schedule and the business "tycoons" in touch with their stock brokers on New York's Wall Street.

Time drug by. Charlie was a smart young man that could manager everything but his own affairs. That is where Lillie took the reins. She could keep Charlie's nose to the grindstone and his pay check in her pocketbook. She took young Teddie under her other wing. She now had two children, a boy that was a toddler and baby girl in the crib. She saw to it that Teddie was clean and well fed. The one thing she asked of Teddie, and with Charlie's support was a simple requirement. Lillie laid the law down.

The small-framed house the Dunn family rented on West Central Avenue that was painted white and tucked in between two large Yankee houses was not large enough for two wives to live under the same shingled roof. To compound the situation, Teddie had no regular job. He was only Charlie's assistant. The third fact was that the town was populated with Yankees and their daughters were off limits to well-reared southern young men and matrimony was out of the question. Teddie listened carefully, and nodded his head in agreement, but remained silent.

Railroad officials were not known for their kind words and understanding nature. They were there to get the jobs done. There is always an exception to a rule, and R.H.. "Bob" McKay was that exception. He was head man up in the traffic department of the AB&A Railroad, and had a lot of pull with the superintendent of the line. His keen eye had noted Teddie Dunn's appearance and dedication to duty, even though he was not yet on the company payroll.

Charlie Dunn had fallen victim to the bright lights and temptations of Fitzgerald's East Pine Street and its den's of iniquity.

Bob McKay had a report from the company auditor that Charlie Dunn's cashbox was short. Charlie caught the next train to Florida. He took Lillie and the children with him, leaving no forward address.

Teddie knew trouble was brewing and presented himself before Mr. McKay. Teddie volunteered that he would repay the shortage, as soon as he had a job. Bob McKay had to make a decision quick. He appointed a friend of Teddie's, Charlie Moore, as Freight Agent. He then gave Teddie Dunn a job as a telegrapher on the swing shift in the train dispatcher's office, and relief operator at the freight house. A for rent sign hung on the little white house on Central Avenue. Teddie moved into the St. James Hotel on the east end of Central Avenue. He was strapped for money until he drew his first railroad check. The twenty-one jewel railroad watch he had obligated himself for at Russell Brother's Jewelry Store was a requirement of his job as a telegraph operator; where could he go but to the bank.

All that Teddie owned was the clothes on his back and a good name around Fitzgerald. He had started going to church with a group of young people and made friends easily. One of these friends was Mark

Mathis, a young clerk in the bank. He negotiated a loan of $25 that P.G. White, his friend from their first day in Fitzgerald, co-signed the bank note.

Teddie tightened his belt. He ate Irish stew at Nick Pope's Greek Café that was doing a good business feeding all the workmen and railroad men plain food that they could afford.

Teddie worked every waking hour, if it was only polishing his shoes.

W.O. Triplett, the Chief Dispatcher, took Teddie under his care as Bob McKay had, and gave him any extra work hours that came along. He was slinging lighting, Nick Pope was slinging hash, and P.G. White was slinging manure. Fitzgerald was lucky to claim such young men as citizens, none of them natives.

Teddie had to scrimp to make his monthly payment to the bank, pay his room and board bill, but he was building wealth, not in gold, but in character.

He associated himself with people that had goals set and turned deaf ears to the call of evil, where ever it existed.

Fitzgerald had its growing pains. The thousands of workmen that had rushed to Fitzgerald to clear the forest, grade and drain the streets, and construct the power lines to transmit the electricity that the generating plant, owned by the city, was supplying power and lights to the industries that had sprung up, even the railroad shops at Westwood.

Italian brick masons, who had paved the broad streets with brick in the uptown district, were gone now. The carpenters that had built the substantial homes throughout the south and west districts were finding work scarce.

The city fathers had a good thing going and intended for the new town to continue to grow and thrive. They created what would come to be some of the first public works projects around. It is outstanding what hundreds of skilled workmen could accomplish in jig time. Lumber, good heart pine lumber, was perhaps the most plentiful resource the area possessed. Many hands, many pine boards resulted in the largest wooden building in Georgia, known as the Lee Grant Hotel.

It dominated the entire two hundred block of West Central Avenue. It soared four stories high and could be seen from the elegant railroad station and Fitzgerald's thriving business district.

The AB&A Railroad had built and bought new passenger coaches that were bringing people from the north to visit and do business in the town. The Seaboard Railroad had a passenger station at the east end of Central Avenue. Seems that people, all sorts of people seemed on the move, and the trains were the mode of transportation.

Teddie Dunn was fascinated by the "Hullabaloo" of the street people. There were aging Union veterans that lounged around the streets, some one-armed, others peg-legged, that enjoyed the warm Georgia sun. No snow to shovel or ice to slip and slide on.

Black people, whose parents had been slaves, were free men. The original southern people tended to be farmers and lumber men. The Yankees were more industrious and tended to business from real estate to banking. The black people lived to themselves on the east side of town. With few exceptions, they were the work force of the white men's industries.

Law and order was here, but graft and disorder had become a problem in Fitzgerald. Crime and the vices seemed to precipitate to certain well-defined areas.

Lower East Pine Street was a place where no lady ventured unaccompanied. Saloons poured whiskey, poker games, and roulette wheels spun to the accompaniment of "Rinkie Dinkie" piano music. Dance halls and their taxi dancers glided with men that were dropouts from the dancing schools.

The black and white people had their separate bars and honkytonks in their neighborhoods. The police seemed to be wearing blinders, and could look the other way if their palms were greased with a little money.

This element of society seemed to regulate itself. Whiskey was shipped in by the barrels full on the railroad. Gamblers, hustlers and their cohorts flowed in and out of town with the arrival and departure of every passenger train. What was wrong with a fellow that had worked hard all week, having a little fun, down on East Pine Street on Saturday night if he stayed in bounds? The law abiding, church going people also had a question…where were the police or the sheriff?

The merchants and preachers knew that things were coming to a head. They had a private meeting one night and over the objections of the Chief of Police, the group decided to hire a constable, a professional lawman that had a lily white reputation, and a fast gun for hire. The city fathers contacted the Wells Fargo Company in Atlanta for a man to suit their bill. Two weeks passed and East Pine Street roared on, the music and whiskey flowed, unabated. "Come on down and have some fun, tomorrow is another day and hell ain't half full."

That law man arrived on the noon train from Atlanta. The passenger train groaned to a stop at the busy station at Fitzgerald. Teddie Dunn had copied a handful of train orders that he was delivering to the outgoing train crew on the station platform.

He was not the only one to notice a small man, dressed in a western suit. This man was wearing a cowboy hat and sharp toed riding boots, and looked either to the right or the left. Teddie wasn't the only person to wonder who the newcomer was. He wore a gun belt that holstered a Mother of Pearl handled pistol that his frock tailed coat failed to completely cover. He was, in fact, a business man. He worked for the peace and quiet business and excelled at it, although he had to relocate often. He stepped into the hack (taxi) that Will Cleveland drove. The redheaded woman that always sat in the carriage knew her business well, also. She smiled at the stranger which was her calling business card. One glance was enough to read the lips of the small man with the big pistol. She chewed a little harder on her chewing gum and spoke next to the driver, "See you round later, Will," as she stepped to the sidewalk of Fitzgerald.

The newcomer spoke in a firm voice, "St. James Hotel, hackie." He slid his grip over to the seat of the street walker had vacated.

Will Cleveland tapped the reins he held against the rump of the old plug horse that knew his way around the new brick paved streets of Fitzgerald, and its "tenderloin district." Why didn't the newcomer go to the Lee-Grant Hotel, as most business men did? The Saint James Hotel catered to workmen. Old Mrs. Muldoon ran a "tight ship" or should I say hotel. Oh well, it takes a lot to shock the citizens of Fitzgerald.

The conductor of the train that hauled the man from Atlanta told the boys around the waiting room that he traveled on a pass issued by the Wells Fargo Company. Speculation was everything from a bounty hunter, to a "trick shot" that was a "front man" for the Buffalo Bill Show that was scheduled to stop here. Time would tell his line of goods.

The next meeting of the City Council, which was dominated by Yankees that intended to rid the town of its vices, was held at the City Hall building. They met Willhiem Smitts, the mystery man that seemed to have himself under perfect control. The commissioners told him what they expected from him, and with little more said, pinned a bronze star on his vest and gave him the title of City Constable, reporting only to the mayor.

Since Charlie Dunn had left Fitzgerald, Teddie felt more on his own. It wasn't that he didn't appreciate his brother's hospitality, and Lillie's home cooking, but he found it hard to work his brother's job, while he was bird hunting or shooting pool, down at the pool hall. But now, he had been left holding the bag, to cover Charlie's debts in Fitzgerald.

He did get a letter from Lillie, that Charlie had landed a new job on the Seaboard Airline Railroad, as station agent at Gainesville, Florida. Teddie thought to himself that Charlie could fall in a barrel of horse manure, and come out smelling like the first rose of spring. Teddie was glad to be out of the picture, as Gainesville was far south of Fitzgerald, Georgia.

The day had not revealed all of its surprises.

Who would be sitting on the front porch of the St. James Hotel, but Bob McKay, Teddie's big boss. He greeted Teddie and asked him to have a seat; that it was time they had a long talk, railroad talk. It seems that there was going to be a vacancy at the Freight house.

Charlie Moore had "bid in" the agents job at the Moultrie, Georgia station, down on the Thomasville branch line of the AB&A. Mr. McKay told Teddie that W.A. Troupe would become agent at the Freight Station now as he "stood" for the job as he had more seniority than Teddie had.

He reasoned with young Teddie that Lightning Slingers were a dime a dozen, and hopped about over the line, that he would be much more secure on the chief clerk's job here in town. He also assured Teddie that he would see to it that the Supervisory of Agency at Fitzgerald would become a positive job and the salary would be higher, not to mention that no one could bump (roll) him. Teddie had a few days to think the proposition over. Bob McKay rose and the two men shook hands.

Teddie redoubled his efforts on the Freight House position. He had his paperwork to handle as well as supervising the transfer operation out on the long raised platform that stretched the entire city block, from Main Street to Grant Street, the through fair of the town that was almost a city in 1912. He was responsible for the cash drawer and the big steel safe.

His two years in Fitzgerald had been busy years. He found little time to socialize, but he was energetic and healthy. He juggled his many duties well enough to manage time for church activities and be initiated into the Masonic Order, now that he was past his twenty-first birthday. There were two other young men in the group of inductees— Nick Pope and C.G. White.

Fitzgerald had matured as well. The streets were safe for women and children. The boomers had moved onto greener pastures. The little constable Smitt had fulfilled his assignment. He and Teddie respected each other from the beginning. They had mastered their trades, one a gun slinger, the other a lightning slinger. Time and fortune waits on no one.

There was a ditch along the railroad track. A bridge spanned Grant Street and the swampy lots below. Smitts rode a high wheeled bicycle over his beat, and would carry a lunch with him, as he was always on duty. After he ate the last of his lunch, sitting on the bridge at Grant Street, he would draw his pistol and shoot snakes that abounded along the water flow. The sound of shooting would draw an audience. His draw was fast as greased lightning, and his eye was sure as sunrise. He would throw tin cans in the air for targets; send them spinning away before they could fall. His reputation became the talk of Fitzgerald. He shot a lot but he never shot anyone.

He and that colt pistol had turned the tide of behavior. The beer was still drunk, the music was heard, but the criminal element had caught the train for parts unknown. A gun slinger never puts down roots in a community. Smitts caught the train one day never to be heard from again.

The second generation of the northern settlers was growing up. Time and toil had thinned ranks of the aging Civil War Veterans. The band that played concerts in the plaza parks of Fitzgerald and on the 4th of July, rode the excursion trains to Andersonville on Yankee Memorial Day, found fewer and fewer members.

The railroads, cotton mills, turpentine stills, and saw mills, manned mostly by southern white and black men were more in evidence as the years passed.

Chapter 22

The Crossing at Grant Street and Tessie

The younger generation seemed more interested in the modern world. They mixed and mingled more. There were two young women that bonded for life, one a Yank the other a Reb. Their school days were happy here in Fitzgerald. One was named Anna Theresa Barwick (Tessie), the other Nettie Day. They had this special relationship, although Tessie as Anna Theresa was known, had a twin sister, Hester Barwick. The three girls were in the flower of young womanhood, as they were seventeen. The Barwick twins lived four blocks north of the railroad track on North Grant Street. Their parents had come south with their grandparents when they were babies in their mother's arms, with the northern colonists in 1896.

Tessie's grandfather, Henry Fisher, had ridden with General Sherman's Calvary as a saddle maker. He was a native of Pennsylvania, the father of Arta, Tessie's mother. Arta Fisher and her father were cooks for a logging camp cutting the last of the original white pine forest in the north woods of Michigan. One day, at the camp, a young man named Charles Daniel Barwick, claiming to be a "lumber jack" signed on with the logging crew. He was different from the Swedes and Germans that were felling the giant trees along the shores of Lake Superior. He spoke with a strange brogue, the King's English. He was tall and muscular, and proudly proclaimed to be a subject of the British Queen. He was an Australian immigrant and told little else of his background, but was good with an ax and a master with the horses and oxen that powered the logging company. Seemed he and his family had been "stockmen" in New South Wales, Australia.

He took a "shine" to the camp cook's daughter, Arta Fisher. She was very close to her father, Henry Fisher, but somehow she was rather attracted to the newcomer. Her father was born in England and he too an immigrant and subject of the British Crown, and as the old proverb states, "Birds of a feather, will flock together."

The last of the northern virgin white pine timber was being cut in the late eighteen hundreds. Charlie Barwick won the hand of Arta Fisher in holy matrimony, there in Michigan. The three returned to the orderly life of the Pennsylvania Dutch farming counties. The winters were cold; Papa Fisher was getting old and he had an inheritance. The newspaper he picked up had an article in it extolling the great new Soldiers Tribune Colony, that a newspaper editor by the name of P.H. Fitzgerald, he himself a Union veteran, was organizing in South Georgia, where ice and snow was unheard of.

Destiny must unfold before humans know how it will touch their lives. Some believe that at the moment of conception, a person's life pattern is set by the position of the stars that hang in the heavens. Gypsies claim to have a special connection with the future, and can look into a ball of crystal glass and see a person's future, for a small fee. Others claim to read the paths ahead from the pattern of tea leaves in a teacup. Be that as it may, no mortal soul has ventured into the realm of the future and returned to tell others of life's joys or pitfalls.

Tessie Barwick had been told, as a child that she had been born with a transparent skin over her eyes; called by the superstitious old midwife that birthed her, a veil. That veil would vanish, but it would in later years allow that person to glimpse into the future. Tessie believed in omens, dreams, and voices spoke to her in the still of the night.

She had watched the tall Georgia pines being cut and burned to make room for streets and parks, the thousands of colonists and laborers that made short work of erecting the fine homes and multistoried buildings that now lined those streets named for Generals of the Civil War, both Yank and Rebel. Some streets were named for native trees that once knew only the calls of birds and animals. Other streets were named for the rivers that drained the wilderness, where now stood a city of ten thousand souls, connected to the cities of America by three railroads.

She had told her girlfriend, Nettie Day, that her future had been revealed to her, that it was only a matter of time until she would marry a southern boy that she had already seen; not in a dream, but in flesh and blood at Andersonville where we go on the excursion train to lay baskets of flowers on the graves of the Union soldiers that died there in the prison camp. He was a cute little cracker boy selling lemonade, older than I am, but small of frame like me. He doesn't know what the future holds for him, but I do. Our stars in the heavens above will cross when the signs are right. She would stare out into space with her blue eyes as if she could see things invisible to others.

The social code of the day demanded that a proper lady did not converse with strange men she encountered on the streets of Fitzgerald. The women that cozied up to men on the street were known as "street walkers," never to be respected. If a young single fellow was moved to acquaint himself with a young lady, he must have a proper introduction by a mutual friend or family member.

Teddie spent much of his workday out on the freight station platform that ended at the Grant Street crossing of the AB&A Railroad. It was a busy crossing for Teddie from the north side of residential Fitzgerald to get to the business district. There was so much traffic that the railroad company was obligated to protect the public from the passing trains that shuttled back and forth over Grant Street crossing.

The company had a man with a red flag stationed in a little track side shack. The crossing flagman was Mr. J.T. Simmons.

Mr. Simmons was peg legged, but active and had spent his days on the crossing warning the public that a train was approaching. He himself had lost his lower leg to a railcar as an employee of the AB&A. The company had no insurance in those days, but would award a life time job to an unfortunate workman that had lost a limb and could still get about. The job as a crossing watchman was a perfect position for such a man.

Mr. Simmons knew many people of Fitzgerald in the course of protecting Grant Street crossing. He also had earned the respect of the older "settlers" of Fitzgerald, among which was Charlie Barwick, Tessie's father. She and her friends would often be in the traffic stopped by a passing train at Grant Street crossing.

Railroad men somehow had gained a somewhat shady reputation as womanizers and flirts. They would wave and whistle at any girl or woman along the line. They were classified with sailors, who were reputed to have a woman in every port.

Teddie and his coworkers would notice the young girls that would only stick out their tongues and look the other way. A proper introduction was a must. Teddie thought he had seen that little red head Yankee girl before, that was always with a group of her school mates and her sister. It left Teddie high and dry when Tessie would ignore him. He would have to try another approach. Cupid was at work at the

Grant Street crossing that day in May, that the sap was rising, not only in the trees and flowers, but in him, as well.

After the train had passed, Teddie stepped over to the crossing guard's shack for a handshake with Mr. Simmons, his friend. He asked him if he knew the parents of the little petite red head that passed with her friends as the young ladies walked to town.

"Teddie," Mr. Simmons told him, as he looked him dead in the eye. I know her and her parents very well. She is the daughter of old Charlie Barwick, and you had best look elsewhere in case your intentions are not honorable as he is a very serious settler from Australia, and would fight a circular saw, he would hold me responsible for any misconduct on your part." Teddie reached in his pocket and produced a silver dollar that he offered the crossing guard. "This eagle is yours if you will introduce me properly to her, and make us acquainted. I don't even know her name."

Teddie found all kinds of business around the end of the platform that afternoon and sure enough the girls returned from uptown, laughing and giggling as young girls will do.

Teddie saw them, straightened his collar and tie, walked down the platform ramp to alert Mr. Simmons. There was no train approaching, and he was nodding in the shack. "Here she comes, please do your best." Mr. Simmons struggled to his good foot, and limped out to greet the girls. He doffed his hat and did a slight bow before Tessie. "Why Mr. Simmons, I hope you are having a nice day. Who is your friend?" "This is the young fellow that has been promoted to the position of Chief Clerk of the Freight Agency, and he had been a telegrapher up in the dispatcher's office above the ticket office back up the track at the big passengers' station. He was raised over at the National Cemetery town of Andersonville.

Tessie shot Teddie a quick glance and laughed a quick reply, "I am pleased to meet you Mr. Dunn. If my memory serves me correct, you and your black friend were serving ice cold lemonade, stirred in the shade, with a spade. Where is your apron? You were the first thing we Yankees saw when we got off the excursion train at Andersonville."

Teddie was set on his heels. He seemed to have trouble finding his voice, but he blurted, "Yes, Miss Barwick, I am the man." "Well, I would like for you to meet my twin sister, Hester Barwick and my closest friend; she is southern as you are. Her name is Nettie Day and we enjoy each other's company.

Mr. Simmons went back to his shack by the tracks to let the young people get acquainted. Tessie was not the least bit timid. Before the girls departed, Tessie told Teddie that she would give him the liberty to address her as "Tessie," as she felt that she had known him before they were introduced formally.

Teddie asked her if he might call on her to meet her parents the next Sunday afternoon. She answered as she left. "I will ask my mother when I get home," and she was gone, but her vision stayed in Teddie's mind.

These were busy times for Teddie, and duties of the railroad came first. The company auditor could drop in on the spur of the moment. The cash drawer had to balance, or he, like his brother before him, would find himself pounding the sidewalks of some city looking for a job.

Railroad stock cars came to Fitzgerald regularly loaded with twenty big mules to be unloaded at the stock pens over on Mead Street. They would be hungry and thirsty after their long trip on the train from faraway Missouri or Tennessee. These critters would arrive at noon or midnight. Who would have to walk a mile at any hour with a crew of black helpers to unload them? You are correct if you guessed Teddie Dunn. All railroad officials were not as kindly as Bob McKay, the General Superintendent, Yard Master, Auditor and others had not been promoted to their high positions on the railroad based on their ability to win friends, but to see how much work they could get out of as few employees as possible, and keep the trains on time. They had no relations with the customers that patronized the company or did they have to collect the freight bills from skin flint merchants and shippers of bulk cargos. Teddie had rather deal with those old Missouri mules over on Mead Street than some shippers.

Time passed, as did traffic on Grant Street. People walked, rode bicycles and horses. Some drove teams that pulled wagons. Men pushed wheel barrows loaded with what poor possessions they owned. It seemed that the northern states were opening its bowels on the south, especially Florida.

Automobiles were appearing on the dirt roads that led to Florida and Grant Street was the roads link through Fitzgerald. Mr. J.T. Simmons was kept busy flagging the trains that passed this parade of humanity, and draft animals.

Teddie had not seen Tessie and her friend walk to town for some days. One afternoon Mr. Simmons waved Teddie over to his shack to hand him an envelope addressed to him. It smelled of powder and perfume, even after it had been in the old man's pocket. Cupid can take strange forms, even appear as a peg-legged railroad crossing guard, but he did!

Teddie's heart skipped a beat as he read the note that had been so carefully folded, as only a girl could do to keep the contents private. The note was addressed to Teddie Dunn, its words were discreet and brief. "It would be my pleasure to have you visit my home located on the five hundred block of North Grant Street on the west side of the street, a two-story Yankee house, behind which is a large barn and stock pen. My mother and father would like to meet you and my twin sister Hester's beau, who plans to come also. Signed...Sincerely, Tessie Barwick.

Teddie would live to make many investments in a long lifetime, but without a doubt, the silver dollar he gave the old peg-legged man that guarded the railroad crossing at Grant Street to introduce him to Tessie would prove to be the most rewarding investment he would ever make.

Chapter 23

Meeting the Barwick Family

Sunday finally arrived, birds were singing, church bells were ringing, flowers were blooming, and Teddie's heart would skip a beat every time he thought of Tessie just budding into womanhood.

There was no message alerting him of livestock movements on the rails. The accounts were balanced, reports sent in to the auditor, and cash was locked in the steel safe in the office. He sat down to the telegraph key and sent a message in Morse Code to the train dispatcher, asking permission to be out of place, as he was always on call and emergencies were frequent on the railroad. The sigh of relief Teddie breathed could have been heard out to the sidewalk where the dispatcher o.k.'d his relief from duty for the afternoon.

Teddie sat down to the dinner table, but he only picked at his food. The other men teased him and said, "What's wrong lad, you must be in love!" He staunchly denied their charges, laying his condition to "spring fever." He pushed his half-eaten plate aside and rushed to his room to dress in his Sunday-go-to-meeting clothes, but it wasn't church meeting he had on his mind, it was a meeting with destiny.

He had selected a new straw hat at Jake Setemeyer's Clothes on Pine Street. It was the latest style hat, a straw "boater" that all the young "blades" were sporting. Old Jake had made him a special price, but the price was equal to a day of his wages, and would be charged until payday. Teddie looked snappy in his suit, collar and bowtie. He stood before his mirror setting his new "boater" hat at different angles on his head until he decided on the best position.

He wondered who Tessie's twin sister Hester's beau would prove to be, as he knew most of the young men that amounted to a "hill of beans" around town. Suddenly he remembered Charlie and Lillie's stern warning about associating with Yankee girls, but he dismissed those warnings, as they were far away in Florida and he was left holding Charlie's debts.

Teddie put his best foot forward as he walked north on Grant Street and tipped his new hat to ladies he met on the paved sidewalk. He remembered the sandy streets and board sidewalks of Pearson, and was glad he was over in Fitzgerald, with its modern conveniences.

The Barwick home on Grant Street appeared to be set in a menagerie of stock pens, house moving equipment, and tools of Charlie Barwick's trade, "house moving." The house was two-story wood frame structure, pieced together from several old buildings that he and the boys, as he referred to Tessie's older brothers, had winched in with the "string" of blind horses. These horses were the stout old Australian man's pride and joy. He termed himself a "stockman" and the place certainly reinforced his title.

Teddie looked somewhat out of place in his stylish clothes, shined shoes, and that straw "lid" set on his head. He did notice that there was a livery buggy, and a sleek horse hitched to the hitching post before the front porch. Teddie swallowed hard as he mounted the front steps and stepped to the front porch. He rang the doorbell on the ornate stained glass windowed front door that seemed a bit out of place on such a decrepit building. The bell worked better than it looked, in fact, it rather startled Teddie. He heard footsteps inside, the lock turned slowly and the heavy door swung open and a whip of a woman braced herself on a crutch in the opening. A slow smile spread on her face. What might your business be young man? Teddie had heard northern people speak with a brogue, but never one this thick. "I was calling on Miss Tessie, I am Teddie Dunn. We were introduced by Mr. Simmons recently. I was invited to call on her, to introduce myself to you and Mr. Barwick. May I come in?"

"Please be seated on the porch, Mr. Dunn, and I will speak with my daughter to see if she's receiving callers" Teddie did not sit down; he just stood at the cracked door with his new hat in his hand. Sounds of piano music and laughter came from inside the parlor. In what seemed to be an eternity, the front door swung open and Tessie and her crippled mother appeared onto the porch.

"May I take your hat Teddie, this is my mother, Arta Barwick and we would like to have you join us and some friends in the parlor and we can all get acquainted."

There were two other young couples gathered around the piano, enjoying themselves and Teddie knew the two young men. To his surprise there was Omar Fairfield, the locomotive engineer that sat at the throttle of the little high wheeled engine that brought the passenger train into the station at Fitzgerald two years ago. The other fellow was Asa Smith, a salesman in a dry goods store uptown. Omar was calling on Tessie's twin sister Hester and Asa was all eyes for Nettie Day, Tessie's best friend. Needless to say, Teddie hoped to become Tessie's object of affection, but it was obvious to see that he would have to make some changes in his opinions of lifestyles. He had never known a man cut on the pattern of Mr. Charlie Barwick, Tessie's father. His piercing dark eyes seemed to look straight through a person. The crook stemmed pipe he cradled in his callused hands seemed to be a part of his person. His tousled hair that seemed unmanageable for tight curls could have stood a clipping. The thing that really caught your eye was his "handle bar" mustache. It was stained yellow from years of tobacco use and seemed to dominate his strong features. His dress was of a laborer, coarse work trousers that hung on his lean frame by strong yellow gallowses, his scuffed boots smelled of the horse lot. Teddie had been around many old men back in Andersonville, both Yank and Reb, but never in his life had he met one with the flavor of Charlie Barwick. He hesitated to shake his extended hand, or run back to the railroad depot. Could this possibly be sweet little Tessie's father? Tessie's mother Arta saved the day when she stepped forward and told Charlie to go back to the stable and leave his daughters to their friends. She then added that he could take the young men to see his horses on another day. Tessie then went to the piano and began to play some popular music of the day. This group broke the "ice" so to say, for Teddie, as he was certainly on strange turf. The tray of tea cakes, and steaming kettle of hot tea that Arta served the young people, settled Teddie's nerves, but that hot tea she poured into a china teacup, set him on his heels, again. Why the poor boy didn't even know how to hold the cup of steaming fluid. Iced tea had been new to him at Pearson, but who in the name of heaven had ever heard of hot tea? Teddie had a lot to learn about northern people of British extraction that had come south with the Fitzgerald colony, only fifteen years past. The other young people laughed good naturedly at Teddie's dilemma, but who do you think snuggled up to him and showed him how to handle the cup of hot fluid in the hand painted teacup. It was Tessie. Little did he realize that through the years to come it would be her gentle touch that would smooth the road that lay ahead of the young couple that stood on the threshold of the door that would open for them for the sixty some years of sorrow, grief, poverty, plenty and happiness, she would always be at his side, in the new life that they would have to create for themselves.

Omar and Asa excused themselves and their "dates" as they had planned to take a ride in the two-seated shay that the boys had rented from the livery stable down on Sherman Street. There was not room in the shay but for two couples, and Tessie's mother had told Tessie that it wasn't proper for a young girl to go out with a fellow she had just met. A parlor date would be more in order.

Tessie was talented musically and had been given piano lessons at Mrs. Berkleman's Music School, over on Central Avenue. She was a German immigrant and colonist, teaching her students violin and piano, classic German waltzes and marches that Teddie was as unfamiliar with as the hot tea. They spent the evening getting to know each other better. Teddie was awestruck at her graceful manner, and talents that included memory of long poems of the day that she could recite, word for word, with an expression that seemed to bring the thoughts right into the parlor of the otherwise rather drab Barwick home.

Where had the girl-woman with the finger curls of red hair across her forehead gotten the taste for the finer things of life? She laughingly explained the crude ways of her father, telling Teddie that he was typical of the Australian "Jackaroos" of the "Outback" of a faraway land that required the strong character that her father possessed, and that Teddie must respect that he was a master stockman, and his talent was training and caring for horses and sheep. She explained that he would never change into a genteel southern gentleman and that he must accept him as he was, as she had.

The evening passed on a pleasant note. The laughing voices of the couples that had returned from their tour of the town and the four mile ride to Minnie's Millpond behind the prancing harness horse that Omar had rented for the evening. Hester and Nettie were full of girl talk to Tessie, of the afternoon's adventure. They had even been treated to a fountain coca-cola and a chocolate candy bar at the concession stand at the popular millpond, where the young couples of Fitzgerald and the area loved to gather, away from the clatter and exhaust of trains and busy streets of town, which did little to create a romantic scene, for "sparking" couples. Lust, not true love, abound on the backstreets of Fitzgerald where female companionship could always be bought at a price at the gin mills and brothels. The price could be steep in both cash and health.   In fact, Teddie was still paying off the debts of the wages of sin that he had inherited from his brother. He was not bitter, as that brother had given him a start on the railroad, here at Fitzgerald.

Teddie bid good-day to Tessie, as the shadows of evening were falling on North Grant Street, and all respectful young ladies would be at home with their families or at evening services at their church.

The young men that had rented the horse and shay invited Teddie to come with them for the ride back to the stable on Sherman Street to return the rig to old man George Gray, the owner. The three young men, clean cut as they were, returned to their rooms before dark. Fairfield would go out on his run to Atlanta that night, and Asa would have to be at the store at daylight, Teddie would have to notify the dispatcher that he was back "on call."

Chapter 24

True Love

Teddie lay in his bed at the St. James Hotel; his mind was in a whirl. He could not get the haunting beauty and the quiet self-assured way that Tessie possessed. She was even smaller than he was, but her thoughts and words had no bounds. She as he, longed to improve their lots in life, neither had been dealt a hand of cards that could win a fortune. They must discard and draw from the deck, as in a poker game, if they were to win in this game of life that lay before them in Fitzgerald.

Time passes quickly for busy young people. Teddie had been given more responsibility at the Freight house. He was being observed by unseen eyes in high positions on the railroad. The foundation of his destiny was being laid well, not only on the railroad, but at the bank and the merchants of Fitzgerald.

Teddie had received a letter from his brother W.T. Dunn. The letter came in the U.S. mail, not in the railroad mail or a telegram. This bothered Teddie as "T" had never written him a letter like this one he held in his hand today. It was postmarked "The Lonesome Pine Sanatorium," Denver, Colorado. Teddie had a pang of sadness strike his heart as he read the words written in the beautiful handwriting of his brother that had been more of a father to him than a brother. He had been diagnosed with Tuberculosis, and sent to the high clear air of the Rocky Mountains, in a hope of curing the dreaded disease that had claimed so many lives. Teddie would have to learn to take bad news in his stride. Charlie's wife Lillie had stayed in touch with Teddie and gave a good report on Charlie Dunn. She had taken over the family finances, and had Charlie's nose held to the "grind stone" and he was performing well. She had a letter from Ida, back in Andersonville. The news was not good from home. Sallie Ann Dunn was in a decline and she often wondered how her baby, Teddie, was fairing out in the world, and if he was remembering the things she had tried to teach him that would be his foundation of success.

Here in Fitzgerald, just as he had found someone to share his thoughts and dreams, he had received the news that two of his most beloved family members were walking through the valley of the shadow of death.

Teddie had today to worry about the responsibility of his railroad job, but the debts he was obligated to settle at the bank came first.

Visions of the red dirt streets of Andersonville appeared in his mind. There in front of Bill Easterlin's store, where the big fine mules that pulled the Standard Oil Company's kerosene tank wagon from Americus, stood flicking their tails at the flies and stomping the ground impatiently. He remembered the initials that were carved in their hooves, J.D.R., their owner's initials that stood for John D. Rockefeller, the richest man in America. Teddie had no mules or wagon, but he had dreams that some day he would struggle toward his goal of financial independence. The definition of a rich man, he had been told, was a man that was happy with what he had in life. Would Teddie remember that advice?

The Barwick children had a way to go places around town. Charlie Barwick had plenty of horses in his lot behind the house. Some were blind, some crippled, and others had harness gall, and spavin disease. Frankly a sorry looking lot of horse flesh. He had brought some remedies, ointments, and poultices from Australia that worked wonders under his expert loving care.

One of these horses was a "burned out" racehorse named "Round About." She was long-legged, blind and gentle, but still could step high when hitched to the surrey that had two seats that would accommodate six passengers. Tessie's older brothers would hitch old "Round About" to the long bodies homemade rig.

Tessie, small as she was, would always want to take the reins and drive across town to school or to visit friends on the outskirts of Fitzgerald. Charlie Barwick felt that the children were safe with a blind horse in the shafts, as a horse so afflicted would never run away and injure the crowd of passengers that would hitch a ride to town.

The old horse was intelligent and knew a person by their odor, and she knew Tessie and trusted her to lead her from harms way. Round About had died of old age, but Tessie always wanted to drive, even when automobiles came along, she would plant her little self at the driver's, seat and away they would go!

Fitzgerald saw much change as the years that passed. Civil War veterans' ranks grew thinner and thinner. The band played less, the Barwick twins no longer went to school. The tall pines had all been cut but for two city parks. Tall buildings and busy streets dominated the business district. Creeks that once flooded low areas had been ditched and drained. Gone were the saloons and speak easies, law and order prevailed. Churches had been built in every section of town. Sleek passenger trains with new coaches sped to Atlanta and Jacksonville. Throngs of people crowded the downtown sidewalks on Saturday, buying the necessities of life. The growing pains of a boomtown seemed to be over, maturity had arrived.

Teddie spent every spare moment he could with Tessie. Things seemed to be changing in the Barwick Family. There seemed to be a rift between Charlie and Arta. He spent more time on the streets and took better care of his horses than he did of his family. Tessie longed to have her own home in one of the tree lined streets in the better neighborhood of town, away from the hustle and bustle of Grant Street.

Tessie's twin sister Hester had left home and married Omar Fairfield, the locomotive engineer. She, as Tessie, was seventeen and had an apartment over on Suwannee Street, not far from the Barwick home place.

Teddie and Tessie were not long following suit. They were married by the Justice of the Peace, Judge Jim Jones one night before Christmas, 1912. They had a few clothes packed in Teddie's suitcase, and a lot of love. They stayed at Hester and Omar's apartment on Suwannee Street until Teddie could find a place of their own. Young people of that day and time seemed to get married on a "shoe string" so to speak, and put their every effort to establish a happy home. Arta Barwick seemed to know her twins were not happy at home, and their choice of sober hard working railroad men could offer them more than she could. Old Charlie blew off some, but seemed glad he had two less mouths to feed. There were only a younger boy and girl left at the Barwick home, and they were big children.

Payday came on the AB&C Railroad and Tessie took Teddie's pay envelope to the bank and opened a savings account in their name. She found a small apartment across the street from the Fairfields. She and Hester went to Mr. Miller's Furniture Store and selected a few pieces of secondhand furniture. Mr. Miller, a long time friend of the Barwicks, took the few dollars Tessie made as a down payment and put the balance on a credit ticket. Mr. Miller sent word to Charlie Barwick to come up to his store and have a word with him.

Who do you think drove up to the sparse little apartment with Tessie's furniture but blustery old Charlie Barwick, driving his team and wagon. He and the "boys," Tessie's older brothers, made short work of placing the furniture as Tessie and Hester hung curtains on the windows.

The kindly neighbors brought in food for the newlyweds. Tessie's heart sang and her curly red hair was in the clouds. She had a husband and a home of her own in Fitzgerald. The sign on the mailbox read, "Mr. and Mrs. Teddie N. Dunn, Apt. #2, 112 East Suwannee Street."

Tessie set the noon day table in their little love nest. She would await Teddie's footsteps in the hallway that served them and the other apartments in the building. The first hurdle to be passed was the northern style food that Tessie had been raised on. The boiled Irish potatoes, navy beans, loaf bread with no cane syrup and the cups of steaming hot tea were so foreign to him. Where was the cornbread, fried pork belly, turnip greens, and the iced tea he had been spoiled on over at Pearson, and yuck…rutabagas. He asked her where the ice was for the tea. Tessie told him, with her sweetest smile, "There was no nickel for the iceman, my dear."

There is a special relationship between twins, even though they are not identical. This was very true with Tessie and Hester. They could chat for hours between themselves, and could live in their own little world and let the rest of the world go by. There seemed to become deep underlying problems in the Barwick family that would not surface.

Could it have been the rearing of the parents?

Arta and her father, Henry Fisher, were very close to each other. The Civil War and the unstable years after it had set a lot of families asunder. Arta and her father had spent years in Michigan, following the logging crews.

Along came Charlie Barwick, an Australian adventurer, good with his hands, and horses, but certainly not a man of letters. He was strong and better with his fists or an ax than he was a pencil.

Charlie had led a rough life in a devil-may-care society on the riverfront settlement along the Murry River in Australia. Charlie had been abused as a lad, and had felt the hard hand of his father on many occasions. He had to be tough to survive in a hard land. On the other hand, Arta's family had a more cultured background. Her father had been raised in England, well educated there, had a trade as a saddle maker that had married a woman that could trace her lineage to an aristocratic family in England, and had been a member of the "May Flower" group of Pilgrims that landed on Plymouth Rock, the Peltons no less.

Arta was a woman of letters that had educated herself. She had lost her mother soon after the family had landed in Fitzgerald. Then, her beloved father died the next year. She bore Charlie Barwick's six children, in Pennsylvania.

The birth of the twin girls had drained her strength. She had delivered Hester first, a fine baby, one evening. The midwife had bathed the child and settled Arta for the night, when in the wee hours of the night, she called for the slop jar to relieve herself. To everyone's surprise, she delivered another baby girl, right in the slop jar. The baby was so small and weak that the midwife shook her head in disbelief. The child was perfectly developed, with a full head of red curly hair. She clung desperately to what breath of life she had bee given, and lived to see the light of the next day.

The midwife told Arta that the small baby had been born with a veil of membrane over her blue eyes, and that legend held it that a child born with the veil had been given a special vision to see into the future.

Arta replied that she didn't hold with omens and such were for ignorant or superstitious people. Charlie Barwick came to see his children that lay asleep in their cribs. He, at a glance, saw that the wee one was a special child, and named her Anna Thresa for his mother in Australia.

He knew of the veil legend, from the native aborigines he was raised among in the Outback. They had influenced him, and he held with omens.

He and Arta agreed on few things, but they both knew that the tiny girl child was special. The way she could look at you, the spirit she displayed clinging to the spark of life she had been given, not to mention the surroundings she had arrived in.

She and Hester bore little resemblance to each other even as they grew up. Tessie, as they called the small one, was the dominant twin, Hester the quiet serious one. Strangers found it hard to believe that the girls were sisters, much less twins.

Be it as it may, the girls enjoyed each other, and were happy young women, married to hard working sober young men that loved them and drew good pay checks from the railroad that had started just as the young couples had, with the odds against them.

Chapter 25

The Fire

One dark night, Tessie sat upright in the bed. She awakened Teddie and told him that she had a dream and in this dream there was an inferno of flames, horses were whinnying and dense black smoke was billowing to the sky. He told her to go back to sleep, as there was no fire in the neighborhood. She lay back down, but sleep would not come to her troubled mind, just you wait and see, she mused.

Several days passed and nothing out of the ordinary happened, but Tessie was not her bright usual self. She confided to Hester that she was worried about things at the home place on Grant Street. Hester did not question her sister's fears. Too often Tessie's eyes had seen things that came to pass.

The young women strolled down Grant Street to visit their mother that was busy in the kitchen. She had slipped on the ice one winter back north, fallen and broke her hip. The country doctor that set the bone had done a poor job and Arta had never gained mobility of that hip, resulting in a bad limp that hindered her mobility. She limped badly and arthritis had set in now. Tessie told her mother of her dream, but Arta was in no mood to listen to her "far-out" daughter as she had two younger children to cook and wash for. She told Tessie to tell her father of the dream as he believed in dreams, and Australians spent much of their time in what they termed "dreamtime" and "walk-abouts" while she and her older boys tended to the every day duties. She then turned the conversation to how they and their lives were going. Tessie knew where her father was and was not satisfied until she and Hester walked the half mile to the fire station on Central Avenue where Charlie Barwick tended and trained the fine team of horses that pulled the fire engine and the firemen to fires that threatened life and property around town. As she had told Hester, there was their father training the horses to run to the parked fire engine and stand beneath their harness that hung on straps from the ceiling to be dropped on their waiting backs when they heard the fire alarm. He was paid nothing for his services, but just loved the horses that much, not to mention his reputation as a "stockman."

He listened carefully as his wide-eyed daughter told him of her dream. He patted her on her red head and thanked her for coming to him with the omen. The two seemed to be closer than the other Barwick children. Perhaps it was because she was so small and in need of his attention, as the sick and injured horses in his big barn behind the home place that his father-in-law Henry Fisher had purchased when Fitzgerald was in its infancy.

That evening Charlie Barwick and his boys turned all the horses out into the small pasture along the ditch that drained that side of town, for no apparent reason. The boys were used to their father's strange ways, notions, and hard hand of punishment, and opened the lot gate and drove the stock into the pasture for the night. The sun sank below the tall pine trees that still stood in the park west of the home place.

Darkness fell over Fitzgerald. Teddie worked late at the depot on the monthly reports. Tessie had left him a lunch on their dining table that sat only two people. As he ate his lunch of homemade bread and butter, washed down with a glass of buttermilk, he was aware of Tessie slipping into the other chair at the table. She had on her nightgown and was barefooted. She didn't weigh a hundred pounds and always walked on her tip toes. She was quite a bundle of charm as she sat with her elbows on the table to support her head of beautiful curls.

Teddie spoke first. He told her that when he had left early that morning he had found a jar of sweet milk, a mold of fresh churned cow butter, and a bundle of fatwood splinters with a crude note with only one word on it, "Tessie." She looked him straight in the eye and spoke, "I know, that was my papa. I had been getting them before you left each morning, but today I was late arising." Teddie's only answer was, "There can't be too much wrong with the old man. He is just a bit slouchy."

Tessie looked away as she talked to him as she was worried about her parent's relationship. They seemed to be drifting farther and farther apart. Her father spent most nights in his hay loft, over the horses. She resented the punishment he would give her younger brother and sister that were still at home. Seems that he worked the daylights out of the two older boys, then he fought with them, to toughen them.

Tessie put her hand on Teddie, and told him how glad she was to be away from that unhappy home, and to please help her to have a home that was predicated on love and respect, in a better neighborhood. Teddie was touched by the plaintive request and took her in his arms and kissed her tears away.

A week later, there was a new moon in the dark sky. Shooting stars streaked through the blackness, while the other stars twinkled in the heavens above. Tessie sat on the porch watching the stars "fall" as she said, "The spirits are restless tonight, it is a bad omen." Teddie told her not to worry her pretty head and to cheer up. She stood upright, again on her toes to look him in the eyes and spoke in an inquisitive voice. "Oh Teddie, are you blind, can't you see? That is the way you southern people are, just so ignorant and happy go lucky." She bit her lips and said no more.

Teddie just laughed and suggested that they go to bed so they would be safe from the evil spirits that were so restless tonight. They fell asleep only to be awakened by the clanging of a brass bell and the frenzied hoof beats of a team of heavy horses on the pavement of Grant Street, just a block away from their apartment.

The voice of a neighbor shouted, "It's old Charlie Barwick's house on fire. Teddie and Tessie ran barefooted to join the crowd that had gathered in the eerie light of the red flames that were leaping into the night sky.

Tessie was desperate as she and Hester searched the crowd to find their parents and kin. "There they are Tessie!" Hester shouted. The twins rushed to embrace their family. Omar was out on his run, but Tessie, barefooted as she was, ran to assist the firemen in saving the barn, behind the house that was enveloped in the leaping flames.

Charlie Barwick was more concerned with saving his barn and stock than he was the house. He smiled and lit his pipe, then he said, "Don't worry fellows, I have been turning the stock out of the lot into the pasture each night since my daughter, little Tessie warned me that the house would burn to the ground. We two are the only ones in my family that hold with signs and omens."

Daylight came, shafts of light tried to penetrate the smoke that had settled over the low pasture and the foundation of what had been the Barwick home. Charlie and the boys caught up the horses, hitched up the wagon with the house moving tools and left the smoldering ruins to cool.

There was a small "shot-gun" house over on Ohoopee Street that was vacant and had been abandoned by a family that had gone to

Florida. Before noon, the home movers had the structure jacked up and on girders, ready to be moved to a lot that Charlie owned just across Alapaha Street from where the home place had set on Grant Street.

The neighbors had pitched in and had a good dinner for the family that had lost everything, but the big old barn and the horses. The twins were with their mother and her younger children up on Suwannee Street.

By the next day, Charlie and the boys had moved the small house on the lot that had been vacant just yesterday. People in Fitzgerald still had the pioneer spirit and would pitch in and help one another in time of need. The home place was never rebuilt. The long narrow house that they had moved was soon renovated and Arta and the young ones had moved in. Charlie and the older boys made a bunk room in the barn that had been saved from the flames. The three men were rough and ready as anyone in Fitzgerald and were right at home with the horses, cows, and chickens that shared their quarters.

Teddie and Tessie dropped a few dollars in the hat that was passed to help the Barwicks get on their feet. Tessie felt some relief that the old place was gone along with some of the arguments and hard words with the smoke.

Charlie had plowed the ashes under, and would salvage the nails and bricks. When spring came to Fitzgerald once more, the Barwicks had one of the finest vegetable gardens, enriched by the wood ashes and manure from the lot that the town had ever seen. Charlie gave vegetables to the neighbors and passersby that he could have sold, but that was Charlie Barwick.

Chapter 26

Social Life and Another Fire

Young married couples found time from their busy lives to enjoy each others company and the natural beauty of South Georgia. Teddie and Tessie joined the Methodist Church over on Central Avenue across from the Lee Grant Hotel. Teddie met with the most promising young business men at the Masonic Hall. Tessie joined the Woman's Missionary Society, played the piano, and sang in the church choir. On occasion they would join other young couples and ride the train to Lucy Lake, South of Ocilla on the Alapaha River where there was a swimming pool, bowling alley, dance hall, and picnic tables.

The Ocilla Southern Railroad was not much of a railroad, only a tram road to serve the saw mills south of Fitzgerald, but they ran a daily mixed passenger-freight train through the fertile farmland and stately virgin forests lands of Irwin County. They had only the one passenger coach, which would be crowded with pleasure seekers. It had a station between Fitzgerald and Ocilla named Minnie's Millpond. It also was a favorite destination of young and old, out on a weekend frolic.

The Seaboard Airline Railroad also served Fitzgerald and had a long depot at the east end of Central Avenue. That line had regular passenger service to Abbeville where it connected with it's mainline from Montgomery, Alabama to Savannah, Georgia on the Atlantic Ocean and Tybee Beach.

The seaboard train stopped at Bowen's Mill. It was also a recreation amusement establishment on House Creek. The large millpond was spanned by a trestle that was a favorite site for swimming in the clear spring water millpond, or the artesian well water of a large swimming pool in case you didn't care for the snakes and alligators that abounded in the millpond. Bowen's Mill was a time honored site for Sunday school picnics and family reunions.

Teddie and Tessie enjoyed the social life that the Barwick family never seemed to care for. Tessie seemed to come to full blossom, and was popular with the best young people, although she lived on East

Suwannee Street, on the wrong side of the tracks. The lives of the happy young couple that seemed to enjoy each other and their new found social life was to come to a screeching halt.

Once more Tessie sat upright in their bed in their one room apartment they called home. She had the same unblinking stare on her face that she had before the Barwick home place burned, but this time she saw two visions, fire and a dead baby. Not a tear would flow from those blue eyes. She knew she was pregnant, but had not told Teddie as she knew he had bills to pay, and their apartment would be a poor place to raise a child.

Teddie brushed off the fire prediction, but was dumbfounded at the thought of fatherhood. He seemed to think that their happy routine of work and frolic could continue until his note at the bank was satisfied and they were older, then a house and a family.

Fate looked at their situation differently. It was just a week later when he and Tessie climbed out a window of their smoke and flame filled apartment that fire was claiming. Once again they stood huddled with their neighbors watching what poor belongings they were still paying Mr. Miller for, go up in smoke, that once again hung over her papa's low pasture. He had no money to help them reconstruct. He had never overcome the loss of the home place, and was living in his barn.

Omar and Hester were their only salvation other than Teddie's good job and the name the couple had established for themselves and the baby she was carrying. They enjoyed the simple things of life, never partook of strong drink or riotous living. In fact, alcohol had never been a problem in the Barwick family.

They just somehow found themselves out of place in a southern setting, among southern people. Tessie had never lived anywhere but in South Georgia, gone to school with southern playmates, and had a deep love for Fitzgerald. She and her papa never had any desire to live anywhere else.

Teddie somehow was doing good on the job. He was not lazy, was dependable and always seemed to protect the railroad's interest. The customers and shippers liked him and he met people well. These qualities put him in line for a promotion and it was not long coming. At age twenty-three he was promoted to Freight Agent at Fitzgerald.

Everything in Fitzgerald was young as was the AB&A Railroad. The broad streets multi-storied buildings were only twenty-seven years old. The only thing old was the original Yankee colonists that had bet their last penny and their lives on and won.

Teddie remembered what his brother "T" had told him what to do when problems arose, was to redouble your efforts, and Teddie did just that. Tessie stood behind him and was by nature thrifty and could make do with what little they had.

Chapter 27

The Dead Baby Girl and Mahue

The next apartment they moved in was larger. Mr. Miller let them have more furniture, even a baby crib, as Tessie was pregnant.

Charlie Barwick kept them in fresh vegetables and firewood. Tessie's friends held baby showers for her and Hester never missed a day that she didn't come over with something for her sister. Hester looked forward to Tessie's baby that she herself would have liked to have, as she and Omar were childless.

Tessie's time had come, she had carried the baby well, but old Dr. Fussell sat by Tessie's bedside all night trying to deliver the child that was stillborn. It was a full-term baby that never drew the first breath of life. There was a funeral. The undertaker came and Arta Barwick let the young couple bury the daughter that they named Dorothy Dunn in the cemetery lot she had bought in colony days out at Evergreen Cemetery, east of town on a lovely hillside. Arta's mother was buried there and her father was buried in the plot where the Union soldiers lay side by side under identical headstones that the government gave them.

Tessie just stared into the distance, with a haunting look out of her eyes, never to shed a tear. She would only say, "I knew it was not to be, all the time."

In a few days she was her old self again. Hester was more grief stricken that Tessie, there again the girls were so different. Teddie was so busy on the new job that he had little time to grieve; besides he now had a doctor and a funeral bill to meet.

The next child Tessie bore was a fine boy baby that was named Mahue Dunn. He was a happy child. Tesse had him walking and saying a few words. Teddie could hardly wait to get home to see him and play with him. He grew into a toddler that would run to meet his daddy. Tessie acted a little strange lately. She seldom smiled, as though a dark cloud hung over her head. Hester insisted that she and Tessie take Mahue to Mrs. Owens photograph studio on Pine Street and have a group picture of the three of them.

Tessie dressed the child and handed him his favorite toy. Hester came in a horse and buggy that Omar had bought her and away they went to the studio.

Hester had to beg her sister to smile, but Tessie just stared into space, as if she was in a trance. The camera snapped and when the picture was developed there was a strange cloud in the background over Mahue's smiling likeness. Tessie told her sister that it was a bad omen. Hester just laughed and said, "You and papa with those omens. It was just the chemicals used to develop the film."

Tessie went about her household duties as if she was in a trance. She would stop what she was doing and clutch the child close to her bosom and quietly whisper, no, no Lord.

Need I tell you that Mahue lay a corpse in Mr. Littlefield's undertaking parlor on Central Avenue three days later. It had all happened so quickly. Hester had bathed Mahue and put him in his little crib. Tessie had cooked supper for Hester and herself. Hester was to spend the night with Tessie as Omar was out on his run and Teddie was working late at the depot. Tessie lay down her knitting and asked her sister to go check on Mahue, who by now should be sound asleep. Hester cried out from the bedroom and came running back with the child in her harms, limp and blue, barely breathing. She was a strong woman, like Charlie Barwick. She was barefoot and dressed in a kimono, but she ran out the door with Mahue in her arms and ran down the dark street to Dr. Fussell's house screaming.

Tessie went to the depot to tell Teddie that Hester and Mahue were at the doctor's house and he must come with her. When they arrived, Dr. Fussell was trying to revive the boy, but only shook his head and pulled a white sheet over the small body that had been so lively only hours ago. Teddie had to be sedated, but again Tessie only stared into the darkness. The horse drawn hearse bore the small coffin out to Evergreen Cemetery once more and Mahue was laid to rest beside little Dorothy, in their grandmother Barwick's cemetery lot.

It was a lonely home that Teddie and Tessie returned to. Teddie again had to redouble his efforts but it was months before he smiled or went to parties or even to church. All this sadness matured Tessie. She quoted the long poems she memorized, and lived in her own dream world, seemingly as if nothing had happened. Teddie seemed to bury himself in his work at the depot, as he now had another funeral bill to pay and he had obligations to meet and there was little time to grieve.

There was a saying on the railroad that if a wreck occurred, as they did, two more accidents would come to pass, before things would return to normal. Would he be man enough to survive a third grief, and see the third loved one be buried beneath the sod of a cemetery? Only time would tell.

Chapter 28

Sallie Ann Dunn's Death

It wouldn't take much time before Teddie's mettle would be tested again. The telegraph key on his desk was calling Fitzgerald Freight Depot. Teddie opened the line and turned to his typewriter to copy the message. His fingers walked the keys, letter by letter to spell out the message that originated at Andersonville from the Central of Georgia agent operator there.

As the message began to take shape, Teddie's world caved in. The words that were formed on the yellow sheet of message paper stated, "With great regret, may I inform you, Mr. Teddie' Dunn's mother, Sallie Ann Dunn departed this life, April 31st 1913. Please accept my deepest regrets." It was Teddie's 24th birthday. He slumped back in his swivel chair. The lightning that had slung that death message went straight to his heart. The telegraph operator in the dispatcher's office had also had his key open and had copied the message and filed a copy to Mr. Bob McKay, Teddie's boss and friend, if such a relationship could exist on a railroad. He sent the messenger boy on his bicycle the two blocks down the path beside the track to the freight house with a message stating that he was relieved of his duties and for him to catch the next train to Andersonville for the funeral.

Who would drive up to the depot in a buggy but Tessie and Hester. Teddie rushed out the depot door to tell them that his mother had died, and wondered how Tessie had known the sad news. She only said "a little bird told me." The sisters took Teddie in their arms to console the poor fellow that had lost so much. They knew he had a special relationship with his mother, as she did with him. He swore that as long as he lived, he would never celebrate another birthday, as his grief would only be renewed.

Tessie hoped she could occupy the void that had been left in Teddie's heart. She lived in two worlds, one of reality, the other of a mystic realm of spirits that only she could see. It was practical Hester that packed that same leather suitcase with a change of clothes and pressed a five dollar bill in Tessie's hand, then drove the couple to the passenger station to board the train to Andersonville. Train connections were good in those days and Andersonville was on the main line of the Central of Georgia Railroad that covered Georgia like the morning dew. It was with a heavy heart that Teddie set foot once more on the red clay street that led to the home that held so many memories of his boyhood. Sweetwater Creek still tumbled behind the store and under the trestle that spanned it carrying the trains on to Americus. The old southern veterans that had held forth at the store had passed on. He and Tessie walked past the spot where she as a budding girl had first seen Teddie at his lemonade stand, trying to earn a dollar. They passed the graveyard where the gravedigger was digging a fresh grave beside the grave of his father, W.T. Dunn, the stern man that had supported his family with a pick and shovel.

Tessie had to put her foot down, as she often said to keep Teddie "in the middle of the road," and not let his emotions consume him. Minnie blinked back her tears and greeted Teddie in her sunny manner commenting on his small frame and ignoring Tessie. Ida was her own self, quiet and efficient, still single. Teddie had not seen Grady since he had left home as an overgrown boy. He was a tall, high cheeked rather haggard looking man that hard labor had left its mark on. Tessie later told Teddie that his brother had the largest hands she had ever seen on a man. W.T. Dunn, or "T" as he was known in the family, was in far away Colorado in failing health. "Where were Charlie and Lillie? Teddie asked. Minnie had taken over the family gathering and the food that the neighbors were bringing in. She told Teddie that Charlie, Lillie, and their three children were due to arrive on the night train from Gainesville, Florida.

Tessie was somewhat bewildered by Teddie's kin and their southern ways. She felt as if she was a visitor in a strange land among strange people with stranger ways. She developed a dislike for Minnie, and her "mouth" that would not go away. Sallie Ann's body was to arrive from Americus tomorrow in the undertaker's black horse drawn hearse in a closed casket. The neighbors invited Teddie and Tessie to spend the night in their guest room. They were the Peak sisters that Teddie had gone to school with, now grown women. They had been good neighbors to Ida and Sallie Ann.

Charlie and his family arrived on the night train. He seemed to be more interested in his comfort, that he was grieved at his mother's passing.

This was the last time the old clapboard house would know a gathering of the Dunns, the house that had known happiness and sorrow, the garden, milk cow, and Grady's red ox, "General Sherman." It had heard the cheerful voice of Sallie Ann as she sang, "December is as pleasant as May" as she cooked the simple meals on the old wood cook stove. Her apron still hung from its peg on the kitchen wall, the scrubbed plank floor, the unpainted dining table where Teddie had lain while the doctor mended his leg that still bore the load of bird shot. So many memories that would end this afternoon.

Ida was leaving for Jacksonville to live with Minnie, as her duties were over in Andersonville when her mama was laid to rest. Sallie Ann's casket was opened in the old houses parlor for friends and family to view for the last time.

She looked as though a great burden had been lifted from her shoulders. The eyes that had seen the horrors of the Civil War, the freeing of the slaves, the kindness of the family that had adopted her and given her a name, the worn hands that had raised eight children to adults, chopped firewood, with that old dull ax, that still was stuck in the chopping block, but rusty now. The hands that milked that old contrary milk cow, churned butter, gave the same loving care to young vegetables in her garden she did to her growing family now lay folded on her waist.

Tessie thought she could see a slight smile on her face, as if she knew she had done her dead level best to make a happy home for her brood.

The graveyard that clung to the side of the ravine beside a log church on the outskirts of the village of Andersonville had an open grave that awaited the remains of a good and faithful woman that had smiled at hardships, over looked faults and short comings of her family and neighbors and encouraged her husband and children. Her two daughters, three of her younger sons, two daughters-in-laws, one a Yankee, the other a southerner that had made it back to stand beside her grave that September day in 1913.

Besides the family there were old friends, both black and white that she had shared her life with. The cool September breeze that swept through the ravine rustled the leaves of the age old red oak trees that had witnessed the nearby Prison Camp where so many battle weary Yankee prisoners had suffered and died. The same breeze tousled the white hair and beards of the few old Rebel veterans that stood with heads bowed, hats in their hands, behind the family group.

To one side stood the black men that had labored on Bill Dunn's track gang, they too were old and bent, but had come to pay their respects to "Ole Miss Sallie." There was a black woman in her Sunday meeting dress named Hattie. She too dabbed at her eyes with a white laced handkerchief. She had always "shown up" when Miss Sallie Ann had more burdens than she could bear.

It was a graveside service. Seems that the Dunns being railroad folks, never had the time or inclination to attend church services, but no more Christian woman lived in Andersonville than Mrs. Bill Dunn. The undertaker from Americus came with the casket that Minnie and Ida had selected. Mr. Bill Easterlin from the store had sent a dozen red roses that bedecked the gray casket that now was suspended on ropes beside the open grave.

The horses that stood so still hitched to the buggies and wagons that had brought the mourners to the graveyard seem to know that death had visited the community. The Baptist preacher stepped forward to read from his Bible, with the ribbon in it, a scripture that told that "The meek shall inherit the earth," and that Sallie Ann Dunn's riches were in heaven, not in Andersonville. Three young girls stepped forward and sang in their clear young voices, "Oh How I Love Jesus." The same breeze seemed to moan a bit as the pallbearers lowered the casket into the red clay soil of Georgia. The tired body could rest in peace beside the husband she had chosen to be the father of her children and the breadwinner that never shirked duty and instilled his children with that same quality.

It was not a long walk back to the home place. Charlie never mentioned the debt he had left for Teddie to settle. Grady told of his children and good wife. Ida was now free to leave Andersonville and had sold her store in the village that seemed to slumber even more deeply as fewer and fewer northern people came to decorate the graves of the Civil War soldiers. This new generation of Yanks had other things on their minds.

Minnie was the best off financially. George O'Niell was well off and their union had not been blessed with any children. She paid her mother's funeral expenses. Teddie was crushed with grief, but Tessie braced him up with her sunny spirit. She had liked Charlie's wife, Lillie, that had been nice to her, but she had reservations about Teddie's sisters that ignored her.

They all went their separate ways, but Teddie left a part of his heart that would remain empty under that mound of red clay where his mother slept.

Tessie waited until they were back in Fitzgerald, tucked in their bed to tell him that she had seen an angel there in the graveyard as the crowd of mourners departed. It was a small angel that awaited to accompany Sallie Ann's spirit to eternity. Teddie told her that Andersonville was a haunted place, and people had seen many spirits and ghosts there about, and could cast a spell, but he had never seen one. They both were silent for a while but sleep didn't come to either of them. Tessie was the first to break the silence of the dark bedroom. She spoke in the tone that Teddie well knew when she was having one of her visions. "My eyes can see what yours can't and I am worried at what I saw. That angel had black wings and the features of our dead baby Mahue. I know our life together will see more trips to the graveyard, those black wings were death!" She then fell into a deep slumber. Teddie said nothing, but arose and walked to the depot and went to work on the stack of papers that awaited his attention. That seemed to be his way to handle grief, work, work, work!

Chapter 29

More Funerals

The close bond between twins had grown even closer between Tessie and Hester. Tessie loved her mother Arta, but she was busy with her younger children over on Grant Street in the "shotgun" house and barely tolerated Charlie Barwick.

He loved the streets of Fitzgerald. His first love seemed to be his horses, just a bit below the drifters and coarse people that called East Pine Street home. He had been quite a "bare knuckle" boxer in his youth, back in Australia and still thought he was the "champ." But, he didn't realize that his reflexes had slowed with age and maturity.

There was always a celebration at the square where Central Avenue and Main Street crossed in the center of town. Charlie was still strong and rough as a corn cob, but fifty-five years had taken their toll. He, encouraged by his cronies, challenged a young policeman that had been raised on Suwannee Street that Charlie had trained to box, to a few rounds at the annual 4th of July celebration.

The match turned into a disaster for the old man. The "kid" beat him to a pulp but Charlie kept getting up off the canvas only to be knocked back down again. Charlie Barwick was never the same. He could not hear it thunder and his speech was slurred. His working days were over.

Tessie could not seem to relax, something was bothering her. Was it the apparition she had seen, the angel with the black wings? Hester did not come tonight as she usually did.

Tessie went over to her house to find her complaining of the side ache. They agreed that she must have eaten something that didn't agree with her. That night Omar took her over to the new hospital on Central Avenue. There the doctor on duty gave her some medicine to ease the pain. By daylight the doctors pronounced her with a ruptured appendix. She died before the sun set. Mr. Littlefield had her body at his undertaking parlor on Central. Tessie insisted on dressing Hester, and she even fixed the dead woman's hair as she had so often done since they were children.

Arta could not believe her daughter had passed so quickly, but she was gone to her rewards at twenty-four years of age. Arta offered her cemetery lot for burial, but Omar bought a half a lot at Evergreen where she was buried the next afternoon. The people on Suwannee and Grant were in attendance at her funeral. Hester could rest in peace as no one could say a word against her.

Arta had a saying that she quoted to Tessie "keep a stiff upper lip." Charlie Barwick sat with his family at the funeral that was held at the Christian church on South Lee Street. He looked bewildered and wept openly. Arta sat next to Tessie to comfort her. She told friends that she always thought that Tessie would be the first to cross the river of life as Tessie was so frail and small. Tessie accepted the fact and once more just stared with unblinking eyes in the trance that she could go into.

Omar said nothing but by morning he was gone back to Indiana, where he had come from, and never came back to Fitzgerald as far as anyone knew. Time heals all wounds, but scars never heal.

Tessie told Teddie that she knew their baby Mahue would be so happy to be with his Aunt Hester that loved him like he was her very own. Time flew by.

Teddie did well on his job. The notes at the bank were settled and the funeral bills were paid. They bought a cemetery lot at Evergreen, close to Hester's grave. Tessie would not go to the cemetery for reasons of her own. Teddie loaded a couple of the black porters that worked at the depot in a wagon he borrowed from Charlie Barwick one Saturday afternoon. He said nothing to anyone. Tessie thought he was on railroad business, but he wasn't. He and the strong young men dug up the two small caskets that contained the remains of his babies and moved them to the cemetery lot he had bought. He didn't even tell the sexton of his intentions. He told the black men that they were his children and he could put them where he pleased. Darkness found two mounds of earth in his cemetery lot, no headstones, nothing but bare South Georgia sandy soil knew where he put them to rest on his lot.

Chapter 30

The Move to Central Avenue

It was some time before Tessie knew what he had done, but she kept her lips buttoned. The authorities that kept the cemetery did discover the transfer and could have caused Teddie trouble, but they didn't.

Fitzgerald continued to thrive and grow. West Central Avenue had been filled and paved where the old blind race horse "Round About" used to have to swim to pull the surrey loaded with school children with little Tessie at the reins. Culverts and storm sewers were built to carry the water under the street.

Tessie set her heart on owning two of those high priced lots on West Central Avenue that were on the right side of the railroad tracks. She walked over to the rich old northern widow's house on South Lee Street to inquire if by chance she would sell the lots to her and Teddie.

Mrs. James had her maid bring in tea and cookies. Tessie made a good appearance and knew how to hold her tea cup.

After some small talk, Mrs. James asked who her parents were. Tessie's heart jumped into her throat as she said, "I am Charlie Barwick's daughter. He has moved some houses for you and I am married to Teddie Dunn, the agent for the railroad here in Fitzgerald." Mrs. James thought for a minute then asked if her father did not have some vacant lots over on North Grant Street.

Tessie said that he did, but she wanted to make her home in a better section of town, below the Lee Grant Hotel. Mrs. James then asked if Tessie had an idea of what those lots were selling for. Tessie smiled and told Mrs. James that they had some money saved and that her husband had a good paying job and had paid off several notes at the bank Mrs. James had stock in.

Mrs. James called for her maid to show Tessie to the door, but she added, you come young woman with your husband, and I will confer with the president of the bank and we will talk business.

That night as the couple ate their simple supper, Tessie told Teddie of her visit with Mrs. James. Teddie thought deeply for a while and told her that he shared her interest in moving to Central Avenue, but there were cheaper lots on Pine or Magnolia Streets. Tessie countered with a flat "no." "I have my mind made up. Mrs. James will help us buy them, and we will have something to be proud of in years to come and we are getting no younger." Hester is gone and I don't think my parents will be here much longer. My older brothers are married now and live on the other side of town. Papa is content living in his barn and walking to town every day. Mama is planning on returning to Pennsylvania as soon as my younger brother and sister finish school. I am tired of paying rent to Mrs. Werner for this little apartment." She didn't tell Teddie that she thought she was pregnant again, that could come later. Teddie agreed to visit with Mrs. James the next time he was free of duty.

A week passed before Tessie dressed in her best clothes, washed and styled her hair the best she could, now that Hester was gone. She walked up Grant Street toward the railroad crossing where she had her introduction to Teddie. The crossing now had bells and a flashing red light and there was no crossing guard.

She walked into Teddie's office to find him reared back in his chair reading a newspaper with one of the porters shining his shoes. The look she gave him brought him to his feet. "O.K. Mr. Big Shot, get your hat and coat and escort me through town over to South Lee Street as you have business with Mrs. James this afternoon."

Teddie complied with her wishes and said under his breath, "Damn Yankees." Tessie could hear a pin drop and answered, "You can call me a Yankee, but never again call me a 'Damn Yankee.' If you know what is best for you, you Rebel son-of-a-gun." He knew when he was whipped and said only "you win again."

Tessie again rang the doorbell on the massive front door at Mrs. James residence. Teddie stood, hat in hand as the maid asked them in. Mrs. James called to the couple to come to her study, where she did business. Tessie spoke first as Mrs. James studied Teddie's face.

"This is my husband, Teddie Dunn. He would like to buy your two lots on West Central, where we plan to build a nice bungalow and call our home." "Yes, yes, Mrs. James said. Those lots are two of the best lots in Fitzgerald and I am firm on my price of $600 each.

Teddie swallowed hard and finally found his voice. "I have only $200 dollars in my account at the bank, Mrs. James and I had hoped we could purchase them both for one thousand and pay you 3% interest on the $800 balance. I have a friend that will sign the note with me. He is a well to do farmer that owes me a favor."

Mrs. James thought for a minute or two and took her reading glasses from her nose. "Teddie Dunn," she spoke, "You have a fine young woman for a wife and I have checked your record at the bank, which I have stock in. You have a good job with the railroad and I am inclined to trade with you. I will notify my lawyer, Colonel Jay to draw up the papers when you take him the $200 dollars."

It was not Teddie that answered Mrs. James, it was Tessie that spoke, "Thank you Mrs. James. He will be at Colonel Jay's office tomorrow."

A year passed quickly. Tessie seemed to handle grief better than Teddie and could pinch a penny. She seemed determined to climb the ladder of success and have something in the life that had started so precarious in a slop jar. Fitzgerald Colony had succeeded and she had her hat set to do the same.

Chapter 31

Lenard Dunn

She and Teddie had a new baby boy they had named Lenard in the cradle where Mahue had slept. He was a bright fine boy baby that seemed to have no problems. His grandmother, Arta, took more interest in him than she had in the other boy. She would come every day to see him and to show him things. Tessie had some reservations about her father to bring Lenard to his barn to see the horses, and letting him drink milk, straight from the cows utter, but Lenard would cry for "warm sweety."

Teddie took him to the depot to see the trains, but he seemed to like the poems and books that his grandmother Arta kept before him. As he grew older he showed little interest in horses or trains, to be sure he would be a scholar. He didn't play rough games with the neighbor boys. He liked to dress up and go with his parents to Sunday school and church. The other children loved him as did the grown folks. He didn't have a piano, but when his mother would play at church or parties Lenard would sit on the bench beside her and sing. He seemed to have inherited his mother's talent to memorize long verses and poems. He was seldom without a book in his hands, and would cry on report card day if he had a "B."

Just to be frank, it seemed that he was an exceptional child. Wherever he went sunshine seemed to follow. Tessie began to wonder if he was too good to live and she seldom let him out of her sight. What was in her premonition that God in Heaven needed another angel up in Heaven? Teddie thought the sun rose and set on him and wanted him to have the best of everything. The years flew by and the lots were paid off.

Teddie was in the mood to build a house on the lots he had paid off over on Central Avenue. He approached Jim Parrott, a friend of Charlie Barwick's that had come to the Colony from Iowa. Charlie had moved houses that Jim Parrott had built as he was a builder. Mr. Parrott told Teddie that he would build him a good two bedroom house and hold only the deed to the two lots that the house would sit on. He knew Teddie would pay him as he had Mrs. James.

A man's name was his bond in those days as an answer to Tessie's prayers, there sat the new house on Central Avenue. The little family moved in, in 1926. Lenard was nine years old. Teddie had not had to go to France in the World War as he had a child and was on an essential job on the railroad. This had given him a chance to save quite a nest egg. He bought Tessie and Lenard a T-Model Ford automobile, new furniture, and even put a telephone in the house.

Good times after the war spawned the "Roaring Twenties" and the country was on a roll.

Teddie was on the Board of Stewarts up at the Methodist Church and taught a Sunday school class of young boys. Lenard was enrolled at Second Ward School, with the best children in town. Tessie took him to school as traffic was bad on busy Central Avenue and there was the railroad to cross. She would run get him at school in the car to join her and Teddie for lunch. They were a happy three as they enjoyed the lemon pie that Tessie had baked in her new oven on the electric cook stove.

Teddie went back to work at the depot. Tessie hurried Lenard into the open Ford car to take him back to school just three blocks away. Her visions had failed her; she was so happy. The school bell was ringing when they arrived at the campus. The children called hurry Lenard or you will be late for class. He jumped out into the street, but Tessie called him back to comb his hair. He, childlike, turned and dashed into the path of a truck that had a load of gasoline that couldn't stop to save running over the boy. He was crushed to death by the wheel of the heavy truck right before Tessie's eyes. She jumped out of the car and gathered his broken body in her arms and ran the two blocks to the depot and cried "Teddie, they have killed Lenard." It took two of Teddie's employees to pry the child's body from Tessie's arms. The whole town wept that sad afternoon. Telephones rang; police and emergency vehicles arrived both at the railroad depot and at the school house.

Tessie's blood stained clothes was all she had to show for the boy that had been vibrant and alive only minutes before. Teddie had to take her into his arms to restrain her. Where had she found the strength to carry a child nearly as large as she was so far? Tessie collapsed beside

Lenard's body. There beside the railroad tracks at Grant Street Crossing, where the couple had first met formally.

Thankfully Mr. Littlefield, the undertaker arrived to take Lenard's lifeless body to the funeral parlor. Tessie's girlhood friend Nettie Day, now married to Asa Smith, was one of the first people to comfort Tessie, unconscious as she was. Her mind was somewhere in the spirit world.

Teddie was angry, vowing to kill the driver of the truck. It was the black men that worked at the depot that restrained Teddie in their strong black arms and spoke softly to him. "Dat little boy done gone Mr. Teddie, he don't live here in Fitzgerald. He with ole massar up in the heaven now."

Nettie put Tessie in her car and took her to the hospital on Central Avenue, just two blocks beyond the Dunn home that only an hour before had heard the laughter of a happy school boy and his father.

The funeral was one of the saddest held at the new Methodist Church, across from the Lee Grant Hotel. School was let out and Lenard's classmates attended in mass.

The small casket was not open as Mr. Littlefield could do little to restore the boy's body. The Barwick family sat with Tessie. Minnie and Ida had come from Jacksonville to be with Teddie, embittered as he was. Tessie was in a trance, her mind on some faraway shore. Many friends crowded that large church that sad day. All of Fitzgerald mourned. The funeral procession to Evergreen Cemetery wound its way to the lot that Teddie had only recently bought, and there little Lenard's body was laid to rest beside the unmarked grave of his departed brother Mahue and sister Dorothy. Yes, there were three mounds of South Georgia sandy soil to mark graves of the hopes and loves of the young couple.

Teddie and Tessie went home to pick up the pieces of their lives that had been shattered. Tessie never to her dying day spoke Lenard's name again as she had buried his memories deep in the most remote recesses of her mind. Those memories were hers and hers alone.

Oh, don't think those memories didn't hurt her, but they were hers alone. She quietly hid his pictures, his Bible, his story books, and poems from his room. Teddie went on a rampage, gathered all of Lenard's belongings, clothes, and play things. With the help of his right hand man, Alzie Kennedy, they kindled a great bonfire on the vacant lot next door. Leaping flames soon consumed the belongings that were so close to the heart that had been stilled by the Standard Oil Company's oil truck. Alzie told Teddie that when the smoke cleared, Lenard's memories would be gone, but they lingered in Teddie's broken heart.

Was it an omen that Teddie should have recognized the day in Andersonville when Teddie had seen the Standard Oil Company's truck, drawn by the big mules with J.D.R. branded on their hooves?

The next day a plowman named Otis Allford and his mule were plowing up those vacant lots, owned by a man in Columbus, Georgia that gave Teddie permission to use them.

Teddie took a few days leave from his job, went to Thomasville, Georgia on the train and bought a hundred rose bush plants that he and his helpers planted, row on row through the ashes of the bonfire. He even put in a water system to irrigate the Red Radiance Rose bushes planted row on row where Lenard had played.

People who passed on the sidewalk would ask how he had the strength to plant so many rose bushes. He would softly reply, "You will never know how many tears I have buried in the fresh plowed soil."

Tessie had her method of dealing with grief. She was now past thirty and maturity had brought out a more mellow personality. She read all of Pearl Buck's novels of hardship in China, "Good Earth" and Then the Rains Come." They seemed to soothe her troubled mind.

It was though Lenard was just a passing dream, and her life lay before her. She did not go to the cemetery with Teddie to place roses on the grave that boasted no slab or headstone, just a mound of dirt. Tessie let Teddie have his peculiarities. It seemed as though she could shed grief as easily as a tree could shed its leaves, during the winter and bud out a fresh in the spring. She closed that chapter in her life and planned on opening another.

Teddie was back to his duties at the freight house, "Slinging Lightning" one more time not through metal wires strung on cedar posts, but in a renewed vigor promoting the AB&C Railroad's business and his own.

One day, some weeks after the tragedy, a fine automobile drove up to the depot and two young men dressed in business suits got out with brief cases under their arms. As the men entered the office door, Teddie arose from his littered desk to greet them.

Little did he know that they were the representatives of the Standard Oil Company that had come to award Teddie and Tessie a cash settlement for the accident that the company truck had been involved in. They hoped to settle the matter.

It struck Teddie wrong as he had not sued the oil company, although the blame had been placed on the speeding truck, in a school zone. Teddie told the lawyers in no uncertain terms that his son's life had not been for sale and that he would accept no "blood money."

He was a hard man to deal with when his mind was made up. A telephone call from Colonel Jay, the lawyer he respected so much, softened him into meeting the company lawyers in his office to settle the legal aspects of the matter. At the meeting Teddie and Tessie endorsed the check for $10,000 dollars to be made out in favor for the Methodist Orphan Home in Macon, Georgia. This agreement was acceptable to all parties concerned, the matter was settled once and for all, but still Lenard Dunn's name was not used.

Teddie still made his daily pilgrimage to Evergreen Cemetery to visit his cemetery lot. He was on the streets of Fitzgerald each day collecting the company accounts and knew every business and its managers.

There was a sewing room next to the bank, operated by an old settler that Teddie had great respect for. She had raised her family sitting long hours at her sewing machine, sewing for the public. She was known as Ma Forbes, known for her no nonsense personality. She had heard that Teddie was going every day to Lenard's grave. In a few days she tapped on the large glass window that faced the sidewalk as Teddie passed and gave a wave for him to come in her shop. She told him to sit down and listen to what she had to say to him as a friend. She told him that he was not the first man to lose a child and that it was time for him to stay out of the graveyard and that people were talking. "Just stop it Teddie, don't let me hear of it again." She never stopped the whir of the sewing machine.

Teddie swallowed hard, but he knew the old Yankee women meant what they said. He put his hat on his head and walked out her door, but he was not seen again at the cemetery, unless he had business there.

Tessie had opened a new chapter in her life. She lived the words of the song she so often sang "Pack up your troubles in the old kid bag, and Smile, Smile, Smile." She had a new friend that would impact her life in the years to come. The large handsome woman that rode a thoroughbred horse side saddle through Fitzgerald was named Mrs. Perry. She had come to Fitzgerald in Colony days with her wealthy husband, a horse and mule trader from Enid, Oklahoma. She was not a Yankee, but was of Southwestern lineage. She was soft-spoken and a member of the Methodist Church on Central Avenue. She was now a widow, rolling in money as people said. She had been taken by Tessie's talents, both at the piano and her recitations at the weekly missionary meeting that they both attended. Maude Perry was childless, lived in a mansion out on South Main Street. Her black housekeeper named Laura ran the house. Maude Perry had put on a lot of weight and wore some of the largest diamonds people had ever seen. She no longer rode horse back, but had a Cadillac parked in a car house on the alley behind her home. Maude Perry was a close observer and her sharp eye, as she had one good eye, the other was glass, had admired how Tessie Dunn could fly around town in that Model T Ford she drove.

The telephone would ring at the Dunn home and it would be Maude Perry wanting Tessie to pick her up; Maude had some plans. Tessie was not saddled with household duties as Teddie liked to eat lunch on the streets of Fitzgerald.

Tessie had a deep desire to have another child and felt that she was too young to approach middle age childless. Teddie was still somewhat bitter on the subject and felt that he never wanted to put himself in the position to be hurt again.

The job demanded much of his time. The railroad had fallen on hard times, trucks and buses were on the newly paved highways. The government had taken over the operation of the railroads during the World War, and had left them in shambles. The AB&C Railroad had been the scene of labor trouble, paralyzed by a long strike that had resulted in placing the company in the hands of its receivers.

The strikers lost their jobs, although Teddie kept his agency job just by the skin of his teeth.

The new home that Tessie was so proud of had to be paid off. They were laughing on the outside, crying on the inside. Teddie had made a mistake when in a moment of temper, which he could display, had questioned Tessie's judgment in letting Lenard get out of the car on the traffic side, which left another scar in her heart. Some things are best not spoken.

Tessie's parents, Arta and Charlie Barwick drifted farther apart. Their children were grown and scattered and good as Arta's word, she left Fitzgerald and Charlie Barwick and went back north. Their lives here in the Colony City had not been a "bed of roses."

Arta had lost her parents and daughter that were buried out at Evergreen Cemetery, not to mention Lenard and Tessie's other two babies. Lenard's tragic death seemed to be the straw that broke the camel's back. Fitzgerald was a place she wished she had never heard of. All these things had left their mark on Tessie's mind. She had lost weight and was only a shadow of her self. She had a secret that she shared with no one. She was pregnant.

Chapter 32

Bryan

The winter passed with its cold north wind and the spring flowers cheered Tessie's blues away. Teddie knew now and made another statement that would come back to haunt him. "I want you to understand that this child is yours, I will be its father and fulfill my duties as a parent, but I will never love it."

Tessie just smiled a sweet smile and told him that she knew that the child that she was carrying under her heart would be a boy. She knew because it was so active in her womb. She had her first labor pains early in June and spent a Friday night that was hot and sleepless. Sometime in the long hours before dawn, a mocking bird lit in a crabapple tree that Teddie had planted beside her bedroom window and sung the sweetest song she had ever heard there in the predawn darkness before any bird had left its' roost.

Tessie took heart and felt that the bird and its joyful song was a good omen sent from heaven above. This boy would survive. Her water broke that Saturday morning. When she called Teddie to come and take her up to the hospital to where Dr. Ware and his head nurse, Mellie Fitch rolled up their sleeve and delivered a small baby boy to a mother that weighed only eighty-nine pounds.

The birth had been difficult and long. The sun was setting at the end of West Central Avenue as Dr. Ware held the child high and announced, "It's a boy." Now if I can only get him to take his first breath, I will feel better.

Tessie, weak as she was, asked the doctor to hold the baby up so she could see his balls and know for herself that the child was a boy and would not have to go through life as a woman.

The baby still hadn't taken its first breath. Tessie shrieked "Take the ice from the pitcher of ice water on the bedside table and rub it up and down h is back. Wouldn't you know, he is too stubborn to breathe, just like a Dunn. Dr. Ware did just as she suggested. The ice no sooner touched the baby's back that it let out a yell and took its first deep breath of life, there on Central Avenue in Fitzgerald. Tessie said nothing but gave a sigh of relief.

Teddie took Tessie and the new baby that Tessie had named Bryan home to be laid in the new crib that she and her best friend Nellie Smith had bought from Mr. Littlefield's new furniture store.

Dr. Ware told Tessie to be patient with the new father, that he would come around in time and that love came with the child in most cases. Tessie and Dr. Ware formed a bond that would last for many years.

She began to eat again, and thrived under the duties of a new mother, although she was thirty-three years old. Teddie buckled down and helped her around the house. He would wash diapers, and bring her breakfast on a tray. He would carry Bryan in the palm of his hand, while he cooked on the electric cook stove, but he didn't show the outward affection that he had lavished on Lenard.

Teddie had always accepted duty and this child would be no exception, but one thing for certain, there would be no other babies to tend to, as he was out of the baby business.

The many friends and associates of Fitzgerald were happy that the couple had another child. The feeling was best expressed by a barber named Walt Owens that walked to work early every morning by the Dunn home. He stated to the crowd that frequented the barber shop. "I was so happy when I heard a baby crying at Teddie's house, as I passed by this morning for two long years there was only silence at 316 West Central." All the comments were not that cheerful. Bryan's grandmother Barwick shared Teddie's bleak sentiment.

Tessie wrote her mother that she was so happy that her baby was a healthy boy. Arta answered her letter only commenting, "Saturday's child shall work with his hands for his living." Tessie only laughed and asked "And what is wrong with that? He is mine and I can see nothing but a bright future for my boy, just you see. Whatever he is, he is mine and I will never forsake him."

Maude Perry, childless herself, never noticed children but showed an interest in little Bryan. When he took his first steps he seemed self-assured and had a mind of his own. Lenard had been so loving and obedient, the apple of his father's eye.

Tessie seemed to revel in the boy's independent spirit. He was his own little man. Teddie Dunn could bump thunder as far as she was concerned. Tessie quietly listened to the first words her boy put together, "Let him do what he wants to do." Tessie had always felt that sentiment, but was afraid to state it so bluntly.

Teddie had always paraded around town with Lenard in tow. The first time Bryan's father took him for a walk, the youngster wanted only to shake the low metal fence that bordered the post office, along the sidewalk. Teddie had to carry him away to his mother. His disgruntled statement to Tessie was. "He is yours; you wanted him, now you can have him! He embarrassed me up at the post office." Tessie smiled and told Teddie that he only wanted to see if the fence was strong and to see if he had the strength to test that fence. The child was strong willed which rather clashed with Teddie's own personality.

Chapter 33

The Depression

Dark clouds were gathering over the financial world. Present Herbert Hoover seemed unable to avoid a collapse of America's economic crisis. The bank in Fitzgerald was shaky. People were withdrawing their savings. Teddie had seven hundred dollars tucked away for a rainy day, and it was raining, not raindrops, but signs in bank doors, where curtains were drawn and signs were displayed stating that they were closed until further notice!

Teddie had been aware of the situation. Just in the nick of time before his thirty-eighth birthday that he no longer celebrated in the year 1929 he had withdrawn his money and tucked it away at home.

The very next day a mob of people gathered at the bank to withdraw their money but found the doors locked and the officials were gone. Who knows what they took with them? It wasn't just the people in the street; corporations were strapped for cash, that didn't seem to exist. The AB&A or rather the AB&C railroad as it was now known, found themselves unable to pay its workers.

Tessie had seen this depression coming. She had been the one that had urged Teddie to take action and bring the money home to her. That was all that saved them from losing the new house on Central Avenue.

Some of their friends that lost everything felt hard at Teddie for liquidating his savings at the bank, but the banks would have failed anyway as it was a national if not worldwide situation. Cotton prices dropped to five cents a pound, stores closed. People, good hard working people, were unemployed. The situation was desperate.

Tessie was no stranger to economic woes, as things never seemed to work out for her father.

Teddie knew no luxury, being raised by a widowed mother that eked a living from five acres of red Georgia clay. The vegetable garden, the milk cow, an ox named General Sherman put simple food on the table.

Her children would spare her a few dollars to pay taxes. Ida was her right hand. Those days were forever gone, but the thrifty habits learned served the struggling couple that called 316 West Central Avenue home, only redoubled their efforts to keep the "man with the lantern" away from their door until things got better.

The necessities of life became so cheap that a man with a job on the railroad, could now meet his obligations and put a few dollars aside. Tessie made do with what Teddie brought in. They made the house payments out of the savings that Teddie had rescued from the sinking bank.

Bryan Dunn had grown into a happy child that his mother didn't spoil, but taught many traits that would serve him well in years to come. Maude Perry took an interest in the serious child that seemed old for his years. He didn't interrupt grown people conversation and always used the key words that Tessie taught him, "please" and "thank you." Teddie began to notice him more and took him to the depot often. Tessie was a good observer and she noticed that Bryan could entertain himself long periods of time with a claw hammer, a pine board and a few nails he would attempt to fashion into toys and tools. He loved his story books that Tessie kept him well supplied with. She had him reading simple verses before most children could tie their shoes.

His mother let him find his own level of learning. She noticed that he was so different than Lenard had been which she never mentioned. He seemed more interested in nature than the church. His father required him to go to Sunday school in shined shoes and formal clothes, which Bryan despised. He made no effort to sing with the other children.

Tessie had moments that she seemed to enjoy when Teddie gave her a report of his poor performance at the things that were close to Teddie's heart. Bryan took to roller skates and bicycle riding like a duck does to water. Teddie tried to interest his young son in baseball, which he had loved. Seems that Bryan never noticed the ball and bat his dad brought him from the "dime store." He had his heart set on a bow and arrow.

Tessie was the one that Bryan could always come to when he had a problem. She would not allow him to shed tears, never to fear the unknown, the value of money, and to respect his elders.

Teddie could see traits developing in the boy that were so much like his brother Grady Dunn, who could build anything. The lack of religious interest, much like Charlie Dunn, and heaven forbid, the untidy dress of Charlie Barwick and the love of animals, that Teddie had turned his back on. It was plain to see that Bryan was going to be no replacement for Lenard. Teddie was going to have to accept the lad that called him Teddie, as he was, and he did.

Fall arrived and Bryan started to school. He was going to a school in a different ward of Fitzgerald, not the one that Lenard had been killed at. The school was a long ways from Central Avenue. The Model T Ford that Tessie had enjoyed so much was gone back to the dealer, a victim of the depression. Teddie was tied to the job. He demanded that Tessie walk to school with Bryan that first day that school opened, but Tessie put her foot down to Teddie. She flat refused, explaining that she had gone with "her" son the route he was to take, showed him how to cross busy Grant Street at the crossing and that a policeman helped children across. She knew Bryan was capable to make the trip to school without her. She wanted "her" child to be self sufficient and that mother would not always be by his side to shield him from danger. How could she bear to see him pedal off on the little bicycle that he could ride so well, where were her visions of the fateful day she had gathered the crushed little bloody body of Lenard to her breast. She seemed to have an inner strength that he would make it in the world, without her. She thought she saw a guardian angel with white wings hovering over her boy as he pedaled away.

Bryan made the trip to school and back home. The teacher was astounded that he could read in his "Dick and Jane" primary book, and could count to one hundred. Had he been given his grandmother Arta Barwick's talent for books and letters? Tessie said a prayer of thanksgiving that night. Teddie only said, "You win again" as he often said when Tessie prevailed and she often did. A red headed Yankee woman can raise "Ole Billie" from the dead, Teddie had learned.

Troubles were not over. She did not dream of the angel with the black wings, but she did dream of the mocking bird that sang a song of good tiding the June night before Bryan was born. This bird sat in a bare tree growing on a desolate plain. It would not sing, and tucked its head under its wing and slept. Tessie had trouble interpreting the dream, but she knew it was a bad omen.

Chapter 34

One More Challenge

Bryan was not his usual self one morning. Tessie noticed a swelling on the side of his neck, and he had a fever. She kept him home thinking he had the mumps. He had little interest in the books he slept with and was listless. The next day Tessie knew he was not improving. The telephone she had enjoyed so much had been taken out due to hard times so she walked to the hospital and met Dr. Ware when he came down the hall. She described Bryan's condition to the kindly doctor that assured her he would stop by her house later and take a look at the boy. Bryan loved Dr. Ware. One glance told the doctor that Bryan was in need of a specialist that he referred patients to in Macon, Georgia, ninety miles north of Fitzgerald. The bad thing was Macon was not on the AB&C Railroad. The trip would have to be made on the highway. Construction that would become the "Dixie Highway," the main route to Florida from the north. Teddie had to make arrangements to take Tessie and Bryan to Macon to Dr. Bershinsky, a well known pediatrician baby doctor. Bryan's little neck had a knot on it as large as a goose egg, and his fever was high. Teddie went around to the Ford Place and approached Mr. Anderson, the owner. He explained his plight. Could he borrow or rent an automatable? The answer was no. Insurance limited loaning cars, but he did have a car that he had taken in on a trade that he could sell him reasonable. It was a 1932 Model A Ford, four door sedan that he would let him have for fifty dollars down, and twelve dollars a month.

Teddie wanted a car and he could afford the payments. Mr. Anderson called his shop foreman to service the blue Ford and fill it with gasoline. Teddie and Mr. Anderson drove to Teddie's home on Central Avenue. He blew the horn as they drove under the car shed that had been vacant for several years. Tessie came running to see who it was. She did a double take when she saw Teddie sitting up under the steering wheel. "Teddie Dunn" she shouted, "You know you can't afford a car." Teddie pleaded for her to calm down and listen to Mr.

Anderson and think of the trip they must make to Macon. She wiped her hands on her apron, ran her fingers through her curls and agreed to listen. Mr. Anderson told her the terms of the trade. The truth was, Tessie wanted a car herself. Teddie got out and offered for her to just drive Mr. Anderson around the block to see how much better it drove than the old T Model that they had. Mr. Anderson showed her how to shift gears and off they went lurching along. Tessie had mastered those gears and was smiling from ear to ear when they came back up the driveway and switched the motor off. She thought a while and looked Mr. Anderson in the eye and told him that she would give him twenty five dollars down and could afford to raise the monthly payment to fifteen dollars. Mr. Anderson laughed and said he should have known better than to try and trade with a red-headed Yankee woman from Pennsylvania Dutch country.

She went in the house and came back with the money, counted it out slowly to the car dealer. They thanked him and he told them that he was glad to know that they had a way to carry the sick boy to Macon. Tessie watched as the two men drove off, feeling satisfied that she had done her best to keep Teddie from going hog wild.

She went to the bedroom and hugged her listless boy that she loved with all her heart. She told him to select the books he wanted to take on the trip and gave him an aspirin tablet to control his fever. She tried not to look at the knot on his neck as she packed the old suitcase with clothes.

She told Bryan that she was going to run up the street to see if Mrs. Burel Richards would go to keep him company and sing songs for him. He liked Mrs. Richards as she was a barrel of fun and could cheer up a hermit. Bryan smiled a weak smile and assured his mother that he would be alright, but to hurry back. Mrs. Richards was the wife of a locomotive engineer that was out on his run and she would be glad to go to Macon.

Teddie arranged with the dispatcher to leave the job for a day. Tessie put Bryan in the back seat on a bed of pillows that left room for Mrs. Richards to squeeze in, as she was a low stout woman. Tessie climbed in the front seat beside Teddie, and off they went to Macon.

The road was paved but the creeks had flooded. The concrete bridges were being built, but were not ready for traffic. The women and child could walk across the water on a foot bridge, but Teddie would drive off into the shallow creek water to mount the far bank. Little

Bryan was terrified to see his daddy drive off into the water in the automobile, but Mrs. Richards would just laugh and cuddle the sick boy and sing "Polly walla doddle all day." Tessie reminded Bryan that brave men never cried and that she had better not see a tear run down his flushed little face.

They finally arrived in Macon and Teddie asked directions to the doctor's office. Macon is a large city and traffic was heavy. Teddie had never driven in the city, but somehow they drove into the parking lot at the Medical Arts Building in the mud splattered Ford car.

Teddie carried Bryan into the waiting room. The receptionist had been told by phone they were bringing the boy, through the country as auto trips were called. The trip had been a strain on them, but they had made it and were so relieved.

Dr. Bershinsky entered the examination room. He was a large balding man with a European accent. He wore a long white jacket, said little as he had his nurse take Bryan's temperature. He then felt around the knot on the sick boy's neck, looked in his mouth and ears. Tessie had already taken a dislike to the doctor who had a rather aloft attitude. He beckoned the anxious couple aside and he calmly told them that he had seen this condition before in Europe and that it was a progressive syndrome that had no cure, that the boys' head would over time grow out of proportion to his body and he would expire in a few years. He was sorry but there was no treatment at present and he would advise Dr. Ware and good day.

Teddie turned pale and asked for the bill, but the doctor told him he would have the bill mailed to him. Tessie refused to believe the doctor. They left the doctor's office in a stupor of unbelief, than even Mrs. Richards could not overcome.

Bryant slept on his pillows but his head jostled with every bump the car hit. They arrived home after dark. Mrs. Richards helped Tessie get Bryan to bed. Tessie took the bad news better than Teddie did. She could not accept a diagnosis like that doctor had made and she would take her boy to Atlanta or somewhere he could be cured.

Teddie spent the night at his depot office on a cot he had in the record room. Bryan slept fitfully in the bed, close to his mother. She prayed until daylight and found great solace in her prayers. She could see a silver lining to the dark cloud that hovered over Bryan's head.

Teddie was exhausted from the trip and the worry. Where was the money coming from to pay Bryan's doctor bills? He had an idea. His friend that had worked at the agency with him had accepted a job in Atlanta with the Railroad Credit Union that loaned money to employees at a low interest rate and his credit was good. He telegraphed his friend in Atlanta of his predicament with the sick child. His friend wired him back not to worry, but to put Tessie and the boy on the train tomorrow for Atlanta. His wife knew Tessie and she would meet the train at the station in downtown Atlanta and take her to the finest doctor in the Southeast, Dr. J.E. Paulin. He had done wonders for their twin boys and he knew he could cure Bryan.

Sims Burns, the flagman that had befriended Teddie on the train that had delivered Teddie to Fitzgerald in the first place had been promoted to conductor now. He assured Teddie that he would see to it that Tessie and the boy were delivered to the waiting room in Atlanta, and he himself would see to it that they arrived to Piedmont Hospital out on Capital Avenue, where Dr. Paulin practiced, just in case their friend did not meet them.

Railroad people looked out for each other, and news had spread around that Teddie had a sick child and had so much sorrow with the other children.

Harry Arrington was at the throttle of the engine that brought the train into the Atlanta station in five hours flat. Bryan's eyes were wide open as he saw the passenger trains loading and unloading passengers. Tessie spied her friend Emavee Mathis standing at the gate where the inbound passengers entered the large waiting room of Atlanta's Terminal Station in the heart of Atlanta.

Bryan cheered up at the sight of the tall buildings and was delighted with the electric street cars that clattered through the streets with sparks falling from the overhead electric cables that powered them with their bells ringing.

Tessie was happy once more to know that Bryan would soon be under the care of Dr. Paulin, a wise and kindly doctor that Dr. Ware back home had told Tessie that she was lucky to get an appointment with such a renowned physician.

Tessie's friend drove her and Bryan out to Piedmont Hospital. She knew a woman that ran a rooming house across Capital Avenue from the sprawling hospital that catered to out patients, and relatives of patients. Tessie took a room for herself and the sick boy with the knot on his neck. She liked Mrs. Morgan, the proprietor of the establishment on first sight. The room and meals were expensive. Three dollars a day, almost what Teddie was paid by the railroad.

Tessie breathed a sigh of relief that she had saved some money for just such an emergency. It was some money she had shaved off the grocery bill each week. She had not told Teddie for fear he would spend it for clothes or coca colas. She was glad when he stopped smoking and chewing tobacco when Bryan was born. Teddie had agreed that the butcher bill could be paid for with what had been going up in blue smoke and brown spittle.

Tessie was up early the next morning. She bathed and dressed herself and Bryan and told him she expected him to be her brave little man and that this doctor would have him back home playing on the sidewalk in no time. She was whistling in the dark, so to say, but never lost hope that she would see this boy to manhood. Hadn't she seen into the future? The sad cemetery would not claim the boy child she had prayed to God in heaven for.

Dr. Paulin made his rounds at Piedmont Hospital that morning. The head nurse handed him a list of new patients that awaited his examination. On that list he noticed he was to see a referral patient of a classmate of his at medical school, Dr. R.M. Ware, down in Fitzgerald, 200 miles south of Atlanta. Dr. Paulin knew this patient, only six years old, had a serious problem. He was a man of compassion, although he was a professional man. His heart went out to the small woman that sat beside the high hospital bed reading a well worn book entitled, "The Adventures of Billy Whiskers." The mother rose to greet the doctor in the white coat with a clipboard in his hand. Tessie knew in an instant this serious man was the answer to her prayers. This doctor was so different from the cold doctor back in Macon, that Dr. Ware had termed "an alarmist." Dr. Paulin spoke in a soft firm voice. "I am glad to meet you, Bryan, and I want to examine you." Bryan told the good doctor that he wanted to be an adventurer when he grew up. Dr. Paulin continued to talk to the boy of his adventures, and assured him that he would soon be home and raring to go.

The knot on Bryan's neck, the doctor told Tessie out in the hall, was a gland that was swollen with poison from his system. He wanted her permission to have Bryan operated on by a noted surgeon, Dr. McCray, who would remove the gland that was diseased and he could examine the tissue under a microscope. He told Tessie that the boy was very sick, but he felt sure that he could bring his fever down and make him more comfortable.

Bryan underwent the operation a few days later and liked Dr. McCray. The surgeon was somewhat of a legend around Atlanta. He came to work on a motorcycle and wore a leather jacket and riding boots when he was not in the operating room.

The operation on Bryan's neck gland was tedious, as poison could be released with disastrous results. The operation went well. Bryan opened his eyes back in his hospital room to see a beautiful young nurse that had been assigned to monitor the patient as he awoke from the anesthesia.

Tessie was across the street awaiting a call to come over to Bryan's bedside when he awoke. She had made friends among the other people at the rooming house. This was the thing that kept her going. Bryan asked the nurse to read to him from his storybook, as his mother did. He was weak and nauseated, but drifted off to sleep again. The next time he awoke, Tessie was there, placing cold rags to his brow. He was a good patient, but ate little and was weak. In the days that dragged past, Tessie did her best to feed her boy and cheer him up, until Dr. Paulin could make his diagnosis that would tell the tale of Bryan's condition.

Early one morning Bryan awoke to see his dad standing by his bedside. Teddie had been on the train all night after a trying day at the depot and looked gaunt and weary. He had not shaved or eaten which only made him appear as a ghost standing there in his overcoat. Bryan looked at his father in disbelief. Could this be the man that was always so neat and smiling? Tessie could see Teddie's anxiety reflected in the boy's face, and stepped forward to break the silence. She told Teddie to go and freshen up and eat and come back later. She told Bryan that his dad was alright, just tired and sleepy. The visit by Teddie was short. He gave Tessie what money he had and caught the next train to Fitzgerald. Bryan, young as he was, would never forget that morning and the look on Teddie's tired face.

The reports were in. Dr. Paulin had a conference with Tessie and Dr. Minix, his understudy. He was concerned that the tumor was growing on the neck gland that had suggested cancer. Tessie gasped, but got hold of herself. She asked, "What next?" Dr. Paulin told her that he would start x-ray treatment on the area that surrounded the gland that had been removed, then only time would tell.

Bryan was annoyed by the bandages on his sore neck, but seemed brighter and his fever was down to nearly normal.

Each morning the orderly would come and lift him onto the rolling table and wheel him to the special room equipped with a giant machine that looked like a rocket ship to Bryan. He could read the funnies in the paper and had marveled at the adventures of "Flash Gordon" aboard his rocket ship. In fact, Bryan made an adventure out of every day activities, with his astounding imagination. The x-ray technician would place a wall of lead bricks around his frail body, then cover him with a heavy rubber sheet to protect him from the powerful, but deadly radioactive rays that would bombard the area on his neck where the tumorous gland had been removed.

The treatments were painless, but ominous for a child. A week passed, the treatment ended, but Bryan's doctors kept him in the hospital to observe him. They were concerned that he still had a low fever that they could not bring down that last degree to normal.

A month passed, Tessie felt that the treatments had been successful. Bryan was cheerful and was eating better. Emmavee, Tessie's friend, would bring her twin boys, Bobbie and Billy to visit with Bryan in a playroom at the hospital. Bryan lost his hair, but it was coming back even more curly than before.

Dr. Paulin stopped by Bryan's room one morning. His trained fingers carefully examined the child's neck, searching for lumps or swelling. A look of satisfaction spread across his sensitive face. He asked Bryan if he would like to go home. The answer was quick and direct, "Yes doctor, if my mama says I can." Tessie beamed, "Lord knows, I am ready to go, if Dr. Paulin thinks you are able." "There is one thing we must see if your fever is normal in the morning, you can leave." Tessie wired Teddie the good news.

Morning came and Bryan gathered his books and play things. The orderly came to get him. Tessie was reserved about his fever as his forehead was warm to her touch. Bryan got his first big disappointment. The head nurse took down his chart, shook her thermometer down, and placed it under Bryan's tongue. She kept her eye on her wrist watch. Her face was stoic as she jotted down 100 degrees. She spoke without emotion, "I cannot dismiss him today Mrs. Dunn, his temperature is some above normal."

Tessie's worst fears had come to pass. Bryan refused to return down that dismal hall to the room he had spent nearly six weeks in.

The tall strong black orderly seemed to share Bryan's disappointment, but stooped to gather the frail boy in his arms. Bryan fought at him with all his strength with his bare fist in the same style of his grandfather Charlie Barwick. It was to no avail, he was overpowered and fell exhausted back in his rumpled hospital bed with all the cranks.

Tessie had mixed feelings. She didn't want to take a sick boy home. Maybe tomorrow the fever could abate. Dr. Paulin heard of the spirit the boy showed. That is the signs I have been waiting for. Bryan has a long fight ahead of him. I have done all I know to do and he and his mother should be at home. He will be more content and his mother will care for him. I am sure she is a fighter in her own right.

Chapter 35

Back Home Again

Tessie was jubilant to hear the news. Dr. Minix told Tessie to keep Bryan out in the fresh air and sunlight, keep him quiet, don't let him run and exhaust himself, check his temperature and come back in a month. All the railroad men knew of the boy's long battle, and many prayers had been said. The train crew cheered when they saw Tessie, Bryan and a "red cap" as baggage men were called coming down the station platform to be loaded on the train bound for Fitzgerald and home.

Bryan was so proud that he waved to Engineer Arrington up in the cab of engine #119 building steam for the run to Fitzgerald, and beyond. Tessie never had felt the sense of self satisfaction she did as Conductor Sim Burns "turned" two seats together so Bryan could stretch out and rest. Bryan seemed to gain renewed strength the closer the train got to Fitzgerald.

Westwood shops passed by the window that Bryan had his nose pressed to. The conductor entered the coach and called, "Next stop Fitzgerald."

The sun was still high in the sky when the train came to a screeching stop before the concrete platform of the fortress like station. There was Teddie and his Porter Alzie Kennedy waiting to meet Tessie and Bryan. Teddie looked like a different man. He was smiling from ear to ear. Alzie took Bryan in his strong arm, with the suitcase in the other hand. Tessie was not one to show affection in public. She was tired, oh so tired, but there was a song in her heart. The happy family loaded into the Ford car and were soon unloading under the carport of 316 West Central.

Teddie had spent his spare time working in his rose garden and yard. He had gone to the country and dug up dogwood and red bud trees that bloomed in profusion each spring and Cana Lilly beds bloomed red and yellow. His yard was a showplace. In the back yard on the south exposure where the cold north wind did not reach, there was the crab apple tree where the mocking bird had sung the night before Bryan was born. Teddie had boxed off an area, filled the space with clean white sand. This was a sandbox for Bryan to play in. He had a little spade to dig with and he fashioned sand castles, frog houses, and fortresses that he would populate with his toy soldiers. He just loved to build things and his imagination knew no end. Tessie encouraged the boy to spend long hours out in the sand box in the sun. He told his mother that he was going to build a miniature Dutch Village. With his paint set he painted oatmeal boxes bright colors, and whittled wind mill wheels from cigar box wood. He dug canals in the sand, and lined the bottoms with tinfoil salvaged from cigarette packages that looked like water on which he placed his toy sail boats. Pastures were formed between the canals lined with green artificial grass. Tessie took him to the dime store where he selected chinaware cows some standing and some laying down that he mounted in the fake pasture.

When he called his mother out to see his Dutch Village, she was delighted with his handy work. When Teddie came home from work he did not share Tessie's enthusiasm for the boy's creation. His statement to Tessie was, "You are just encouraging him to be a workman like my brother Grady, just look how soiled he is." Tessie shot him a look that he well knew. "And what is wrong with being a builder Mr. High and Mighty?" She replied. Teddie just retreated to his rose garden.

Bryan did not attend the first grade the rest of that year. Tessie conferred with Bryan's teacher, Miss Barfield. She laid out a work schedule for the boy, gave Tessie his books, and papers to study just as if he was in class.

Teddie did not come home at noon; he ate at a boarding house uptown. Tessie ate like a "bird" but was careful to see that Bryan had a good diet. Dr. Paulin told her to make syrup candy for him to eat each day for the iron content of the cane syrup. She gave him orange juice between meals. In fact, she spent her time nursing her son back to health.

One day in the spring the postman rang her door bell. He had a bundle of letters, all addressed to Bryan Dunn. Tessie opened the bundle, and there were 26 letters written by Bryan's classmates. They all sent their best wishes and how they missed him and hoped he would be in the second grade with them next fall. He loved his classmates, and eagerly read each one of the letters so painfully written by fingers that had just learned to write. Bryan studied hard at his mother's knee and was doing work well beyond many of his classmates. He loved to read, study maps, and draw pictures of birds and animals. On occasion Tessie would take him to school, after classes, and Miss Barfield would test him. She was pleased with his progress and wrote on his blank report card. "This work has been made up and he is progressed to the second grade."

The time had arrived for Tessie to take Bryan back to Atlanta to have a checkup at Dr. Paulin's office in the Medical Arts Building out on Peachtree Street. Teddie saw them off on the noon train to Atlanta. Bryan loved the sounds of the train, the smoke, the bells ringing, the steam whistles, and the powerful drivers that made the wheels turn on the steel rails. He was fascinated by the men in their uniforms and goggles.

When they arrived in Atlanta, Bryan was strong enough to help his mother with her bags, and be her little man, as she complimented him. They caught a streetcar that carried them out Peachtree Street to the tall building where the doctor's offices were located. They rode the elevator up to the tenth floor where Dr. Paulin's waiting room was. Bryan had a long scar on his neck that had healed well. He was suntanned and had grown. When his name was called, he and his mama went to meet the doctor. The doctor greeted them as he would an old friend and was surprised to see the progress that Bryan had made since he had dismissed him from Piedmont Hospital.

His fever was normal and he was bright and happy. Dr. Paulin showed Bryan the distant mountain range out the window and pointed out Stone Mountain to him. Tessie was so proud that the doctor told her that she had done a job that he had his doubts about when they left the hospital, but low and behold the boy had outgrown the malady that had brought him to death's very door.

Teddie had the bills to pay. Dr. Paulin had sent a doctor bill of $1,000 dollars, which didn't cover the hospital bill. Teddie wrote Dr. Paulin that he could not raise that much money and hoped he could see fit to reduce his bill. The reply was not long in coming. It read, "Mr. Dunn, I realize that times are difficult, and money is hard to raise. I will reduce m y bill by one-half and if you cannot afford that amount, I will half the amount again."

Chapter 36

Tightening Their Belts

Tessie came into the picture. She told Teddie to return the automobile she enjoyed so much to Mr. Anderson this very day. He could arrange a loan with the bank and the Railroad Credit Union. She told him she had a few dollars set aide from the household money, and he would have to cut out hamburgers and coca-colas on the streets and come home at noon and eat black-eyed peas and rice that she would prepare.

He would cut back on church donations since charity began in the home. The couple spent most of the night haggling over money. She went so far as to tell Teddie that she was tired of watching him trying to be a "big fish in a little puddle." Bryan heard those conversations and it shaped his attitude toward thrift and money management. Two days later, Teddie wired Dr. Paulin five hundred dollars by Western Union.

Teddie seemed to turn in his best performance when he was under stress. He was a changed man; he had no funeral bill to pay. His health was excellent, and was a dynamo of energy. He was a Lightning Slinger, but in a very different way.

Tessie had suggested that they rent out the front bedroom to a single gentleman. She could clean the room and make the bed. The twelve dollars a month rent payment would buy groceries. Teddie and Alzie dug up the crab apple tree and Bryan's sand box and scabbed on a bathroom with a concrete floor and a drain for a shower. The two men would work on the weekends, even by electric lights Teddie strung himself. He had the Dunn talent to build and knowledge of electricity.

Bryan watched his father and helper with great interest. The boy was now eight years old, but he knew how many shovels of sand, cement, and gravel that had to be mixed together to create cement. He even held the water hose as Alzie mixed the ingredients. He watched as the men raised the frame to create the walls and rafters that were cut by a sharp hand saw on "saw horses" Teddie built.

Little did he know that Bryan, with his talent for creation, was learning things and skills that would mean far more to him than the lessons he was getting in that stuffy old classroom at Third Ward School. Teddie had a green thumb, but he never dreamed the seed he was sowing in the fertile ground of Bryan's mind would one day grow and thrive to bear fruit that Teddie never dreamed of.

As soon as he had the bathroom operating, they built on a screened in bunkroom. He and Bryan would sleep there in the fresh air for several years leaving Tessie the bedroom that wasn't rented out.

The economy improved somewhat in the late thirties. The doctor and hospital bills had been paid off. The one thing that Tessie missed was an automobile, but her friends had been good to come by and pick her up to go to Missionary Meetings that she loved to attend.

Teddie and Bryan took long bicycle rides on Sunday afternoons, even to Bowens Mill, ten miles away. The exercise was just what Bryan needed; in fact, he seldom came in the house, summer or winter.

Tessie had her privacy. She would build a fire in a small coal grate fireplace that kept her room warm. Now that they had a bathroom in the rear of the house, she, not Teddie, decided to rent the front living room, dining room, and kitchen out as a furnished apartment.

Teddie hired a black carpenter named Coleman Ellis to help Tessie convert a back screen porch into a kitchen with a small letdown table they could eat their meager meals from. The rent from that front apartment made the monthly payments on the nice house. The little family made out very well for the duration of the depression. The house was so close to town that just a short walk would put you at the railroad station, the freight depot, the Methodist Church, the library, or the movie theater. Bryan's hospital bills were slowly paid off.

Tessie would write a weekly letter to her mother Arta that lived with her oldest son Robert. They would move around often to find work. Robert was a mason and sometimes he would be in the Northeastern cities and sometimes in Miami, Florida. Life was not easy for Arta, being crippled and living on what Robert would bring in. Tessie would make sacrifices to put a dollar bill in each letter and would send Bryan on his bicycle to mail it in the drop slot of the rolling post office car on the afternoon passenger train. She kept in touch with her father that now lived in the shotgun house that Arta had vacated. He walked all over town, deaf as a post. He would pick a bouquet of wild flowers, or some from the flowerbeds in the parks that he would bring to Tessie's side door. She, for reasons of her own, never let Bryan associate with him, as he set a poor example for a child. Perhaps it was because of Lenard's memories.

.

Chapter 37

Bryan's Education

Bryan was fascinated by the trains that thundered past and the men that piloted them. He would laugh at the clouds of black smoke and hot cinders that the laboring steam locomotives belched from their smoke stacks. The rhythm of the exhaust, the powerful driving rods, and the whistles, were to Bryan, what the hymns of the children's choir had been to Lenard.

Bryan dressed in a pair of khaki pants, leather moccasins on his feet. Shirtless in the summer and was tanned brown as a berry. He wore no hat in the summer, but a strong leather belt with a sheath knife in the leather scabbard strung at his side. He was healthy and that was the thing that Tessie was so proud of.

Teddie had hoped for a son that would shine in the academic world, a professional man that would walk the corridor of some university in a far off city, as he would have liked to have done. Bryan had rather have some minnows in a jar or a turtle in a dish of pebbles that he could feed flies that he swatted.

Tessie had been his professor, the streets of Fitzgerald and the surrounding creeks and ponds his classroom. Things were slow to change in Fitzgerald, although the trains still ran through town. Teddie managed to stay on the job at the Freight Depot.

Tessie enjoyed her home and son. Bryan went to the picture show on Saturday afternoons with the neighborhood kids. The vacant lots by the house where Teddie had grown so many roses grew up in broom sage. Somehow bamboo got started in the fertile moist soil and had developed into a cane break.

Bryan mowed the grass in the yard. He took the garbage to the alley and "laid" fires in the fireplace. For his efforts, Teddie paid the boy fifty cents, half of which he could spend, the rest he put in a savings account at the bank. The little bankbook with his weekly deposits recorded and tallied seemed to fascinate him. It gave him great pride to have money in the bank.

His tenth birthday was a milestone that Tessie reveled in. Her faith and efforts had paid off. Teddie gave him a stamp album to mount the postage stamps he collected. He had a collection from every country that had a postal service. He would spend hours studying maps, identifying countries, their rivers and mountains. He cared little for games or contact sports, but he was a whiz at geography and natural science. Tessie observed his developing personality, and was rather amused at the channels his mind was taking.

But then it happened right out of the blue summer sky. Teddie bought an automobile. Mr. Williams knew Teddie very well, being the owner of Williams Chevrolet Company, right across Main Street from the Theater. Teddie walked by the front of the automobile agency with its showroom full of new 1939 cars painted in all colors.

He stopped to pass the time of day with the aging business man. After a friendly greeting and a handshake, Mr. Williams invited Teddie into his office. He told Teddie how slow business was and how he needed to move cars out of his warehouse, where they were gathering dust. Mr. Williams leaned back in his swivel chair and lit a cigarette, blew a cloud of blue smoke and spoke. "Teddie, you need a car, and I am going to make you a deal you can't turn down. You bring your wife up here this evening when you get off work and let her pick out the color and model she likes and tomorrow morning I will have my men service, wash it and put it under your carport with a full tank of gasoline."

Teddie was dumbfounded by the offer and thanked him adding, "But how can I pay for a car? You know I am struggling to get on my feet from the house I have bought and the doctor bills with Tessie and the boy." "I know all that," Mr. Williams continued, "Take the car for $600, nothing down, but your signature, pay me monthly what you can, and we both will hope for the best."

Teddie left, walking on thin air. He was a splurger, and he thought he would never get a better deal.

That day he burst into the little kitchen and took Tessie in his arms. "What are you up to now, Teddie Dunn? I know you too well. You are only trying to get me to sanction some extravagant idea you have concocted," Teddie knew her weakness and played his ace. "You and Bryan need a car to go places and see people. Mr. Williams is practically giving me a car." Tessie shook her finger in his face, "Whoever knew of a car salesman giving a car to a poor man like you?" He explained the deal and Tessie began to weaken some. She agreed that the boy did need to get out more and go places now that good paved roads were connecting Fitzgerald to the rest of the country.

Tessie deep down inside her bosom, was thrilled at the idea of a car of their own, any car, any color, just so long as it had a steering wheel and a horn.

She told Bryan when he came in from school and his eyes got wide with excitement. "Our own car, Mama! Can we go to Ossiwissee Springs, Lake Beatrice, Bowen's Mill or maybe even to the beach, where the waves come in and I can see the seagulls and fish?" They walked the three blocks to meet Teddie that evening at the car warehouse. Tessie picked out a blue two-door standard model car that would be her "magic carpet."

The next morning, before noon it was sitting under the carport at 316 W. Central. It was the talk of the neighborhood that day in June. Teddie had a garage built on the alley behind the house to protect it from the weather, and not to bother the tenant that lived in the front of the house.

Bryan told all his friends and playmates that his dad had bought a car and he and his mama could go places, and see things. Teddie told Tessie that he would arrange for her to get a tank of gas a week at Jim Weaver's Filling Station and that he would ride his bicycle to work or walk as usual. He explained that they had earned a little pleasure in life and the dark days were over.

Tessie was not long in mastering the controls of the new car. Gone were the square body styles, the canvas tops and isinglass side curtains. The driver could start the engine inside the machine. There was room for six passengers. The gear shift was up on the steering column and could that be an electric cigarette lighter? The streamline body and smooth running engine could whisk along a paved road at 60 m.p.h., with all the comforts of home.

Tessie relented on her hard fisted financial program somewhat. The next Monday afternoon who came driving up to Missionary Meeting with several ladies that she had rode with when she had no car. Her girlhood friend, Nellie Smith was sitting right beside her.

All that summer, she would take Bryan and his friends to Bowen's Mill or Ossiwissee Springs to swim in the clear water. Bryan took to the water like a duck. If he saw a person doing something he was quick to follow. He made his first big adventure in the water when he swam by himself over the deep, boiling spring at Ossiwissee.

Tessie held her breath until he stood triumphant on the far bank. She always encouraged him to achieve the things that were a challenge.

Teddie had to stay on the job at the depot. He seldom sat down at the telegraph key. Telephones were replacing the rattling instruments. The day of the Lightning Slinger was slipping into the past. The two pictures that Teddie kept on display under the glass plate of his desk at the depot was his school teacher back at Andersonville, Professor Clark. The other was a likeness of Dr. Paulin, Bryan's doctor in Atlanta. Both men were dead now, but Teddie never forgot either.

His outlet from the long hours he spent serving the AB&C Railroad Company was the flower beds and the almost weekly fish fries that he held in his backyard. He would buy speckled sea trout, cleaned and ready for the pan, for 12 cents a pound from his friend he met the first day he arrived in Fitzgerald, Nick Pope, the proprietor of a thriving Greek Café down on East Pine Street.

Teddie loved a crowd of people, and Fitzgerald never seemed to be short of people of all levels of society. He let the people that enjoyed strong drink and riotous living, have their fun elsewhere. Tessie's father Charlie Barwick lived in his own silent world over on North Grant Street or with a crowd of old timers down at the blacksmith shed behind the mule barn. A young woman called "Goldie", the mother of a boy around the age of Bryan had moved in the now decrepit shotgun house with Charlie. All that was left of the Barwick property that Tessie had once called home when she and Fitzgerald were young, the blind ponies, aging race horses, milk cows, and the barn that had sheltered the old man from Australia was grown up in weeds and vines. Tessie had blotted that early life from her mind, just as she had the loss of her babies and her twin sister. She and Teddie had left their troubles, as the song they once sang, were packed away in that "old kid bag." The only family member she treasured was Arta, her mother, and they lived in different worlds.

Maude Perry was Tessie's best friend. Nettie Day had met a tragic end in an automobile accident. It seemed that the graveyard had claimed so many of her childhood friends.

Maude Perry had a vacation home on St. Simons Island on the Georgia Coast. She would include the Dunns in her guest list, especially at Thanksgiving season. Teddie would load Tessie and

Bryan in the Chevrolet, go by and pick up Laura, Mrs. Perry's maid and cook. He would drive like a demon, Tessie by his side, barely missing the herds of free ranging piney woods cows that lay on the pavement. Bryan and Laura sat on the backseat, with all the groceries and linens. Tessie acted as copilot, pointing the way through Waycross, over the Satilla River, onto the salt marshes of Glynn, and over the humpback bridge to Brunswick.

Bryan seemed to know every creek and river on the route. He loved Laura, with her turbaned head, clean apron, and the smells of asafedity and snuff.

He would be the only child there. Mrs. Perry was not that fond of children, but Bryan was the exception. His manners and quiet nature pleased the rich old dowger, wonder of wonders. Teddie would reluctantly walk with him to the banks of the Dunbar Tidal Creek where he would catch fish and crabs that Laura would prepare for the table. Teddie would not touch a fishing pole or crab basket, claiming that his brothers, Grady and Charlie had drug him along the banks of Clearwater Creek as a boy. Why, he wondered was his son so much like his brothers, and so little like him, the clerk and businessman? Tessie would smile with satisfaction at Bryan's catch, only wishing that she had been with him on the banks of Dunbar Creek that murmured with the changing tide under the age old live oak trees, festooned with Spanish moss.

Chapter 38

The AB&C Railroad Problems

There had been changes on the AB&C Railroad in the last ten years. Growing pains had played the fledging line with financial panic. The great depression, labor troubles and the all consuming demon fire. Probably the line would have ceased to operate, as others did if it hadn't been for the foresight of the founding civil engineer, Mr. Bonner. He surveyed a route from Waycross, Georgia to Atlanta through Fitzgerald that would prove to be the shortest and best link between Florida and the heartland of the nation. These connections would prove to be the redeeming factor in the railroads future. Fate played into the hands of the line when a devastating hurricane demolished the "over seas" route of the Florida East Coast that connected Miami with Key West. That company had designed a locomotive that was fast, powerful, and could operate on light rail and over wooden trestles. They no longer needed this fleet of locomotives and put many of them on the auction block at Jacksonville, Florida.

Twenty of these light Pacific engines found a new home at Westwood Shop, just beyond Fitzgerald. The engines were converted from oil burners to coal. They replaced the worn out engines that were retired from the AB&C mainline, fitted with "foot boards" and put into yard services as switch engines.

Other powerful locomotives were purchased from the New York Central Railroad that were powerful enough to handle heavy tonnage on the grades that existed north of Fitzgerald to Atlanta and Birmingham.

Through passenger trains now connected with the cities of the north, bidding for the Florida tourist trade. Other things like train wrecks, competing lines, lack of capital to operate the road, were constant problems. Fire seemed to strike Fitzgerald with regularity. The spacious freight depot and the platform that reached from Main to Grant Street and twenty-two cars of merchandise went up in flames one night in the early thirties. The heart pine structure fueled a fire that by morning had consumed everything on that block. Only ashes and twisted steel frames of boxcars remained the next morning.

Teddie no longer had an office. An army of workmen cleaned the ashes, and rebuilt the tracks, but the company had no funds to rebuild the depot. A nearby cotton warehouse was rented and remodeled to serve as the Freight Depot until better arrangements could be made. The cubbyhole office cramped Teddie's style, but the pay check was the same.

About the year 1939 Teddie found himself able to buy an automobile, the Railroad Company broke ground to build a new Freight Depot on the sight of the old wooden depot. This building was constructed of scrap steel rails for a frame, formed and poured with concrete walls and a flat roof. There wasn't enough wood in it to build a good fire to warm by on a cold morning. Only the doors and a partition to wall off the office and restrooms were of wood. The finished building was termed "fireproof."

Bryan seemed to feel at home at the Freight house. The clerks and porters took up time with him and his dad let him go with them over the track yards and town. Lots of days when he would leave school on his bicycle, he would pedal to the ballpark and play ball with the other boys, then pedal to the Freight Depot, watch the switch engine as it shuttled cars from loading docks of other warehouses or to the "team track" where watermelons were being loaded by farmers. He soon knew the whistle sound of different engines and the crewmen that operated the trains.

Teddie had much rather he had taken as much interest in his school books than in the operation of a railroad that was struggling to pay off debts. How could Teddie or Fitzgerald survive if the railroad ceased to operate?

Tessie and Bryan didn't worry about the railroad; they just took it for granted, just like they did the pine trees and the rivers and lakes. They spent many happy days fishing in House Creek where it emptied into the Ocmulgee River. Bryan didn't realize those activities were a part of his therapy that was agreeing with him so swell.

He always had an eye for a way to earn some money to put in his savings account. Tessie would make candy for him to sell on the uptown streets on Saturday afternoons and would run home with the coins jingling in his pant's pockets. He would sharpen Tessie's butcher knife on the concrete back steps and cut the bamboo canes that thrived on the vacant lot next to the home place. The branches were removed by trimming at the joints with great care and skill. The fishing poles that were hung to dry during the winter were displayed out front in the spring and summer for sale. He could sell all he could cut and cure for 10 cents and 25 cents each. The canes would sprout back and renew themselves, and another crop would ripen and harden on the first frost of winter. Bryan's income would be as much money as Teddie made at the Depot some days. Teddie didn't say much about Bryan's fishing pole business, but it didn't seem to fit to well in the programs that Teddie wished to see the boy pursue. Tessie even thought that Teddie was just a little put out that the boy not yet twelve years old was making money on fishing poles. Bryan seemed to turn a profit on several things that Teddie thought was below his dignity. The stacks of clean newspapers Bryan would sell to Nick Pope to wrap fish in, the scrap iron and copper the boy seemed to accumulate and sell to Ashley Dowling at the junkyard only added a hefty balance to Bryan's bank account. Tessie would let the enterprising boy stay out of school to trim fishing poles, if he would keep his grades up and he did.

Chapter 39

Pearl Harbor and War

These idealic days could not go on forever. Then one Sunday morning it happened. The thing that would change the world forever. The thing that Tessie had feared and every mother fears, the clouds had gathered over Europe and had erupted into war on June 7, 1941, one day before Bryan's twelfth birthday the Japanese bombed Pearl Harbor. The United Sates declared war on the Axis powers, Germany, Italy and Japan. President Roosevelt came on the radio to announce that the country must mobilize its men and resources.

Tessie wondered where her boy was on that beautiful Sunday morning, she just wanted to hold him in her arms. He had slipped off from Sunday school and was fishing at Bowen's Mill. Another boy, some older than Bryan, had called him to the old railroad trestle that spanned the mill pond and told him as he sat in a leaky old boat the tragic news. Bryan strung his fish, paddled to the bank and rode his bicycle back to town to check in with his mother, before Teddie returned from church.

He knew that Pearl Harbor was in Hawaii, and told his mother that it was a long way from Fitzgerald, and they would be safe. Teddie came in all excited. He had missed the first World War and thought he was too old for the Second World War, but he, like Tessie feared that their only son could become "cannon fodder." Only time would tell.

Bryan got the twenty-two caliber rifle he wanted for his birthday over his father's protest. Teddie had shot himself in the leg with just such a gun, and now he was giving Bryan a gun. Tessie had prevailed, even asked Dr. Ware for his opinion of Bryan having a firearm. The doctor told her that under the circumstances, he knew Bryan was capable to handle the gun safely and was a responsible kind of boy.

The war was raging worldwide. Sacrifices had to be made by the people back home. Gasoline, sugar, meat, shoes, and even coffee went to the war effort and were rationed to people left on the home front.

They sat down to many meals of game and birds that Bryan's rifle had brought down.

Ammunition was hard to find, but Bryan had friends in the "home guard" that would slip him a carton of bullets that were intended for target practice. Gas for the little blue Chevrolet that was allotted only three gallons per week was supplemented by gas from the barrels that the Railroad Company shipped in to power its motor cars and trucks somehow got to Teddie, and the "gospel car" as Tessie called it.

Bryan was too young to answer the draft call, and Teddie was over the age limit to serve in the Army. He and his brothers were never inclined to join the armed forces or be interested in politics. They dedicated their every thought and effort to the railroad, which was so vital to the war effort. Troop trains and ammunition trains rumbled through Fitzgerald day and night.

Chapter 40

Bryan's Efforts to Excel

Bryan did manage to finish high school the year the war ended. Teddie was disappointed that Bryan was not among the honor students and made many comments after graduation night. Teddie was reprimanded by Tessie on the way home. She told him that she doubted that any of those outstanding scholars had as much money in the bank as "her son" had.

The next day Teddie told Bryan that they needed to take a long walk down the track together. Bryan knew that always meant a lecture on the facts of life. He wisely never argued with his father as his mother would.

Teddie began by telling Bryan that he loved him and would help him, although it was evident they had chosen different courses of endeavor. I have saved some money to send you to college, but you show no interest in becoming a professional man of letters, in fact, you are a wild one. I have decided to invest the money in some lots out on West Pine Street and build rental units. He continued before Bryan could comment that the property was his and he would receive the rent payments. Then Teddie turned a little more charitable to the boy and stated "your mother has dinner each day, if you are hungry, come in and eat with us. Your bed on the porch will remain there if you are tired and feel welcome to use it, but never ask me for a thin dime, as my pocketbook is closed."

Bryan nodded in agreement. The next morning he presented himself to the train master in his office at the big station that had been his home away from home. He told the train master that knew him from childhood that he wanted a job as a fireman on the railroad which needed men to meet the traffic of the postwar boom. The train master smiled and asked if he was a high school graduate and twenty-one years old, which he wasn't twenty-one. He then pulled a desk drawer open and handed Bryan an application to fill out. Bryan knew all the rules and regulations of train operation by heart. He filled in the application and completed the rule book examination in short order. He was then sent to the property protection officer that was one of the men that had taken him bird hunting and taught him to shoot straight and true. There he was finger printed and had his police record checked, which was clear.

Bryan had no car but he had bought himself a motor scooter that he rode out to Westwood Shop and went into a training job as a hostler helper. The job was hard and hot, he had to shake the grates of the steam engines, clean the ashes from the engines ash pans, and throw the switches to head the engines to the turntable and the Hostler that drove the engine around the engine house. He was so much more contented than he had been at school.

Teddie didn't have to tell Tessie how her son had gone to work at the shops. She knew every move he made by her telephone and the "clothes line" gossip system the town wives operated around the clock.

Bryan stayed at home just as his father had offered, and was made welcome.

He soon qualified as a fireman on the mainline. He would hang out the gangway of the engine he was firing and wave to Tessie that would be standing on the corner where they used to stand for him to count the cars of passing trains when he was just a child. Teddie seemed to relax that the boy was happy and doing what he wanted to do. He also seemed to know what train to look for Bryan to be on.

Tessie's papa, Charlie Barwick died where he had chose to live, over on North Grant Street in the "shotgun" house that Teddie had been paying the taxes on. The county buried the old "stockman" on a lonesome plot at Evergreen Cemetery. She was left alone, here in Fitzgerald, where she had been brought as a baby in Arta's arms. Arta lived all over the United States, but mostly in Miami, Florida still with her oldest son Robert.

The war had brought new prosperity to Fitzgerald and the railroad that spawned it. Changes were not long in coming on the railroad. The AB&C Railroad had been taken over by the Atlantic Coastline Railroad. The steam engines were replaced by diesel electric locomotives and passenger trains were abolished. Cars and trucks had ended the package freight. The Westwood Shops were moved to Waycross. Bryan managed to hang on to his job on the strength of the many work trains that were busy rebuilding the mainline.

Teddie still held his agency position, but had more duties saddled on him. He had pyramided the apartments he built with the money he and Tessie had saved for Bryan's education into twenty odd rental units that he rented. He didn't own any mules with T.N.D. branded in their hooves, but he had lifted himself up by his bootstraps to a level that he and Tessie could relax, but would you believe that they continued to live just as they always had in the little scabbed on apartment at 316 W. Central, with Bryan sleeping on the screen porch, when he was off his run.

Teddie had traded the little 39' Chevrolet for a 1954 model that he drove Tessie around town every evening. He still rode his trusty bicycle when the weather permitted.

Bryan announced that he was planning a wedding. He was 27 years old, and like h is mother knew how to pinch a penny. He had a side job with the Department of Agriculture and had bought several small farms and never was without a herd of cattle. He had been drafted during the Korean War but deferred to continue work on the railroad. He sold a farm for enough profit to buy a new Buick automobile that he would go to Irwinville to see his intended when he was in off the railroad. She was a school teacher, just a few months younger than he was named Gladys. Gladys was to become the daughter Teddie had longed for, and never had. She had a mind of her own and set Bryan straight to start with. She told him she would marry no man that had no house to take her to and she would give him a year for him to prove his intentions were as good as his promises. She put her "bit" in Bryan's mouth. He brought her a large diamond ring that he paid cash for. Teddie had to get into the act. He owned two vacant lots out on the highway to Irwinville. He propositioned Bryan that he would deed one of the nice lots to him and Gladys after the wedding next June, if Bryan would have a house built on the lot. It was a deal, Bryan drew the plans for the new house, got a building permit, and traded with the best self-employed carpenters around. He dug the foundation on his off days from the railroad. He and that carpenter set in to work. Bryan and a black friend of his named Henry, cut pine timber on Bryan's land with a hand powered "crosscut" saw, hauled logs to the saw mill, and swapped logs for finished lumber. A black brick mason that had been working on the railroad laid the foundation for the new home on Teddie's lot. He would drive by and look, but was astounded at the progress that the men were making. He had contracted his houses built, but Bryan just had to get into the work.

Teddie told Tessie at the supper table that Arta Barwick was right in her prediction that she made the Saturday Bryan was born. "Saturday's child will work for his living." Bryan was possessed to do the hardest, dirtiest work he could find.

Tessie smiled and reminded him of the struggles they had had to raise the sickly child that the doctor in Macon had predicted to be afflicted even if the survived. Teddie agreed with her and never again did he mention his disappointment in the route Bryan had taken. Tessie smiled and told Teddie that he had better start filling out one of those blank deeds that he kept in his desk drawer to the new owner, Bryan Dunn and his bride. Teddie snorted and said, "You win again Tessie," but he is like my brother Grady that worked himself to death for a thankless railroad. Both Grady and "T" Dunn had filled early graves. Ida and Minnie had died in Jacksonville, leaving no children.

Gladys had finished her class year and had her four year B.S. Degree from college and would receive her MRS. Degree at a country church on June 9, 1956. Teddie was at the wedding with Tessie. The newlyweds left on a trip to Nassau in the Bahamas, and Bryan didn't owe a penny to anyone.

The years passed, Tessie began to show the strain and heart ache she had suttered off as a young woman. She had a sense of satisfaction in giving "her" son to Gladys, as he needed a good woman's guiding hand as his father had.

Bryan, unbeknown to his father, had bought five vacant lots for a song, and he sung it, just below the bridal house. Teddie drove by in his little car one morning and saw Bryan unloading lumber on the bottom lot. He stopped and got out, pulled his britches up, straightened his necktie that he always wore and asked Bryan what he was doing. Bryan smiled and told him in a joking manner, "Why don't you ask Tessie? She knows more about our business than we do. I'll bet she could tell you the answer to your question. No, Teddie, I have been cut off the extra board out at Westwood. In fact, I am 23 times cut off. I am going to build a house on my lot with my labor and my money and hope to rent it as you do yours. Teddie stiffened as if lighting had struck him. "You are just going to ruin a pile of good lumber. You are no contractor, much less a carpenter. Don't come running to me when you need help." He turned and slammed his car door and drove to the depot.

Other neighbors and tradesmen shared Teddie's views of Bryan's
capabilities. The foundation was laid by Bryan and his black helper.
Brick masons shouted insults as they passed and carpenters sneered at
him. Bryan had the house "dried in" and it looked good. He would
work from daylight till he couldn't see to work any more. The
neighbors circulated a petition that had many signatures on it; the best
people in town resented an individual bypassing the tradesmen. To add
insult to injury, the house was being built on a tax deed lot that the
bank would not lend a penny on. Bryan had a builder's permit duly
issued by the fire chief, but he never dreamed that Bryan would build
the three bedroom house by himself in a fashionable neighborhood, but
there it was, sticking out like a sore thumb on the main highway. Bryan
felt trouble brewing but good as his word, he hadn't called on Teddie
for a thin dime or any advice. He was into this alone and he had to
prove himself to his doubtful father that would have liked to domineer
him. He had heard some rumors that the petition was going to be
honored by the city officials that morning and he would have to stop
work and lose the hard earned money he had tied up in an unfinished
house and be at the mercy of the unhappy neighbors. Bryan had rather
have died than to stop building that house he had going so well. In
desperation, he picked up his Winchester shotgun and took it down to
the unfinished house and leaned it in the jam of the front door frame,
just in case he needed it in a hurry. He told the two black helpers
nothing of the trouble that was brewing uptown in the city hall. The
helpers were up on the roof gable nailing on sheeting, their hammers
clipping in the nails that held the boards to the rafters. About three
o'clock Bryan heard doors slamming in front of the house, lots of
doors. Bryan knew his hour of truth had arrived, it was now or never.
He sat down in the open doorway to face the delegation. He knew
every man in the crowd. There was the mayor, the city attorney, the
sheriff, the jailer, two city councilmen, an architect, and two carloads of
well-to-do neighbors striding onto the sidewalk in front of the
unfinished house. Bryan reached behind the door frame and brought the
shotgun across his knees. He pumped a shell into the gun's chamber in
one quick motion, and pulled the hammer back as he said in a firm
voice. "Don't step off that sidewalk onto my property unless you have a
warrant for my arrest." A silence fell; the men on the roof stopped their
hammering. No one spoke until Bryan told them to continue working
until he told them to stop, that the job was going to continue. He never

pointed the loaded gun at the crowd, but they stopped in their tracks. The wise old attorney addressed Bryan. "We are here to advise you that your project is a nuisance to the neighborhood and that you have no contractor's license." Bryan firmly answered the city attorney. "Colonel, I am not a contractor, I own this lot outright, I am building with my own material that I have bought and paid for with my own money and I have a building permit issued by the city building inspector, paid the fee, and that permit is in date and posted here on the job for all to see. A murmur went up, the sheriff stepped forward, but the city attorney took him by the arm restraining him. He turned to the disgruntled crowd and addressed them. "Mr. Dunn is within his rights, now go home and leave him alone."

Chapter 41

Teddie and Gladys

About that time school was dismissed and Gladys came by in the Buick car he had bought her. She did a double take and swerved when she saw Bryan, with the gun on his lap and the crowds of dignitaries. She sped up and drove straight to the depot where Teddie sat at his desk. She blew the car horn and motioned for him to come quick. Bryan was in trouble with the law out on the "job." Teddie jumped in the car wit h her and they sped to see the crowd dispersing and Bryan still holding his ground. Teddie and Gladys came to his side. No one said a word but Teddie. His voice was low and firm. "I am so proud of you boy, you were right and my brother 'T's' spirit must have been in you. That gun is going to get you in trouble yet. Put it away." No more was said, but the house was always referred to as the Winchester house. Bryan never went back to the railroad, but one by one, he built seven nice houses in that neighborhood over the next few years.

Gladys went on teaching school, and Bryan paid their bills from the rents that poured in on investment of land and cattle sales. Tessie had always helped Teddie to pay off his debts. She had spent several years giving up small things like new curtains on the windows, a new oilcloth table cover, or even a new dress or a pair of shoes. The day came that Teddie's last note came due at the bank and the mortgage note could be burned. Two more rental houses would be theirs and she could get the things she wanted. That day at noon when Teddie came in and sat down at the little drop leaf table, she happily asked if he had paid off the houses. He glibly assured her that the note was settled. She breathed a sigh of relief and started to list her desires. Teddie ate in silence. A moment of tension followed, then she asked in a low serious tone, "You haven't borrowed more money from the bank, have you?" Teddie kept his composure, took a swig of ice tea and replied, "Now Tessie, you know a businessman has to do business with his bank. I did, today float a small load to keep my credit line alive." "How much did you borrow you numbskull?" Teddie rose to leave the table, wiped his mouth on a napkin and found the voice to blurt, "Twenty thousand dollars." Tessie fainted dead away.

The years seemed to fly. Bryan and Gladys had no children. They traveled in the summer when Gladys was on vacation. Bryan built a boat in Glady's kitchen and bought a small camper trailer that he refurbished. They went camping along the rivers of South Georgia. Gladys cooked the fish they would catch, and the game he would bring down with the gun he had gotten on his twelfth birthday and the Winchester shotgun that had backed up his brave word that afternoon he had to stand his ground with the city fathers of Fitzgerald.

The Atlantic Coastline Railroad still ran many trains through Fitzgerald, but a freight depot was no longer needed as a package business had moved to trucks on the highway system that had proliferated after the wars were over. Teddie retired after fifty-seven years of service on the railroad at Fitzgerald. Tessie began to drift into failing health. She once again stood beside an open grave at Evergreen Cemetery. Arta Barwick had died at ninety-six years of age at a nursing home in Americus, Georgia. Tessie once more stared straight ahead as she always did at a funeral. She seemed to give Bryan to Gladys, as her job was over. Bryan was a man. They would drive to where Bryan and Gladys were camping and seemed to enjoy the camp suppers Gladys would prepare. On one occasion down at a campsite at Lucy Lake on the Alapaha River, where Teddie had courted Tessie so many years ago, Tessie insisted on taking Bryan's fishing pole, and demanded that he bait "her hook" and as the sun set Tessie struggled to land a fine red breasted perch that glistened in the last rays of the setting sun. That was the last fish that Bryan would take off the hook for her, but he would never forget the pure look of rapture she had on her face, the wrinkles and gray hair seemed to fade away in the fading sunlight and there instead stood the vibrant mother that had taken him fishing so many times in the long, long ago.

It was not long until Tessie was confined to her bed and rocking chair on the side screened porch at the little apartment in the rear of their house that they had lived in since they moved from Suwannee Street in 1926. There had been many happy times there, many flowers grown, and a sick boy had regained his health. There were no more notes to be paid and no more demanding railroad officials to please. Teddie gave Tessie the attention she so desperately needed. Parkinson's disease had attacked her with its debilitating effects. The steady fingers that had played the piano wrote letters and crocheted table clothes and bed spreads quaked uncontrollably. The eyes that could look into the future had dimmed. The red hair that once cascaded down her neck in perfect waves had thinned and was sprinkled with the frost of many winters. The finger-curl that she wore across her fair head still tried to cover the brow, was now furrowed with wrinkles. The feet that once tipped around the house on tip toes were drawn and twisted with arthritis. The lips that once recited poems and bible lessons were stilled. Her eyes had seen unbearable grief that she had bared, happiness and love.

Not once had her lips spoken the names of the children that had been snatched from her arms. There was something buried deep in her mind that remained there concerning her father and the breakup of the Barwick family that had scattered to the four winds. She just sat there on the porch in that old green rocking chair, staring into the distance. The only name she called was "Teddie." They had fought the battles of life together, and sailed the stormy sea of matrimony for sixty years. She had been his "balance wheel" in the times when the world had rested heavy on his shoulders and had been his pillar of strength.

Now the tables had turned, she needed him. Bryan found it difficult to accept the changes that had crept like morning fog over the mother that had given him life and hope. He also had memories of his childhood. The happy days they had spent at the sand pile under the crabapple tree. The time he had been at the depot when an abusive railroad boss had been "Walking Teddie's log," Bryan had attacked the man and kicked his shins until he had to be carried outside by the black porter.

That evening Teddie told Tessie that he was going to give Bryan a good thrashing. Tessie put her arms around her boy and quietly told the angry father, "No, he was standing up for you, and I admire his spunk." Then there was the time that Teddie felt that he could no longer bear the pressures at the railroad job and came home in the middle of the morning and threw his hat on the sofa and told Tessie that he could take no more, and was quitting his job.

Tessie picked his hat up, crammed it on his head, and headed him to the door saying, "Teddie Dunn, you don't have the luxury of making that decision. You have a wife and child to support and I married you for a fight to the finish." Back to that depot he went, sat down at his desk and was "cat of the walk" until he was seventy-five years old.

In her latter days, Tessie wrote a note to be read at her death. She had tucked that short letter among her personal things. It read, "I married a penniless southern boy when I was seventeen years old. At times I had to bite my lips and speak my mind both to Teddie and my son. I loved to see Bryan rebel, and set his own course in life. I gave him to God almighty when he was born, and it was he above, not me that saw him to manhood. He is now a grown man and I have once again given him to a girl I like. She looks well enough and must have loved him to put up with him as I did."

The day came that Teddie told Bryan he could not meet the needs that age had bestowed on Tessie. The dream world that served her well as a young woman was now consuming her every thought. She would still call out in the dark hours before dawn, "Teddie, Teddie," but never Bryan.

Teddie and Bryan had a conference out the back steps of the home place near the spot by the crabapple tree where the mocking birds once sang and nested. They agreed that Tessie had spent her last night on the lots that she had wanted so badly. The doctor had told Teddie she needed to be where she could be given the care she so desperately needed, the nursing home. Thankfully, her mind never let her realize she was no longer at home. She lingered a few months there under sedation. Teddie would ride his bicycle to the nursing home each afternoon to sit at her bedside. Bryan thought he could reach her somewhere in the dream world she lived in, and was frustrated when he couldn't. He had thoughts of the times he had felt the wrath that she could display at an instant notice. The only time he could remember tears on her cheeks was the day that he shot, with his unerring aim, the rifle she had wanted him to have, a mocking bird that was singing its heart out in the crabapple tree. It fluttered to the ground, squawking its last notes. Tessie came to the back door with tears in her eyes. He would never forget her words, "Lord in heaven, what have I brought on this earth to kill the bird that helped me bear the birth pains I suffered when he was born." Then there was the time when he was still in high school, that he failed to have the little blue Chevrolet car in its parking place out on the side yard by 11:00 p.m. Tessie had positioned herself behind an azalea bush, dressed only in her nightgown, with the wet mop that hung beside the back door firmly held in her grip. She said nothing as she, with all her strength hit her boy in the face that sent him reeling to the ground. She shed no tears this time, but her words hurt worse than the mop. There she stood in the moonlight of the wee hours of the morning. She spoke from her heart. "I had rather see you dead, than to see you lay out all hours in my car with the scum of the earth." Teddie slept through that scene, but Tessie never slept until she heard his footsteps on the steps.

Chapter 42

Death Claims Tessie

Teddie was digging in the yard, age had been kinder to him than it had been to Tessie. He was still alert and strong, even though he was 80. Bryan and Gladys had moved into the home place and made home in the apartment since Tessie had gone to the nursing place. Bryan was sliding his boat into its shed when Gladys came to the back door. She had answered the telephone that was ringing off its hook. She quietly took the message from the nursing home to Bryan. "Get your father in the car, your mother is not expected to live through the afternoon." It was a message that all three of them had expected. They arrived to find the head nurse waiting in the hall for them. Tessie was beyond a doctor's care. She was struggling for her last breath. The doctor was by her bedside trying to ease her. She once more called for Teddie in a faint voice from somewhere out in the distance world that she was leaving. Teddie took her hand with the gnarled fingers that jerked in their last spasms. Bryan's heart went out to her, but he saw the last look from her set eyes. "You were mine, not your father's." Her breathing stopped, and then she gave one last final gasp and was gone. The nurse saw that Bryan needed something to settle his mind and handed him a glass half filled with a milky liquid that soon had him in a dream world. Teddie took the death in his stride and planned her funeral. Bryan was only there in body, but his mind was somewhere else. Gladys was all that Teddie or Bryan had to lead them back to reality. Teddie's friends had passed on to their rewards; Bryan sat at Gladys' side. There was no other family, only the three heard the words that were spoken over her grave there beside her babies that had so long ago gone on. Bryan had to be led away by Gladys. His only wish was that he could shovel the dirt that was piled behind the bank of flowers onto Tessie's casket. They had done so many things together over the years, that in his mind she would have liked for him to have shoveled that special dirt over the grave that had taken her from him. That same independent feeling that had been instilled in him to overcome his sickness by Tessie seemed to be once more calling him.

Teddie had no one to turn to but Bryan and Gladys. He made them welcome to stay with him at the home place. Teddie told Bryan that Tessie had never spent a dime of her share of his railroad pension that she had left. Bryan suggested that he spend the money on a new Chevrolet automobile and truck to pull a nice travel trailer. Teddie readily agreed that the three of them needed to get away from Fitzgerald and see the country. The next ten years were happy times for Teddie. He no longer drove the car, but Bryan took him on trips to Florida and places that he had never seen. Bryan still brought in fish and game that Gladys prepared for the table. His taste for birds had never diminished, and the biscuits she cooked just topped them off. Teddie bought new clothes and shoes that he wore to church every Sunday. He told Bryan that he wanted to go back to Andersonville and Americus, "the old country," he called it. He took Bryan to the Dunn burial plot on the side of the red clay ravine. There he pointed to the crumbling graves of his mother, Sallie Ann Dunn, father W.T. (Bill) Dunn, brothers Henry, Grady, and Claud Dunn. Bryan had never known his grandparents or the uncles that lay sleeping beneath the moss grown concrete slabs and failing brickwork walls. Time had again taken its toll. Bryan was taken by the words on his Grandmother Dunn's grave slab, "Sallie Ann Dunn—a good and faithful wife and a friend to all." Those words seemed to transpose themselves into Bryan's heart. Teddie showed his "children" where he attended school, Ida's store, Mr. Bill Easterlin's store, the abandoned Railroad Depot, where Miss Maggie had taught him the Morse code and how to "Sling Lightning," when he was a barefoot boy in knee pants, and the row of tumbled down railroad section houses they had called home until his father died. They walked over to where his mother moved to the little clapboard house with the mulberry tree beside it, where the red ox would stand and bellow in his deep voice, the place where he lay for weeks after the gun accident seventy years ago. He could almost hear his mother singing, "December as pleasant as May" and see her coming from her garden, as the sun rose, wet to her waist from the night's dew. As they topped the steep hill, Teddie was bewildered. There was only a yawning cavern in the red clay and a sprawling processing plant located on the track of the Central of Georgia Railroad. A big sign read "Malocca." Bryan laughed and teased his dad. "Teddie ole boy, you didn't remember way back when that lawyer from the Malocca Corporation came to your desk at the depot wanting to buy a quick claim deed to your mother's farm and you told him that he would be glad to sign any claim to that washed away hillside where you tried to plow that stubborn clay that would weld itself to the plow point? Well, you were right, it was the toughest clay in America that when ground to powder and mixed with a resin was indestructible and could withstand the heat of a rocket ship reentering the earth's gravity. Well, that ridge of clay was to become some of the most valuable real estate in America, and you gave it away." Teddie's words struck Bryan like the lightning he used to sling. I don't care what they get for it, I still would be glad to see it gone!" Gladys laughed at them and suggested that they go over to the National Cemetery and the prison park, where the Dunn boys played and drank the water of Providence Spring.

Teddie seemed to be glad to get back to Fitzgerald and the home he had built on Central Avenue. He spent the next five years collecting his rents, and riding his bicycle on long rides into the country side. Bryan was told that his dad was once more pedaling to the cemetery to visit Tessie and their children's graves.

Bryan decided not to say anything about the trips to the cemetery, but he told his dad that he was going to place a headstone at his mother's grave with the words, "Tessie Dunn, beloved mother." Teddie objected as he despised headstones with the names of his loved ones engraved on them. He told Bryan that Minnie had those words engraved on his mother's grave, unbeknown to him. Bryan told his father that Tessie was his mother, as well as the wife of Teddie and he did place a simple headstone at Tessie's grave. Teddie never commented, but accepted the stone as Bryan's wishes.

Teddie's health held out till he was eighty-six years old. His small body seemed tireless. He could jump out of the bed at any hour, but he began to fall and hurt himself. Bryan had taken his black men that had stayed by his side for twenty years and cut timber and sawed lumber to build Gladys a nice home on a five-acre tract near where he had played in a creek as a boy, and built the "Winchester house" some years past. Gladys deserved a better home than the little apartment Teddie loved so much. In the years that followed Bryan would go at night back to the home place and sleep in the room next to Teddie's bedroom. Teddie had a bad fall and fractured his skull. Bryan and Gladys nursed him back to health, but he was confused. His body was strong, but his mind just got worse. Gladys was the only person that could reason with him. Teddie still thought he had to compete with his son. They would take him on picnics, which he enjoyed. One night, as she calmed him for the night she asked him if he wanted to go on a picnic tomorrow and he answered, "If you are going, I want to go." Before Bryan turned the light out for the night Teddie inquired of Bryan, "Have you put the switch list in the way bill box at the depot?"

Chapter 43

The Grim Reaper Claims Teddie

Those were the last words that he would speak. Bryan fell into a deep sleep that night and realized it was daylight and his father had not called him. He sprang to his feet and saw his father laying in disarray covers slung aside, staring with unblinking eyes stiff and dead. Bryan pulled the bed sheet over Teddie's body, picked up the telephone and called Gladys before she left for school. His words were slow and measured, "Well, Teddie has gone to be with Tessie and their babies. I am so happy that he got his last wish to die in the home they had worked so hard to build and pay for." He lacked only three months of living ninety years and had slung a lot of lightning, buried his family, seen hard times, good times, left no debts, influenced a lot of lives. He had a good name and his word was never broken.

The funeral was planned by Gladys. She had grown close to Teddie. He had no daughter nor had Gladys known her father that died when she was a small child. Bryan felt satisfied that he had done his best to make his father's last years as comfortable as possible. He had devoted the last three years to feeding, bathing, and entertaining Teddie. He tended to the business that Teddie had built and his own and Gladys always brought a smile to his face. At times things didn't go as smoothly as at a nursing home, but they got by.

Teddie expressed his wishes for the last years that he wanted to be buried at Tessie's feet, not by her side. He said he felt that he wanted to humble himself to her misery. The girl he paid a dollar to be introduced to, the one that had bore his children. The one that was strong when he was tired and discouraged. His other wish was that he would never be put into a nursing home.

Gladys took over the funeral arrangements. She went to the dry goods store and bought Teddie a new suit of clothes, a white shirt and a beautiful neck tie. She wanted everything to be new because she knew he loved to dress up and put his best foot forward.

The night of the viewing at the funeral home, there was barely standing room. Teddie had outlived his brothers and sisters, as he was the youngest Dunn child. The age group that he had known and worked with were long gone. None of Tessie's people were there, but the young men that he had taught in Sunday school, took on hikes and swimming parties that were now middle aged, came to view his remains. Many friends of Gladys and Bryan's brought food to their new home.

Bryan could only look at his father's hands that now lay beside his still body. He thought of the lifetime they had served him, the old contrary milk cow he had milked, the plow lines they had held, the wood they had cut for the cook stove, the train orders they had taped out, the flowers they had planted and picked, the shoes that they had half soled for him, and the morning he held him as a baby as he cooked breakfast, the diapers he had changed and washed, and the dollar bills he had collected for the railroad and himself. Then he thought of the cheerful way he approached his later years and his tireless efforts to make life more comfortable for him and his mother. They had not always agreed, but Teddie was quick to forget the unpleasant moments and move on.

He was gone now to be once more with Tessie and the babies that awaited his arrival on the other shore of the river of life. Bryan was alone with Gladys now in a new house. He caught up on the things he had put aside to take care of Teddie.

Chapter 44

Bryan and the Spirit

Twenty five years passed quickly, times changed, Gladys retired after thirty-eight years in the classroom. She and Bryan both drew a pension, he from the railroad, she from the state of Georgia. They both stayed busy, Bryan continued to preserve his pine tree plantations and cattle trading. He no longer fished and hunted as he once did. He hung up his guns and fishing tackle. He was now in his late sixties, still active and strong. The only gun on the wall was the 22 caliber rifle he had gotten on his 12th birthday that hadn't been fired for many years.

He decided that he wanted to go back to Brunswick and St. Simons Island. He ended up buying a few acres on the Satilla River. He started building houses there when he was sixty-nine years old, just as he had done when he was young and built the Winchester house. This time he wanted to drive every nail, cut every board, lay every stone for the huge stone fireplace.

He would go every week for three days, camping in a trailer that he and Gladys bought in Waycross. It took him three years to complete his rustic house and surround it with flowers and bushes.

He enjoyed the project so much that he started another house, this time a long house. Seems he was like his Uncle Grady and had good use of his hands. Bryan was seventy-five when he finished that log house that fall. He had moved a family in it and was proud of the new income that the two houses generated. He was told to slow down but he just laughed and spent his time sawing and stacking lumber for another house. A load of logs had been carried to a saw mill close to Bowen's Mill, where he and Tessie had spent so many happy days. He set in on a cold January day with his heavy chainsaw to length his logs to the dimensions he wanted the lumber sawed.

He was alone, there in the mills log yard sawing away as he liked to work, ten miles from Fitzgerald when it happened. He broke out in a cold sweat and an ominous pressure in his chest. Could you believe he was having a heart attack! He threw the saw in the back of his worn out truck and decided he could make the trip alone to the hospital. The old truck ran good and he soon was approaching the traffic of Fitzgerald. He knew every minute counted, but his mind was clear as was his vision. He only hoped that there would be no long train over the railroad crossing between him and the hospital.

Luck was with him as he drove to the emergency room and strode to the desk. A young woman asked if she could help him. He told her that he hoped so as he was having a heart attack. The door flew open and he collapsed in the arms of nurses and a young doctor he didn't know. They went to work on him and soon had him "stabilized." The next thing he knew was late that night when his doctor sat on the side of the bed and told him that he was being transported to Macon. The next morning Gladys and her nephew followed the ambulance to Macon where Bryan was to spend the next twenty-eight days in the hospital. The operation, quadruple bypass went well, but complications set in, and his lungs were full of fluid. The doctors worked on him constantly, Gladys stayed by Bryan's side for the entire ordeal. He nearly slipped away twice, but Gladys saved the day, bringing help.

Bryan was sent home to recuperate. He was weak and depressed. A young couple tended his cows, Gladys tended to his business, but he just somehow couldn't return to his old lifestyle.

Nearly three years passed before Bryan had a feeling that he must return to Andersonville. A friend drove him up there one day before Thanksgiving. The leaves were turning their fall colors, Sweetwater Creek was flowing, and the old village still stood much as it did when Teddie was a boy. The trains still ran. The noon hour came and they were directed to a café across town. It was to Bryan's delighted to see the old building where Teddie had attended school, just beyond the graveyard beside the old log church. Bryan felt hungry and ate a big dinner prepared by a black cook.

After dinner the two men walked across the ravine to the Dunn's burial plot. There the line of graves was still intact, after all those years. Bryan felt that he must sit down on his Grandmother Sallie Ann Dunn's grave slab. He read the inscription on her grave that he already knew.

Suddenly a strong energy entered his body, the hair on the back of his neck tingled, as he went into a trance, and felt as though he had a great awakening. He told his friend that some strange power had moved into his very soul and that a spell had been cast upon him.

Andersonville seemed to be an enchanted place, inhabited by spirits and angels that guarded over the graves of Union Soldiers that never returned to the arms of their loved ones. Bryan had heard as a child of the haunting voices in the night. The warm breezes that brushed by mortals on cold mornings. Teddie played among those graves that still marched row on row over the red clay hills.

Bryan's entire life passed before his eyes. He thought he could see Teddie, cheering him on, they were all there not in the flesh, but their spirits awakened a new vigor and strength in Bryan. Was Teddie still slinging lightning?

Bryan left that graveyard and the grave that had been there since the year of 1913. He returned home to Gladys and told her of the experience at the graveyard. Bryan never again lacked for spirit even though he was the last of the Dunns. He knew where to find the strength to face the trials and tribulations of old age, he would never be alone.

Printed in the United States
219167BV00002B/3/P